D0256739

FOR RENEWALS TELEPHONE 0114

Developmental Dyspraxia

Identification and Intervention

A Manual for Parents and Professionals

Second Edition
Madeleine Portwood

Illustrations by John O'Neill for Max Baker (1992–1998)

David Fulton Publishers
London

David Fulton Publishers Ltd,
414 Chiswick High Road, London W4 5TF

www.fultonpublishers.co.uk

First published in Great Britain by David Fulton Publishers 1999
Reprinted 1999 (twice), 2000, 2001, 2002, 2003
10 9 8 7

Note: The right of Madeleine Portwood to be identified as the author of this work has been asserted by her in accordance with the Copyright, Designs and Patents Act 1988.

Copyright © Madeleine Portwood 1999

British Library Cataloguing in Publication Data
A catalogue record for this book is available from the British Library

ISBN 1–85346–573–9

All rights reserved. The materials in this publication may be photocopied for use only within the purchasing organisation.

Typeset by FSH Print & Production Ltd, London
Printed in Great Britain by Ashford Colour Press Ltd, Gosport, Hants

Contents

Foreword

Madeleine Portwood's first edition of *Developmental Dyspraxia* has been a major source of information and help to parents, carers and all those involved in the education and treatment of children with dyspraxia.

In this, her second edition, the author has built on her well researched, evidence-based practice to refine and develop intervention programmes which can be used by parents and teachers alike. Madeleine Portwood possesses a unique gift - the ability to impart knowledge and information in the kind of straightforward language which neither patronises professionals nor 'blinds with science' parents and carers.

Developmental Dyspraxia spans all ages from the early years through to primary and secondary education. A welcome addition is the chapter on "Information for adults with dyspraxia". Many adults, undiagnosed and untreated in childhood, now have difficulty obtaining relevant information and help. Provision for adults with dyspraxia is sketchy but professionals such as Madeleine Portwood and voluntary groups such as the Dyspraxia Foundation are working towards raising awareness of the condition and an achievement of adequate, appropriate resources.

Madeleine Portwood has been working in a professional and voluntary capacity, helping children and young adults with dyspraxia for some ten years. The Dyspraxia Foundation is privileged to have her as a Trustee and Chair of the Education Committee. Her warmth, humour and no-nonsense attitude make her a popular and valuable committee member.

I wholeheartedly recommend this book, as an indispensable resource, to all who are involved with the development and education of children and young adults with dyspraxia be they teachers, therapists, family or friends.

Tricia Pullen
Dyspraxia Foundation
January 1999

Foreword

'Clumsy' is a miserable label to live with, and 'clumsy kids' suffer from an accumulating social handicap throughout their schooldays, the later toll of which has not even been estimated in terms of adult disadvantage and despair. Disappointment and humiliation associated with everyday drawing, writing, gym or team sports can be compounded if attentional disorders, language problems or learning difficulties are also associated with *developmental dyspraxia* (or 'developmental co-ordination disorder'). In our experience a constellation of problems is often associated with more severe cases of dyspraxia.

It is these severely affected children who are probably first noted in checks by primary health care nurses and then assessed systematically during screening by the school medical service that are most likely to benefit from this book. Those who care for them, in the family, the school or the clinic, should find it a spur to developing better and better practice for their *effective* rehabilitation.

Past practice left a great deal to be desired. A 'clinical audit' by community paediatricians established a need to improve the recognition, referral and treatment of dyspraxia. Above all, there was a need for a better understanding of the condition among health service and education professionals and especially parents struggling in a maze of contradictory advice or changing fashions in treatment.

These concerns were not restricted to Cambridge. When I submitted a short note on dyspraxia to the journal *Physiotherapy* in 1994, I was astonished by the subsequent flood of mail from professionals all over the world. Most of this was along the lines of, '*Are you really seeing children like ours? What works? How soon can you let us know?*'. In 1995 the Child Development Centre presented a very preliminary picture of our randomised controlled trial of treatment at an Anglia & Oxford Regional Health Authority conference: there was standing room only. We were also able to study patterns of handwriting thanks to a small grant from the Nuffield Foundation for a psychology student project. Well, when it came time to outline that modest project at a regional dyspraxia study day, we had to turn people away who wanted to squeeze into that session. Undaunted, we just kept booking bigger venues – often with two or three of us presenting the results in turn.

The Cambridge conference, Changing Perceptions, has just reviewed the growing body of evidence which indicates that providing therapy can make a real difference. The College of Occupational Therapists has even suggested that treating dyspraxia could become their key contribution to the government's new initiative for *Our Healthier Nation:* Healthy Schools. Two crucial themes emerging from this are 1) the *participation* of families as equal partners in determining both policy and practice and 2) *reducing social exclusion,* that is creating imaginative opportunities for disadvantaged children to play a full part all through their schooldays and later on in life. The good news is already beginning to emerge, in the following chapters based on extensive practical experience in Durham. Children with severe dyspraxia have specific needs. In observable, measurable ways, they do respond to specific treatments. 'Clumsiness' is not an indelible label.

Dr. Woody Caan
Head of Research and Development
Lifespan Healthcare, Cambridge
November 1998

Preface

The first edition of *Developmental Dyspraxia* was produced to offer parents strategies to help their children. Some parents had known, almost from birth, that their child was having difficulty achieving expected developmental milestones. My experience suggested that access to 'professionals' who would 'diagnose' dyspraxia was problematic and therapy in many instances unavailable. The way forward had to be to provide intervention programmes for parents.

Since publication in 1996, more than 10,000 copies have been sold, not only in the UK, but in many other countries including the US, South Africa, Australia, Iceland, Greece, China and Singapore. More than half have been purchased by professionals, mainly teachers who have designed and implemented school-based programmes to develop the skills of their pupils.

As more research information becomes available we are able to achieve a greater understanding of the nature of the condition and refine and implement more successful interventions. This new edition details the experiences of parents and professionals who have been involved during the past few years in developing these programmes, and discovering which strategies are most effective.

In a perfect world every child and adult would have access to the appropriate professionals, including paediatricians, psychologists, physio- and occupational therapists and speech therapists, but resources are limited. This manual is for those involved in working with the children on a daily basis – parents, teachers and friends – and it is through their commitment that youngsters who in the past have been undiagnosed, and labelled behaviourally difficult or poor achievers, can begin to reach their potential.

Such involvement must come sooner rather than later to prevent the frustration, disaffection and distress that the condition can generate.

Madeleine Portwood
Durham
January 1999

Acknowledgements

I would like to thank all of the children, parents and professional colleagues who provided the information discussed in this manual.

I have benefited from the continuing support of the Educational Psychologists in the Durham Service and the Director of Education, Keith Mitchell.

In this second edition I would like to acknowledge the additional contributions made by school staff throughout the country who have embarked upon school-based intervention programmes.

Finally, I thank those directly involved with the production of this material:

Peter Chislett for his sensitive editing
Margaret Clay for preparing the manuscript
John O'Neill for his illustrations
John Portwood for producing computerised images
Chris Ridley for extending intervention programmes
Peter Withnall for his examination of content

1

Since the publication of my first manual in June 1996 a great deal of research has focused on external factors such as nutrition and the effect of the environment on the developing child. My own studies during the past two years provided access to a greater sample population of children and young adults and have clarified my thinking about the condition termed *dyspraxia*. This second edition encompasses much of the recent research evidence and its implications for parents and teachers.

I became interested in the subject in 1988 after attending a seminar to discuss the increasing numbers of research papers suggesting that a high proportion of youngsters with emotional and behavioural difficulties showed evidence of significant neurological immaturity.

I was employed then by Durham Local Education Authority as Specialist Senior Educational Psychologist for children with emotional and behavioural difficulties, and screened 107 youngsters aged between 9 and 16 in the county. All had been identified as having special educational needs and allocated day or residential provision for their extreme behavioural difficulties. In that sample, 82 (77 per cent) of the pupils showed symptoms of neurological immaturity.

Research suggests that between 5 and 10 per cent of the general population would expect to have similar immaturities but with this elevated figure of 77 per cent in the sample assessed, it would be reasonable to assume that this factor must be significant in the development of subsequent unacceptable behaviours.

Many of these pupils had experienced failure from an early age. Delayed language development, poor social skills and a lack of co-ordination had forced isolation within their peer group. Many had become the victims of more assertive pupils. For some of the youngsters there were additional problems in their home environment. Some had suffered extreme emotional and material deprivation, others had presented as extremely difficult youngsters from birth with parents resorting to respite care and/or medication to enable them to cope.

There are occasions when environmental factors form the sole basis for explanations about a child's behaviour. It is important to take a more detailed overview and explore factors within the child before reaching any conclusions.

In my original sample of 107 pupils, 12 were selected from the identified 82 for intervention. Their intellectual ability was assessed using the Wechsler Intelligence Scale for Children – RS (WISC-RS) and found to be in the average range despite a number of very low scores in some of these sub-tests. In addition these youngsters had spelling ages of at least three years below their chronological age and their handwriting ranged from barely legible to illegible. In the sample, nine had reading ages, assessed using the Edwards Test, which were at or above their chronological age.

Members of the school staff agreed to supervise individual motor-skills programmes which were provided for each child and followed daily for 20 minutes. Progress was evident by the end of the first month, but within six months there was improvement, not only in language and handwriting skills (see Figure 1.1) but in concentration and behaviour. It was apparent that these youngsters had 'failed' in the educational system because of their inability to perform to expectation. Their frustration had led to displays of uncontrolled emotion which had resulted in significant behavioural difficulties. It seemed certain that, had the 'problem' been diagnosed at a much earlier stage, many of these children would not have been labelled as behaviourally difficult, and they would not have been placed in an educational environment away from their mainstream peers.

The 'symptoms' identified in the previous paragraph characterise the condition defined as *dyspraxia*. My confidence in stating this comes ten years later after being involved with more than 600 children and young adults with similar difficulties.

In 1990, after working extensively with youngsters who had been offered alternative educational provision, my next area of study was to consider approaches to identify and prepare intervention programmes for those within the mainstream sector experiencing similar difficulties, and probable candidates for such provision in the future. Pupils referred for psychological

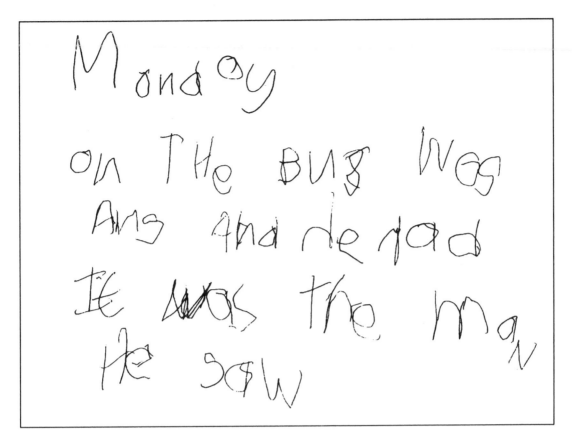

Figure 1.1a Handwriting of Andrew, aged 9, before intervention

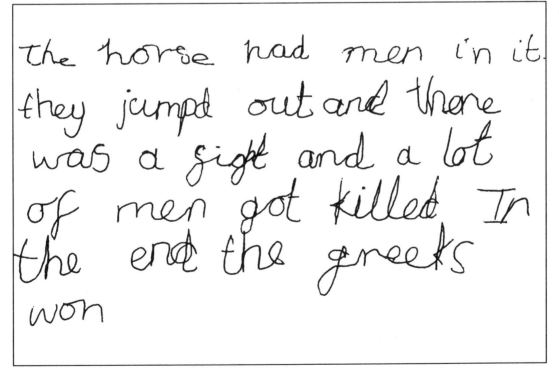

Figure 1.1b Handwriting of Andrew, aged 9, after intervention

assessment usually exhibited recurring displays of unacceptable classroom behaviour, although a minority of the youngsters appeared to be extremely withdrawn. Most of the youngsters were aged between 8 and 11, with the sample heavily skewed to the older end because of the fear that 'although we have managed to "contain" him here, he will never make it in secondary school.' After identification, the youngsters were given access to a series of graded motor-skills activities. Programmes and methods of determining the children's access points are detailed later. Within the primary sector I was given access to data collected by other educational psychologists in Durham and this greatly increased the size of the sample.

The assessment techniques developed for use by teachers to identify dyspraxic youngsters in school were tested between 1988 and September 1993. I embarked then on a control study with children aged between 5 and 7, as research has shown that the earlier the diagnosis, the greater the impact of any intervention programme. This study was undertaken at an infants school in the county and included eight pupils aged between 5 years 3 months and 6 years 8 months. The results of the programme were extremely encouraging.

The research was then extended to older pupils as I believed it was important to develop access to programmes in secondary schools. My initial assumption was that, given the differences between the primary and secondary school environment and the age of the pupils, success would be the exception rather than the rule. I had made a total misjudgement: on the whole the pupils themselves were more committed to remediating their difficulties than the younger children.

This research was published in 1996 and attracted a great deal of media attention. I was approached by Sheilagh Matheson, the producer of the BBC2 programme *Close Up North* who was interested in the relationship between dyspraxia and juvenile delinquency. She arranged access to Deerbolt Young Offenders Institution in Barnard Castle and I screened 69 of the youngsters aged between 15 and 17. More than 50 per cent of the youngsters assessed showed varying degrees of dyspraxia.

The programme also followed a youngster who was 4 years of age and due to enter reception class. He had been identified by a speech therapist six months previously as a child who displayed the symptoms of developmental dyspraxia. His progress was filmed over a period of eight weeks to determine the success of the intervention programme. The extent of my research, which is from birth to adulthood, is outlined in later chapters.

As more research evidence becomes available the term *dyspraxia* becomes more complex.

2 Development of the brain and the significance of diet

Dyspraxia results when parts of the brain have failed to mature properly. To understand the complexities of the condition it is important to consider the early development and subsequent functioning of the brain.

Five weeks after conception cells within the developing embryo specialise to form the nervous system. As the brain develops, cells move, cells die, connections are made and broken as the brain assimilates information from sensory input. Eventually the brain develops into a network of 10 billion cells with 1 million billion connections. The brain adapts the body to the environment, through a process of natural selection reinforcing the connections between nerve cells which are most advantageous to the individual.

Esther Thelen, a developmental psychologist at the University of Indiana, has completed an extensive study of babies and produced strong evidence that selection plays an important role in the development of human behaviour. A month-old baby is able to fixate on a suspended object in its line of vision. At 2 months the baby is able to make anticipatory movements towards the object with a closed fist. At this age the child does not know how to co-ordinate movements. In Dr Thelen's study, motion sensors were attached to babies which tracked and recorded their movement in space. This movement was monitored to determine how skills are acquired. By the age of 6 months the child is able to reach and grasp appropriately.

Conventionally, it was believed that skills such as learning to reach are genetically programmed and the brain directs the body to perform certain activities. However, her research discovered that each baby has to solve for himself the sequence of instructions which will result in reaching towards the object. The baby has a range of movements and has to select from these the ones which work. He must locate the place in space to grasp the toy. The baby produces a large repertoire of random movements, making facial grimaces as well as flapping his arms and legs, while grasping at empty space. Occasionally, by chance, he will make contact with the toy. Over time, repeating this variety of movements, the repertoire is narrowed down to enable the action to produce the desired contact. The child is beginning to be able to exert some control over his environment. The next question must be: how does the brain produce this controlled behaviour?

Gerald Edelman, a biologist who won the Nobel Prize in 1972 for his theory that the immune system works by a process of natural selection, has suggested a possible explanation. The source of this information is his book *Neural Darwinism. The Theory of Neuronal Group Selection* (1989). His thoughts are extended in *Bright Air, Brilliant Fire on the Matter of the Mind* (1992).

There are over 200 types of cells in the human body and one of the most specialised is the nerve cell (neurone). It differs from other cells because of its electrical and chemical function and the means by which it is connected to other nerve cells.

The brain is richly supplied with these nerve cells which are interconnected via complex neural systems. There are two kinds of nervous system organisations, which are very different, even though both are made up of neurones.

- *The brain stem and limbic system* have evolved to understand the signals within the body. They respond to feelings such as hunger and anxiety and are connected to a variety of body organs, the endocrine system and the autonomic nervous system. These systems are responsible for regulating heart beat, respiration and digestion. They also determine the body's sleep cycle.
- *The thalamo-cortical system* which consists of the thalamus and the cortex acting together to receive signals external to the body. The cortex is adapted to receive signals from the sensors which respond to sight, touch, taste, smell, hearing and the body's awareness of its position in space.

Within these two systems the greatest area of interest is the cerebral cortex where much of the higher brain function takes place. Thoughts and actions are the result of signals travelling between nerve cells and, if the cortex is magnified, each region shows millions and millions of cells. Thousands of new cells are interconnected to produce a complex network. The cortex contains billions of specialised neurones and their function is to transfer signals from one part of the nervous system to another.

The neurone comprises a cell body, projecting from which are a number of short branches called dendrites (see Figure 2.1). The dendrites receive messages from other neurones and the message is transmitted through the axon, which is a tubular extension of the cell. Nerve impulses can travel only in one direction across the junctions (synapses) between neurones, so the axon of one neurone takes position close to the dendrites of another. A single neurone can receive messages through its dendrites from many other neurones which are transmitting via the axon (Figure 2.2).

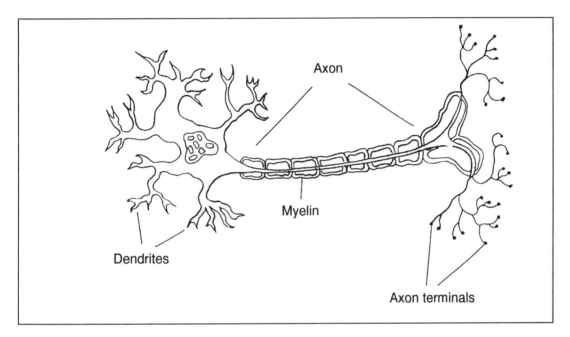

Figure 2.1 Diagrammatic representation of a neurone

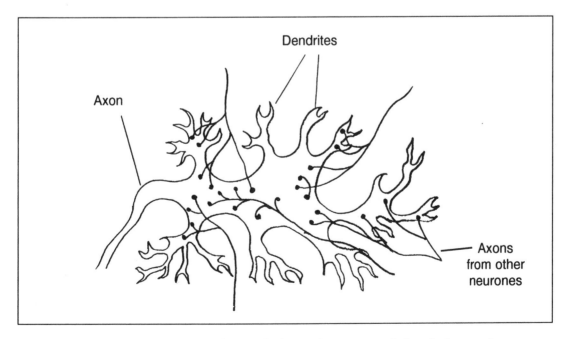

Figure 2.2 The transmission of signals from the axons of closely located neurons

The synapse is the point at which the message is transferred from one cell to the next. It is a specialised structure in which electrical activity passed down the axon of the pre-synaptic neurone leads to the release of a chemical (a neurotransmitter) that in turn induces electrical activity in the post-synaptic neurone (Figure 2.3). As a result, nerve signals in the form of electrical discharges occur at the membranes of the neurones. The synaptic junction is where the signal transfer takes place and the neurone discharges or 'fires' when it is stimulated to a specific threshold. Their sensitivity to stimulation can be altered by a variety of different chemicals, including the neurotransmitters at synapses, and drugs.

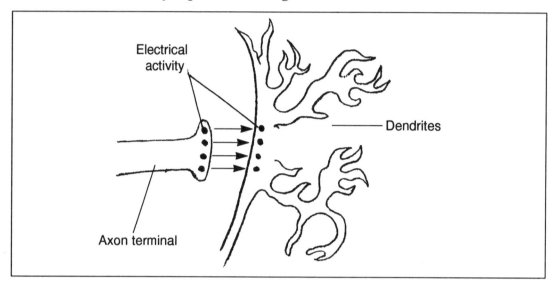

Figure 2.3 Electrical transmission through a neurone

The production of purposeful movement

As mentioned previously, the brain has 10 billion cells and a million billion connections: as many cells as there are transistors in 10,000 Pentium processors and as many connections as the memory capacity (in bytes) of a million hard disks. These connections, in turn, produce a vast number of pathways along which messages can be transmitted. Many of these pathways will serve no useful purpose. By the time the child is 3 years of age a third of these neural pathways will be 'pruned'.

It follows that the brain must have a means of selecting only those pathways which produce useful behaviour. If we look again at the early movements in infants, the grasping response is the result of 'firing patterns' or messages transmitted between nerve cells in the cerebral cortex. When the firing pattern produces a successful outcome, such as grasping a toy, the connections used to achieve that outcome will be reinforced, and other connections which have not been utilised may disappear altogether. The strength of the connection between neurones that are in place rises or falls, increasing the likelihood that the 'stronger' synapses are usually selected. As the infant builds more and more levels of action and thought, each action achieves a satisfying objective.

Implications for the dyspraxic child

The motor movements of the developing infant determine which connections in the cerebral cortex are reinforced. Comparisons can be made between the neural pathways of a 6-week-old child and one who is 6 months (Figure 2.4).

At birth the template for interconnecting neural pathways is present. Observation of a 6-week to 2-month-old child indicates that when a toy is suspended in the line of vision, instinctively all four limbs thrash around wildly as the child seeks to make contact with the desired object. Every so often, just by chance, the child is able to:

- fixate on the object
- extend from the shoulder
- move elbow appropriately
- extend fingers
- touch object.

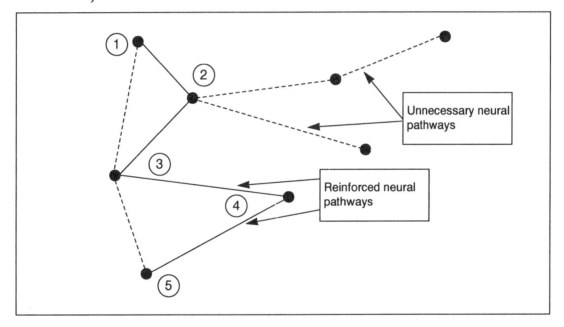

Figure 2.4 Simplified representation of neural pathways at 6 weeks

The track of the simplified message response is outlined in Figure 2.4. Observation of the child, however, shows messages going to all four limbs and this is the result of transmission along unnecessary neural pathways.

By the time the child is 6 months of age he is almost 'reflexively' able to reach and secure a dangling ring, hold small cubes and assist with holding a feeder cup. There has been further reinforcement of appropriate neural pathways, and those which have remained unused are beginning to disappear. In Figure 2.4, the 6-week-old child has to transmit messages between five nerve junctions. In the 6-month-old child (Figure 2.5) this is reduced to three. There are five operations in the younger child compared with three in the older child: therefore not only is the speed of information processing greatly increased but it is much less likely that information will be misdirected.

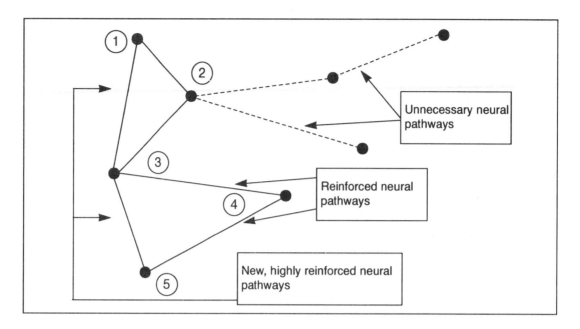

Figure 2.5 Simplified representation of neural pathways at 6 months

Usually, between the ages of 8 and 12 months, the infant has learned to co-ordinate not only his hands but also his feet. The child is able to crawl and can operate hands and feet in opposition. High kneeling follows and soon the child is able to achieve a standing position and walk independently.

There is evidence to suggest that in the case of the dyspraxic child, reinforced interconnections between nerve cells in the cerebral cortex are reduced in number. The cortex persists in a state of immaturity which varies greatly between individuals.

It seems reasonable, therefore, to suggest this is the possible explanation for some of the difficulties encountered by dyspraxic youngsters. Not only do they require additional time to process information, but messages directed towards specific limb function are passed to all four limbs. The vast majority of dyspraxic youngsters do not go through the crawling stage but prefer to bottom-shuffle, and then walk. It is necessary to be able to co-ordinate all four limbs independently to crawl successfully, so it is probably much easier for them to miss out this stage and walk independently as this requires the co-ordination of only two.

If we consider the function of the brain beyond the cerebral cortex, it is possible that there may be other factors which explain some associated behaviours of dyspraxic children. The cortex controls the body's sensory systems, its motor responses and the complex behaviours of thought and language. The cortex surrounds the limbic system, which is the 'instinctive' part of the brain responsible for the automatic responses within the body (Figure 2.6). It is also closely involved in emotional behaviour. The cortex serves to 'dampen' the effect of the limbic system. If this were not the case, the individual would present as highly excitable and over-emotional, with inappropriate responses to differing levels of sensory input. Although the comorbidity of conditions such as dyspraxia, dyslexia, attention deficit and

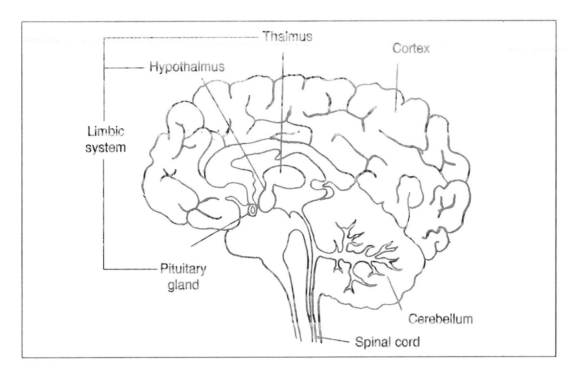

Figure 2.6 The limbic system in relation to the cerebral cortex

hyperactivity disorder (ADHD) and sometimes autism, is high (35–40 per cent), it can be very difficult to obtain a specific diagnosis.

If ADHD results in high levels of excitability, then it is expected that the origin is the limbic system. If this is the case Ritalin (methylphenidate) is extremely effective in 95 per cent of the cases. Ritalin is a stimulant which increases the electrical activity within the cortex, increasing the dampening effect that this has on the limbic system. The excitability of the individual is therefore controlled. In the case of a dyspraxic youngster, it is the cortex with its reduced number of reinforced neural connections that is not sufficiently dampening the limbic system. Although the prescription of Ritalin will increase the electrical activity, this cannot be directed along appropriate neural pathways and therefore the dampening effect on the limbic system appears to be significantly reduced – by perhaps 80 per cent. Although the behaviours of children with dyspraxia and attention deficit and hyperactivity may be similar, i.e. high levels of excitability and poor concentration, the origins of each are very different.

The significance of diet on the effectiveness of neural transmission

My research has led me to believe that dyspraxia is the result of neurological immaturity in the cortex of the brain. However, in my sample of over 600 children and young adults 18 per cent did not appear to have the expected developmental history (to be discussed in later chapters). I was concerned that for such a large group of individuals I could offer no explanation as to the origins of their difficulty. In recent years there has been a great deal of research considering the importance of the maternal diet and its relationship with significant feeding problems in new-born infants. Some of this research has provided a possible explanation.

In the mid-1980s research focused on the production of a specially formulated milk product for babies who were premature or small for dates and could not be breast fed. This pre-term formula milk was higher in protein, carbohydrate and fat content than the readily available formula milk. In 1990 Professor Alan Lucas reported on the results of a study in Glasgow which compared the development of pre-term and small-for-dates babies who were fed either pre-term or the usual formula baby milk. As expected, the results showed that youngsters having access to pre-term formula milk showed a significant IQ advantage at 18 months. Another feature of this intervention highlighted the significance of appropriate feeding up to four weeks after birth. Youngsters who had been fed pre-term formula milk in excess of this four-week period did not show any greater advantage at 18 months than those fed up to four weeks. However, the youngsters who had access to the pre-term formula for less than four weeks after birth did not show the same advantage. The study concluded that pre-term formula milk had significant advantages over the usual formula milk.

In 1992 Lucas reported on a similar study where a comparison had been made between pre-term babies fed either mother's own breast milk, donor breast milk or pre-term formula milk. The youngsters were assessed at the age of 8 and it had been anticipated that those having access to pre-term formula milk would show the greatest advantage. This was not the case. The youngsters who had mother's own breast milk were those who achieved the highest scores in indicators of intellectual ability. It was evident from this study that although there were some advantages with the improved nutritional content of pre-term formula milk, mother's own breast milk offered the best start in life. Further investigation showed that the significant factor was not higher concentration of protein, fat and carbohydrate, but another essential nutrient, docosahexanoic acid or DHA (a long-chain polyunsaturated fat).

The brain is 60 per cent fat, 25 per cent of which is DHA. Further research by Makrides, Neumann and Gibson (1996) highlights the importance of maternal docosahexanoic acid throughout pregnancy and particularly the first four weeks following birth. Some studies have attempted to measure the DHA content in the cerebral cortex from birth through to 2 years of age. They are: Neuringer et al. (1988), Makrides et al. (1994) and Farquharson et al. (1995).

In the fifth week of pregnancy when the cell division of the embryo is most active and again in the last trimester, the DHA content of the cortex increases to between three and five times its normal level. The higher scores on developmental tests achieved by breast-fed infants in comparison with their formula-fed peers prompted an investigation into the relationship between the development of the brain and long-chain polyunsaturated fatty acids in the diet.

The cortex of the brain was analysed by capillary gas chromatography and this determined that breast-fed infants had a greater proportion of DHA in the cortex than those who had been formula-fed. The proportion of DHA increased in breast-fed infants (but not formula-fed infants) with age, and the level continued to be monitored for two years following birth. This higher concentration of DHA in the cortex of breast-fed infants may explain the improved cortical function, as it is possibly integral to neurotransmission.

In the pre-term infant the blood levels of DHA are below what is expected at term (Crawford 1996). Post-natal follow-up suggests that, two weeks after delivery, the DHA level has fallen farther, to a third of the proportion the baby would have had as a foetus. For these youngsters, it is crucial that they have access to appropriate nutrients, high in DHA.

Where breast-feeding is not a possibility or there is a requirement to supplement with formula milk, the nutritional composition, which is detailed on the product, should be checked. One of the well-known brands in the UK states:

> X is a complete food for your baby. It has been specially formulated to be nutritionally close to breast-milk. It contains DHA which is a special blend of long-chain polyunsaturated fatty acids or LCPs, used to help brain and visual development.

With this information I re-examined the developmental histories of the 18 per cent of youngsters in my original sample of 600 pupils who did not appear to follow the usual pattern of early development. In that group, 70 per cent of the youngsters had significant feeding problems from birth and many mothers reported failure to gain weight appropriately during their pregnancy. It appears from this research that there could be two explanations for the evidence of symptoms of dyspraxia. In the vast majority of cases there is evidence to suggest that there are insufficient reinforced neural pathways in the cortex: there are immaturities. However, for 18 per cent of the youngsters in the sample it may well be that the neural pathways are appropriately placed but there may be a problem transferring the message across the synapse via the neurotransmitter.

Many youngsters and adults in my survey have considered supplementing their diet, and long-chain polyunsaturated fatty acids are readily available in evening primrose oil and fish oil. Some parents have reported immediate improvements in their children's co-ordination and ability to process information. It is important at this stage to include a note of caution: where youngsters and adults have shown elevated levels of electrical activity (diagnosed epilepsy), introducing high concentrations of long-chain polyunsaturated fatty acids into the diet has resulted in an increased number of seizures. Where epilepsy has been controlled, interference with the neurotransmitter is likely to affect the overall electrical activity in the cortex.

The importance of the left and right hemispheres of the brain

To understand in greater detail the learning difficulties associated with dyspraxia, it is necessary to consider how information is processed in the cortex. The brain comprises a right and left hemisphere, and they function in different ways. The left hemisphere is described as analytical because it processes information sequentially and it specialises in recognising the parts that make up the whole. Although it is most efficient at processing verbal information, language should not be considered to be 'in' the left hemisphere. The motor component of speech is situated in the right hemisphere. The left hemisphere is able to recognise that one stimulus comes before another, and verbal perception and subsequent generation depend on the awareness of the sequence in which sounds occur.

While the left hemisphere separates out the parts which constitute a whole, the right specialises in combining the parts to create a whole (Figure 2.7). Unlike the left hemisphere, which processes information in a linear manner, the right

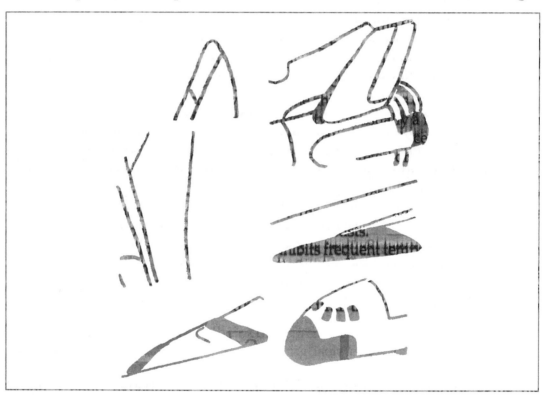

Left hemisphere

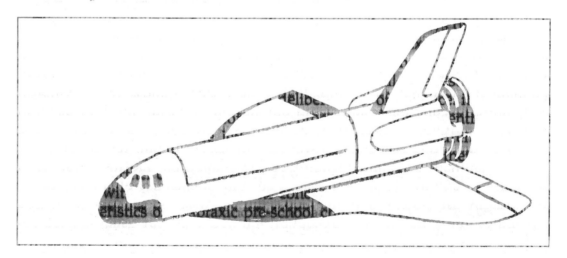

Right hemisphere

Figure 2.7 A visual representation of the functions of the two hemispheres

hemisphere organises simultaneously. It specialises in a method of processing which perceives and constructs patterns. It is more efficient at visual and spatial processing (images). Its language capacity is limited and words play little part in its functioning. While both hemispheres process sensory stimuli, it is thought that non-verbal stimuli are processed primarily in the right hemisphere.

Research into the specialisation of the right and left hemispheres shows that the effective processing of information requires access to both, as they work to complement each other (Figure 2.8). The dominant hemisphere operates to utilise the non-dominant hemisphere appropriately. Problems occur when a child is unable to utilise fully either or both hemispheres. By the time pupils reach secondary education they are expected to absorb more information from books and verbal discussions with their teachers. They work, in many instances, almost exclusively with words and numbers. Youngsters with dyspraxia have very poor short-term auditory memories: consequently they are less able to process verbal information and are required to learn in a way which is excessively difficult for them. By understanding how information is transmitted and interpreted, we can begin to examine assessment techniques which identify difficulties evident in this process that are experienced by dyspraxic youngsters.

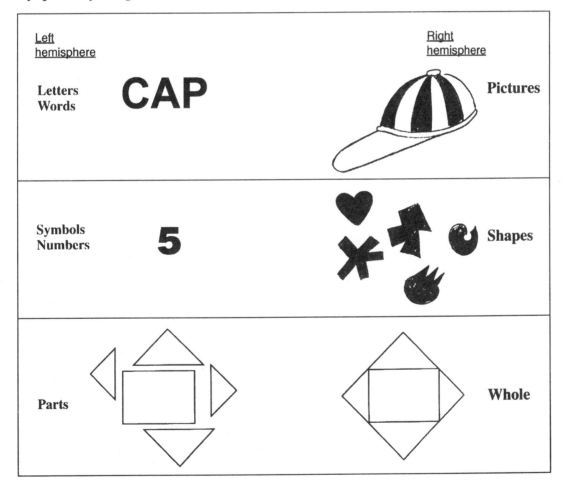

Figure 2.8 Processing differences between the left and right hemispheres

3 | What is dyspraxia?

The *Diagnostic and Statistical Manual* (DSM-IV) of the American Psychiatric Association uses the term *developmental co-ordination disorder*. There are five criteria for diagnosis which are:

(a) There is a marked impairment in the development of motor co-ordination.
(b) The impairment significantly interferes with academic achievement or activities of daily living.
(c) The co-ordination difficulties are not due to a general medical condition, e.g. cerebral palsy, hemiplegia or muscular dystrophy.
(d) It is not a pervasive developmental disorder.
(e) If developmental delay is evident, the motor difficulties are in excess of those usually associated with it.

The manual also lists associated features, which can include phonological disorder, expressive language disorder and mixed receptive-expressive language disorder.

Developmental dyspraxia describes youngsters who have co-ordination difficulties but who also, in the majority of cases, show evidence of significant perceptual problems. Confusion can arise when the word 'dyspraxic' is used in its literal form, i.e. unco-ordinated, and used to describe the symptoms evident in conditions such as hemiplegia.

Developmental dyspraxia is currently applied to youngsters who present a wide spectrum of difficulties. However, a word of caution is recommended by Mary Lobascher, the Principal Clinical Psychologist at Great Ormond Street Hospital for Sick Children. In her introduction to the first edition of *Praxis Makes Perfect* (Dyspraxia Foundation) she says:

> It is hoped that the diagnosis of dyspraxia does not suffer the same fate as that of dyslexia so that every child who may be a little forgetful, disorganised and clumsy is diagnosed as dyspraxic.

The rate of a child's development varies from one individual to another and some youngsters never develop good physical skills. However, when we are able to identify problems with co-ordination together with other behaviours characteristic of dyspraxia, then it is possible to begin making a diagnosis. We need to acknowledge that these youngsters can be able children who have bright and enquiring minds. Their never-ending questions continue almost to the point of exhaustion. Listening to instructions and remembering them is very difficult, and so they require a high level of verbal feedback to facilitate retention of the information they seek.

The youngster with dyspraxia is soon singled out, even in the pre-school environment, as a child who is different from the rest of the group. Their frustrations are evident when they have:

- poor articulation
- difficulties with dressing and feeding
- limited concentration
- inability to follow instructions
- heightened sensitivity to sensory information, e.g. differences in noise and changes in lighting
- poor figure–ground awareness, always falling over and bumping other children
- an inability to record anything on paper.

They are always the outsider in a group and the last to be chosen as a partner.

From the research evidence now available it appears that, in dyspraxic youngsters, parts of the brain are not sufficiently mature to allow the child to follow the path from action to response without the transmission between the nerve cells breaking down or becoming an unacceptably lengthy process.

The definition of the condition offered by the Dyspraxia Foundation, I believe, describes accurately the observable behaviours: 'Dyspraxia is an impairment or immaturity of the organisation of movement. Associated with this there may be problems of language, perception and thought' (*Information*

17

for Parents leaflet produced by the Dyspraxia Foundation). The word 'dyspraxia' is taken from two Greek words: 'dys' - meaning ill or abnormal, and 'praxis', doing.

The focus of this chapter is to determine if there are identifiable characteristics evident at key stages of the child's development which would lead to a probable diagnosis of developmental dyspraxia. This information is based on my individual assessment of more than 500 children and young adults aged between 2 and 28, interviews with their parents wherever possible and access to additional information from the assessment of more than 100 pupils by other educational psychologists, speech therapists, occupational therapists and physiotherapists. Specific research information is documented in Chapter 5.

Obtaining a developmental history

It is important to obtain as much information as possible regarding the child's development. We know from studies already mentioned in Chapter 2 that factors during pregnancy can have a significant impact on subsequent development. Some studies (Gubbay 1985) have suggested that in perhaps 50 per cent of cases of diagnosed dyspraxia there are significant factors evident during pregnancy, labour and birth. However, the parental interviews regarding the youngsters in my own population sample highlighted difficulties in 82 per cent of the cases.

Although interviews with parents gave a great deal of general background information, some details were difficult to record. With this in mind a parents' questionnaire was produced to ensure that accurate, comparable data was available from every interview (Table 3.1: *see also* Figure A.1 in Appendices).

Pre- and post-maturity were recorded as categories for birth before 38 weeks and after 42 weeks. Information regarding critical periods in utero, i.e. five weeks after conception and the third trimester, proved significant. Maternal weight gain during pregnancy was also noted and whether the child had any significant feeding difficulties. Some parents reported achievement of the usual developmental milestones until about approximately 14 months of age, when there appeared to be some deterioration in abilities.

Table 3.1 Parental questionnaire

Background information

Is X your first child? If not, what is his position in the family?
How old were you (mother) at the time of birth?
Is there any family incidence of learning difficulty, e.g. dyslexia, dyspraxia, autism, ADHD or diagnosed genetic condition?

Personal details

Can you remember whether you had any illness during your pregnancy?
Did nausea persist beyond the third month?
How did your weight progress?
When did you have your scan and was it repeated later during pregnancy? Were there any concerns?
Was there anything unusual about the last trimester (6–9 months in utero)?
Did you maintain a good diet?
Did you smoke during pregnancy?

Birth details

At what stage of pregnancy was X delivered, e.g. 34 weeks, 42 weeks?
Was X induced and if so what was the method of delivery?
Was there any indication of foetal distress before the birth?
How long was the labour? Obtain additional information regarding the second stage if possible.
Were there any concerns immediately after the birth?
What was the birth weight?

Developmental profile

Child presentation within the first four weeks.

- Levels of activity (e.g. hyper-, hypo- active)

- Feeding – was weight gain appropriate? Any evidence of lactose intolerance?

- Sleeping – settled quickly or very irritable with very short periods of sleep?

Motor skills

- Sitting independently at –

- Crawling at –

- Walking independently at –

Social skills

- Finger feeding at –

- Co-ordinating a knife and fork at –

- Toilet trained at –

Language

- Able to say 20+ distinguishable words at –

- Used 3+ words to construct simple phrases at –

Were there any other difficulties during the first 12 months?
Suggestions may be:

a) raised temperature/convulsion

b) jaundice

c) infections

Is there anything else you can remember that was of concern?
Has your child been assessed by anyone, e.g. paediatrician, speech therapist, physiotherapist or occupational therapist?

In order to determine whether there are areas of concern, it is important to have some general guidelines regarding expected developmental profiles.

The cells which will divide and subsequently form the nervous system are present five weeks after conception. The brain continues to develop throughout childhood, and its ability to process and interpret information is not complete until the child is at least 8. Although the brain develops in an orderly manner, there are significant differences between boys and girls in the early stages. The left hemisphere (language centre) appears to become more specialised in girls from the age of 2. Meanwhile, boys are developing their perceptual skills (predominantly right hemisphere) and enjoy constructional toys such as Lego and Duplo. It is necessary to take into account these developmental differences before deciding whether there is any significance in the delayed acquisition of a particular skill.

Between the ages of 5 and 6, thinking skills progress in a more predictable sequence. The developing sensory and motor systems are the foundations for the development of verbal and abstract thought. Skills such as reading and writing require complex co-ordination of these systems, and children who have not achieved sufficient sensory motor integration will experience learning difficulties. For any youngster whose neural system is developing more slowly than those of his peers, psychological barriers to progress are in place before formal schooling begins.

As the child progresses towards recognised developmental milestones, some features emerge which are indicative of dyspraxia. It is important to recognise that statements which are true in the majority of cases may not apply to every individual. It is crucial that all aspects of the child's development and achievements are considered before any diagnosis is given. The following tables describe expected behaviours of a child at 6–12 months, 24 months and 36 months. Characteristics evident in youngsters given a diagnosis of dyspraxia are listed alongside. Descriptions of the child refer to 'he' rather than 'he/she' because the incidence of the condition is so predominantly male-biased.

Table 3.2 Observable behaviours at 6–12 months

Social skills	
Expected behaviours	**Indications**
Easily comforted by voice or adult physical contact	Takes time to be comforted Can present as very irritable
Feeds well, contented after a meal	Feeding difficulties, colic reported after 3 months and milk allergies
Enjoys a variety of foods	Diet can be quite restricted
Adapts to good sleeping routine by 6 months	Sleeping difficulties. Seeks constant adult reassurance
Drinks from a feeder cup and finger-feeds	Food and other objects frequently mouthed
Enjoys having a bath	Can become distressed and show early dislike of water (up to 6 months)
Not distressed when left to play alone	Requires constant adult attention
Gross motor skills	
Rolls from back to stomach Sits unaided Crawls on hands and knees	Usually 'bottom-shuffles' and either does not go through the crawling stage or passes through very briefly
Pulls up to standing position	Sometimes cannot sit unaided at 9–12 months
Makes purposeful arm and leg movements, e.g. moves to pick up toy and then spends time actively playing with it	High levels of motor activity Repetitive arm and hand movements
	Sometimes additional repetitive head movements – 'rolling' and 'banging'

Fine motor skills	
Expected behaviours	**Indications**
Able to pick up small toys with either hand. Uses thumb and first finger in opposition to do so	Picks up objects using palmar 'fisted' grip
Passes toys between hands	Finds it difficult to locate small objects and is unable to manipulate a toy in each hand
Able to point with index finger	Uses right hand for activities on the right side of the mid-line and conversely the left

Language skills	
Enjoys listening to music. Responds to adult requests like: 'show me the ball'	Responds with distress to high noise level
Some single words	No evidence of emerging language skills
Listens to adult conversation and responds by making appropriate eye-contact and sounds	Is easily distracted from receiving verbal information without a high level of visual input

Reasoning ability	
Lifts toys from table and manipulates in direct line of vision Shows interest by smiling or making babbling sounds	May pick up a variety of toys but with fleeting interest: moves from one to another after only a few seconds
Shows awareness when toys are obscured from view, e.g. object hidden under a cup: child removes cup and shows understanding of the 'game'	Becomes irritated with 'hide and seek' game, has difficulty understanding the 'rules'

Table 3.3 Observable behaviours at 12–24 months

Social skills	
Expected behaviours	**Indications**
Assists with dressing: is able to remove shoes and socks and can take arms out of an unfastened coat	Shows no interest in dressing
Drinks from a handled cup appropriately and feeds with a spoon	Feeding continues to be messy Limited control of spoon
Eats food with variable texture.	May require food to be processed to remove the 'lumps'
Bladder control emerging, usually dry during the day	Often does not achieve toilet skills until 36+ months
Bladder and bowel frequency appropriate	May have problems with bowels: stools often hard and difficult to pass
Begins to share toys and work co-operatively with other children	Happy with his own company – isolated play Exhibits extreme uncontrolled temper tantrums
Gross motor skills	
Walks competently backwards and forwards and jumps from a low step, feet together	Often walking is not achieved until 18+ months Is not able to jump
Runs and is able to climb up and down stairs	Appears to be unsteady, falls easily and may move with a wide gait
Can kick a ball with either foot	Unable to lift one foot without overbalancing
Shows interest in pedal toys, e.g. cycle	Prefers sit-astride toys which do not need the co-ordination of hands and feet
Can throw a small ball with either hand	Difficulty directing movement

Fine motor skills	
Expected behaviours	**Indications**
Starts to show preference for right or left hand	May not establish hand-dominance until 4+ years
Plays constructively, building towers of 6+ bricks or stacking beakers.	Shows little interest in constructional activities. Finds tower building very difficult.
Replaces pegs in pegboard	Problems manipulating pegs and takes longer to complete the task
Enjoys water play, pouring between different containers	Enjoys water play but usually pours from container back into trough
Enjoys scribbling with crayons on paper	Has difficulty holding the crayon
Can make horizontal, vertical and circular strokes	Grip may be unnecessarily 'tight'
Language skills	
Vocabulary comprising 20/30 words Makes simple sentence construction like: 'There is the car'	May make initial sounds like 'mm' but has difficulty saying single words. Difficulties with articulation rather than comprehension
Enjoys listening to stories and likes looking at books. Makes 'singing' noises and actions to some nursery rhymes	Interest in books may be fleeting Listens to nursery rhymes but finds it difficult to make appropriate actions at the right time
Reasoning ability	
Enjoys completing popular form-boards with 3 insets. Can replace ○, □ and △	Has great difficulty manipulating shapes into the correct position Becomes very frustrated and distressed
Enjoys completing simple jigsaw puzzles	Completely avoids this type of activity
Constructs large 'Lego' pieces	Dislikes or avoids these activities

Table 3.4 Observable behaviours at 24—36 months

Social skills	
Expected behaviours	**Indications**
Uses a spoon and fork appropriately	Feeding continues to be messy: prefers to use fingers
Beginning to form social relationships and play co-operatively with other children. Uses language to communicate, with additional use of gestures	Limited social communication: disadvantaged because of language difficulties. Continues to be emotional and easily distressed
Makes demands but accepts a verbal explanation of refusal	May exhibit prolonged periods of distress which are a response to high levels of frustration
Shared and singular activities extend to period of 15 minutes	Unable to stay in one place for periods in excess of 2–3 minutes
Sleeps undisturbed for 10-12 hours	Sleeping difficulties may persist
Gross motor skills	
Balance improves: child can stand on one foot for 6-10 seconds	Unable to balance on feet separately
Walks on tiptoes with arms moving loosely at either side	Walks on tiptoes with poor balance and hands showing associated mirror movements. (Arms move outwards and hands bend backwards from the inside)
Able to ascend a climbing frame with confidence, placing one foot on each rung	Dislikes climbing activities Can be anxious about heights
Performs running and jumping activities with arms held alongside body	Runs in unco-ordinated manner with arms above waist level.
Can pedal a tricycle and change direction appropriately	Exhibits high levels of motor activity
Uses language in conjunction with increased activity when excited	Continues to have difficulty co-ordinating handles and pedals May engage in repetitive behaviour such as hand clapping or vigorous rubbing of thumb against forefingers of both hands when excited

Fine motor skills	
Expected behaviours	**Indications**
Able to copy simple shapes such as ○, □	May still be at the scribbling stage. Tends to avoid using writing implements
Able to thread a sequence of large beads	Unable to co-ordinate this activity
Can cut out large shapes with scissors	Difficult to use as hand-dominance is not yet established. Look for associated movements with other hand

Language skills	
Sentences extend to 6+ syllables 'My dolly is called Meg'	Developing a single-word vocabulary: may frequently use the same sentence to generalise meaning, e.g. 'Want drink' which may refer to any type of food
	Uses gestures to convey meaning
Able to repeat some nursery rhymes and make appropriate actions	Unable to co-ordinate actions with rhyme
	Loses interest easily
Enjoys looking at books and understands that the words convey meaning	Concentration presents major difficulties
Can follow commands such as 'Put the car on the box'	Confuses 'on', 'in' and 'under'

Reasoning ability	
Extended play with constructional toys Enjoys 6+ piece formboards and simple jigsaw puzzles	Any activity which has a motor skill component is difficult and usually avoided
Beginning to have some concept of numbers. Can select the 'big' toy from choice of 2 or 3 items	Conceptual understanding is usually age-appropriate but communication of ideas presents problems

Table 3.5 Summary of behaviours at 0–3 years

- irritable and difficult to comfort – from birth
- requires constant adult attention to alleviate anxiety
- feeding difficulties: milk allergies, colic, reflux problems, tolerates a restricted diet
- sleeping difficulties: problems establishing routine, requires constant adult reassurance
- delayed early motor development: sitting unaided, rolling from side to side, does not usually go through crawling stage as baby
- high levels of motor activity: constantly moving arms and legs
- repetitive behaviours: head banging or rolling
- sensitive to high levels of noise, or changes in light intensity
- continued problems with development of feeding skills
- toilet training may be delayed sometimes with evidence of bowel problems
- avoids constructional toys such as jigsaw puzzles and Lego
- delayed language development: single words not evident until age 3 – problems with articulation not comprehension
- highly emotional: easily distressed, frequent outbursts of uncontrolled behaviour
- concentration limited to 2/3 minutes on any task

Parents are aware almost from birth that their child is having difficulty acquiring particular skills. The majority of youngsters will have had significant feeding problems, presented as very irritable babies, poor sleepers, and constantly demanding adult attention for reassurance. The development of gross and fine motor-skills will have been delayed. Many parents report that they were made to feel they were worrying without good cause and were 'over-anxious'. Parents usually have greater insight into their children's behaviour than 'professionals' and too frequently their concerns are minimised. Parents have witnessed the extreme difficulty and distress experienced by their children trying to acquire basic skills such as feeding and dressing themselves.

Often, when the youngster finally transfers into a structured setting, like nursery or play-group, staff who are able to observe the child as he settles into the routine confirm parents' anxieties. Parents are usually relieved by this acknowledgement as in many instances they really believe that it is 'something much worse'. A diagnosis is of benefit to the child and the family so that information regarding the nature of the condition can assist those involved with the child to understand his difficulties. Without intervention, a dyspraxic child grows into a dyspraxic adult.

The assumption that children 'simply grow out of it' has not been supported by the past 20 years of longitudinal research. There is strong evidence that in the majority of cases, problems persist well into adolescence and beyond. My own research (Chapter 9) suggests that adults who have not had their dyspraxia recognised 'grow into' many other associated conditions. Early identification must reduce significantly the emotional and psychological distress that the condition can generate.

Observable behaviours between 3 and 5 years

Objective observational assessment can be undertaken if the child attends regular provision away from home. In the nursery environment the child is presented with a series of structured and more complex activities. The child's responses in a variety of settings can be recorded.

Social skills

Children with dyspraxia present higher levels of motor activity and limited concentration. Many continue to experience difficulties using the toilet, which is often the result of dietary problems. Some are unable to effect adequate muscular control over their bowels. Finger feeding, which can be a source of embarrassment to parents is often the only method by which food can be safely transported from the plate to the mouth. These youngsters are often excluded from co-operative games enjoyed by other children because their behaviour is too erratic.

Remembering more than two or three instructions is very difficult, so they cannot always follow the rules. Excitable behaviour is perceived by other children as immature and intentionally spoiling the game. Sensitivity to touch is poorly developed and dyspraxic children may be viewed as deliberately rough or aggressive. They have difficulty determining their position in space and easily bump into others. This can be very irritating to other children in the group. The need to change activity frequently often results in wanting access to materials which are being used. Turn taking is a problem because these children require immediate gratification. The disputes which follow remove the dyspraxic child farther from gaining acceptance within the class group.

Gross motor skills

The dyspraxic child may bump frequently into static objects. He may trip easily and appear accident-prone. Associated movements will be evident when motor activities are performed. The child is unable to separate out messages and direct them to particular limbs. Consequently, when running, both arms will be raised and the movement will appear unco-ordinated. Jumping and hopping also produce associated hand movements. Difficulties with hand-functioning can be observed. If the child is required to throw or catch a large ball he will be unable to stand still while doing so. If one hand only is involved in the throw, the other performs similar movements – like a six-week baby attempting to reach and grasp using both arms, although the toy is located on one side of the body. Even when he is seated to perform manipulative tasks, like building or measuring, leg movements such as feet tapping or swinging are characteristic of a dyspraxic child.

During outdoor play sessions the child prefers not to sit on the pedal toys as he will find it impossible to co-ordinate the required leg movements. The climbing frame is another source of anxiety as the child has poor figure–ground awareness and cannot gauge the height of the equipment. It may appear that the child is totally unconcerned for his safety as he launches himself from the uppermost level of the apparatus, but this apparent absence of fear is because at this stage he does not perceive the potential danger.

Fine motor skills

The snack table can be a distressing experience for the dyspraxic child if a routine is not established. Eating and holding a cup for drinking can still present major problems. Frequently the child is singled out by other youngsters because the drink always ends up either on his clothes or dripping from the edge of the table on to the floor. Jigsaw puzzles, formboards and other constructional toys are avoided as they are a major source of frustration. Although the child knows exactly how the pieces fit together his hands are unable to manipulate them. Dyspraxic youngsters have difficulty achieving a good pencil grip, so drawing and colouring skills are immature. Copied shapes such as a circle and square are recognisable but are usually not joined, e.g. drawings of people are recognisable but immature (Figure 3.1). Laterality is usually not established until 5–6 years; when tracing around objects the dyspraxic child may draw round the right side of the shape with his right hand and then change to his left hand to complete the figure. He has difficulty crossing the mid-line: activities set out on the right side of the body will be performed with the right hand and conversely the left hand executes tasks positioned on the left.

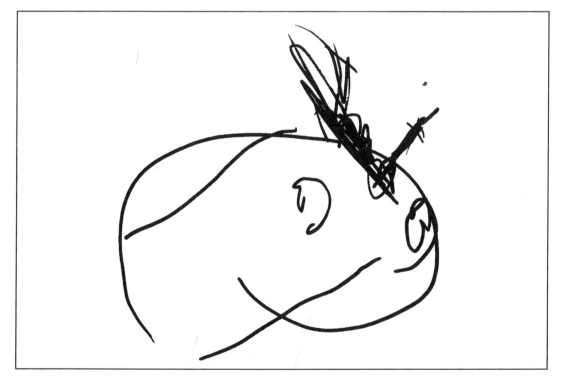

Figure 3.1 Drawing of myself by William, aged 5

Threading beads and using scissors to cut around large shapes are skills expected of a child transferring from nursery to reception class. Mastery of these tasks is not usually achieved by a dyspraxic child until 6–7 years.

Language skills

Verbal communication skills may be significantly delayed. Parents will express concern that speech cannot be understood by unfamiliar adults. The child may still be at the single-word level and even these words can be indistinct. The child will try to convey meaning using gestures and will become frustrated when they cannot be interpreted. Dyspraxic children have poor sound discrimination and will not be able to separate out verbal instructions if there is a high level of background noise. Voice-tone may vary. Some children will appear to 'shout' most of the time and the pitch may alter if the child becomes excited.

Where there is evidence of language difficulty, it is usually a motor problem in the way the lips, tongue and palate co-ordinate to produce the sound. The product is therefore indistinct and can often be interpreted only by those who are familiar with the child. The content itself is usually age-appropriate: e.g. one 5-year-old child said: 'e-d, I ,-a, -a,-i-d, -a-d' meaning: 'Yesterday I had a birthday party'. Where there are problems with the content, and the language is disordered, it is probable that another condition exists.

The dyspraxic child is emotional and exhibits frequent temper tantrums which reflect the mismatch between the child's understanding of the surrounding environment and his ability to operate control over it. Language development is slow and problems may continue to be evident until the child is well into primary education.

Reasoning ability

When a child experiences difficulty with perceptual and motor skills his reasoning ability is affected. It is important to recognise that the performance of these youngsters does not reflect their true intellectual ability.

The transmission of information along the neural pathways of a dyspraxic child, is a lengthy process; consequently the youngster executes instructions more slowly. If the children is are asked to gather together for story-time, the dyspraxic child will continue to play in the water while the rest of the group responds to the request. This is not a deliberate act of defiance: it is merely a problem with the speed of information-processing. Poor concentration skills persist and many tasks are left unfinished. Dyspraxic children often lack creativity in play and this is yet another feature which isolates them from their peers and is further compounded by additional language difficulties.

Problems with sequencing and the conceptual understanding of 'time' are also characteristics of dyspraxic pre-school children. Events are described in the present tense and they may not understand the notion of 'morning' and 'afternoon'. If they are asked to sequence several shapes ranging from small to large, a random pattern will often result. Sequencing picture cards to make a story will highlight similar problems. It is the organisation of the task and knowing where to begin which are the greatest obstacles. In addition the need

Table 3.6 Summary of behaviours at 3–5 years

- **Very high levels of motor activity**
  - feet swinging and tapping when seated
  - hands clapping or twisting
  - unable to stay in one place longer than 5 minutes

- **Very excitable**
  - voice loud and shrill
  - easily distressed, temper tantrums

- **Moves awkwardly**
  - constantly bumping into objects and falling
  - associated mirror movements, hands flap when running or jumping
  - difficulty pedalling tricycle or similar toy

- **Poor fine motor skills**
  - pencil grip
  - use of scissors
  - immature drawings

- **Poor figure–ground awareness**
  - no sense of danger, jumps from inappropriate heights

- **Avoids constructional toys**
  - jigsaw puzzles
  - building blocks (Lego)

- **Lack of imaginative play**
  - does not enjoy 'dressing up' or playing appropriately in the home-corner or Wendy-house

- **Limited creative play**
  - isolated in peer group
  - rejected by peers, prefers adult company

- **Laterality still not established**
  - problems crossing mid-line

- **Language difficulties persist**
  - children often referred to speech therapist

- **Limited response to verbal instructions**
  - slower response time
  - problems with comprehension
  - limited concentration, tasks often left unfinished

- **Continues to be messy eater**
  - often spills liquid from drinking cups
  - prefers to use fingers to feed

- **Sensitive to sensory stimulation**
  - dislikes high levels of noise
  - dislikes being touched or wearing new clothes.

to engage constantly in motor activity – swinging legs, clapping hands – distracts the child from successfully completing the task.

The dyspraxic child is deemed to be failing long before he reaches the age of 5. Motor development and language skills are implicit in any assessment process at this age. Any test of cognitive ability relies heavily on the child's ability to respond verbally or execute the task manually. To score in a standardised assessment under the heading 'Reasoning skills/cognitive ability', the child is required to:

0–12 months	Hold cubes Manipulate objects Click bricks together Find a toy under a cup
12–24 months	Open boxes Put lid on box Open a screw toy Complete three-piece formboard
24–36 months	Identify 'big' and 'little' Discriminate between two coins Complete six-piece formboard Repeat three digits
4 years	Build a bridge Complete 11-piece formboard Count to five Compare two weights
5 years	Build a gate Talk about the concept of time: yesterday, tomorrow Count 15+ bricks Manipulate blocks to complete a pattern (time-limit)

Consequently he will appear to have delayed cognitive skills if his ability is assessed using tests which have a bias towards language and motor skills to determine cognitive functioning. There is further discussion relating to cognitive profiles in Chapter 4.

Observable behaviours between 5 and 7 years

Problems which may have been identified previously by parents or teachers become more apparent and other difficulties may emerge. On entry to full-time education the child becomes part of a much more structured environment. Activities which might have been avoided in the nursery are an integral part of the daily routine.

Social skills

The routine itself may present significant problems for dyspraxic children. They find it difficult to sequence events and do not always remember to dress themselves in outdoor wear before going into the playground. They cannot understand why all the other children move back into school when the whistle is blown. The rest of the class is seated and ready to begin work with pencils out and pages opened before Danny returns from the cloakroom after spending ten minutes struggling with his coat. He is upset anyway because he wasn't allowed to join a game of tag. He has been publicly rebuked: 'You can't run, you just push and spoil the game'. Danny is questioned about his lateness: he can't find any reasons, his eye-contact is poor and he stares at the ceiling wondering perhaps what is on the menu for lunch. He is accused of not listening, and instructed to go to his seat.

Gross motor skills

While trying to listen intently to the next set of instructions he swings too far backwards on his chair. The class is disrupted again and Danny's 'behaviour' is becoming increasingly concerning for the class teacher. Unfortunately, everyone has been directed to the hall for PE. Danny hates PE. Everyone laughs at him. The unintentionally sexist directions are given which emphasise still further his failure to conform. 'When the music starts I want the girls to walk around the outside of the hall and the boys to jump on the spot. When the music stops all change, boys walk round and girls jump'.

The music starts and Danny enthusiastically begins to move with a quick marching step in a clockwise manner. He slowly realises that he is the only boy doing so. He slows down, trying to merge with the group in the centre, and starts to jump. He hasn't realised that by this time the music has stopped and only the girls are jumping. The children are then divided into pairs. It has to be done that way because no-one would ever choose Danny as a partner. It is to be a simple catching game. A large soft ball is thrown from one child to the other. Danny can't properly judge the ball's position in space and the speed at which it travels. He stands with his legs in a wide, awkward stance and almost falls before the ball is thrown to him. His tongue is protruding and he licks his lips anxiously as he waits. The ball arrives and he flings his arms wildly into space. His arms cross somewhere in the region of his chest and his attempt to catch has sent the ball to the opposite end of the hall.

Fine motor skills

Danny is pleased to change out of his PE strip. He puts on his trainers, with Velcro fasteners (he thinks he will never be able to master the skills required to tie shoe laces) and thinks it will be easier to tie the sleeves of his jumper around his waist than attempt to put it on. Back in the classroom he picks up his pencil to complete the maths, which is still unfinished. Danny knows how many fish to add to the line to make 14 but they look more like tennis balls than sea creatures. His hand aches because he grips his pencil so tightly. Sometimes there is even a slight tremor when he has to write or draw for a long time. His work always looks messy. The pencil seems to make smudge marks all over the page. Even when the teacher writes 'good work' or places a 'sticker' at the end of the page he knows she doesn't really mean it because it always looks so untidy. Sometimes Danny becomes so angry with his written work that he rips it up and scribbles over it before anyone can see it. His name was barely legible, a mixture of upper and lower case letters. He just can't master the shapes.

Thank goodness it's lunch time! He supposes he will probably be at the back of the queue. Danny finds it impossible to stand still and is always being accused of deliberately pushing into other children. Once, he fell against the fire bell and the whole school was evacuated. When Danny started in the reception class he had enjoyed sitting down to eat with the other children. By the end of the first term no-one wanted to sit next to him. He was unable to co-ordinate a knife and fork and his food was usually scattered over the rest of the table. The problem was avoided when he changed from school dinners to packed lunch: sandwiches, crisps, an apple and a boxed drink with a straw presented fewer problems.

Language skills

Danny's verbal communication skills had improved considerably after having regular access to speech therapy. He was referred when he was three because his vocabulary comprised ten indistinct words. His articulation was now age-appropriate but he would easily lose the thread of a conversation if more than three ideas were contained in a sentence. He still confused words when speaking quickly, like 'I'm taking my school to bike,' and sentences were taken literally. For example, when asked to stand on his toes, he placed one foot on top of the other.

Reasoning ability/cognitive skills

Danny's class teacher thought he was lazy. Written work was never completed in the allotted time. His concentration span at best varied between five and ten minutes, depending on the task and he constantly wandered around the classroom. He did not enjoy the privilege of taking messages because he could never remember them.

Although he gave good answers in class discussion, his ability was measured mostly by the responses he was able to commit to paper. He was unable to set his work out appropriately on the page. His writing was illegible to anyone but himself, although he could read back stories from several months previously (see Figure 3.2).

The best part of the day for Danny was the session in the afternoon after play. That was the time for individual reading. His measured ability was two years above his chronological age, but despite this achievement Danny was unable to excel. When reading aloud his tone was flat and monotonous. His pitch varied from line to line and the words were usually pronounced at varying speeds.

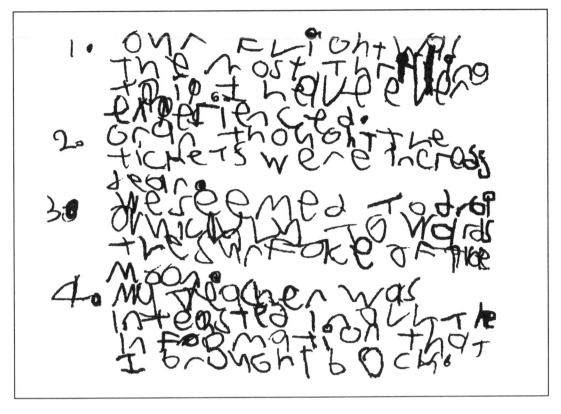

Figure 3.2 Sample of Danny's handwriting, age 7

Behaviour out of school

At home Danny's parents were observing more difficulties. He was constantly on the go, and appeared restless even when watching his favourite television programme. He was very excitable and when a 'funny' character came on the screen he jumped off his seat and clapped his hands vigorously. Danny had always had erratic sleeping patterns and a bedtime routine had still not been established. He frequently woke during the night complaining of nightmares.

Although he was tolerated by his 4-year-old brother, he had no friends of his own age. Temper tantrums were becoming more frequent and he was irritated by the labels in the back of his clothes. His parents were very concerned that he spent most of his time at home alone in his bedroom, reading or using the computer.

He refused to join in games of Snap or Picture Lotto and would not help his brother build models with Lego or Mega Bloks.

Standardised assessment of children aged between 5 and 7 years

Although many observable behaviours are evident at the pre-school stage, many dyspraxic youngsters are not referred to outside agencies until they reach 6 or 7 years. As discussed earlier, it is often the confirmation by teachers when the child is in a more structured setting that results in further investigation of his difficulties.

Opinions differ as to the proportion of dyspraxic youngsters in the population. Laslo and Bairstow claim that 10 per cent of all 7-year-olds are affected. Gilberg offers a more conservative estimate of between 1 per cent and 3 per cent being significantly affected. My research suggests that probably nearer 6 per cent of all youngsters have difficulties sufficiently significant to require intervention.

In Scandinavian countries, where great emphasis is placed on developing gross motor skills up to the age of 7, the incidence of dyspraxia is reported as only 1 per cent – 2 per cent of the population. In Sweden, full-time state nursery education is available for children from 12 months of age. In recent years there has been a government initiative to take up sport. While incentives are offered to older pupils, encouragement is given in pre-school provision where children have access to extensive outdoor play equipment.

Among diagnosed dyspraxic children the ratio of boys to girls is 4:1. However, this ratio is not reflected in the number of youngsters referred for assessment. The ratio alters depending on the age of the children, and this is discussed in Chapter 5.

Observational assessment of the child's behaviour will give a general profile of ability. Social, motor, language and reasoning skills can be recorded at home and in the classroom. In addition, when a child is aged between 5 and 7 it is important to obtain more detailed information about cognitive ability and motor development as appropriate standardised assessments become available.

Youngsters with dyspraxia often have difficulties with ocular tracking – the motor-movement of the eye as it scans words or pictures. This can affect the child's ability to read fluently, particularly when speaking aloud. A specialist assessment should be sought if there are concerns.

As outlined in Chapter 2, motor movements reinforce the connections along selected neural pathways. Therefore it is the child's ability to execute specific motor tasks which gives an indication of the functioning in the cortex. As scans become more sophisticated they will enable clinicians to obtain specific information about particular areas of the brain. However, at present the usual clinical approach to the study of brain functions remains the neurological examination. Information is obtained by examining motor patterns and responses to testing of specific muscle groups. There are many standardised assessments available. The *Movement Assessment Battery for Children* (Henderson and Sugden 1992) is most commonly used. Children scoring below the tenth centile should be considered to exhibit a significant level of difficulty.

In addition, a full cognitive assessment should be completed. The Wechsler Intelligence Scales are standardised to be used with all school-age children and adults and give the required information. However, many articles state that the single most important factor in the diagnosis of dyspraxia is the comparison of the scores between performance and verbal IQ, the latter being significantly higher. Sydney Chu, in his article *The Diagnosis of Dyspraxia 1991*, expresses reservations with this 'diagnosis' as the test was not designed for this purpose. My research, which is detailed later, confirms the limitations of the discrepancy model of IQ scores. It is unhelpful to give the accumulative scores for verbal and performance IQ because that disguises the particular strengths in the child's cognitive profile. In addition the scaled scores in some of the sub-tests vary depending on the age of the child at the time of the assessment.

What is important is to assess whether there are significant discrepancies between individual sub-test scores. Those which are consistently lower in dyspraxic youngsters are arithmetic, digit span, coding and block design. Even then, there are some dyspraxic pupils who do not fit this pattern of development, and the final diagnosis depends on the experience of the clinician.

Table 3.7 Summary of behaviours at 5–7 years

- Problems adapting to a more structured school routine
- Difficulties evident in PE
- Slow at dressing – unable to tie shoe laces
- Handwriting barely legible
- Immature drawing – including copying skills
- Limited concentration and poor listening skills
- Literal use of language – problems with articulation
- Remembers only 2 or 3 instructions
- Classwork completed slowly
- Continuing high levels of motor activity
- Motor stereotypes – hand flapping or clapping when excited
- Easily distressed, very emotional
- Problems co-ordinating a knife and fork
- Unable to form relationships with other youngsters – appears isolated in the class group
- Sleeping difficulties – wakes during the night and reports nightmares
- May report physical symptoms - migraine, headaches, feeling sick.

4 Observable characteristics

Parents have concerns about their child's development from a very early stage, usually before 6 months. Friends and professionals will want to offer their reassurance but parents would benefit more from an acknowledgement of these difficulties.

From birth, it is probable that dyspraxic youngsters will present as hyperactive and extremely irritable, and have some feeding problems. They may have bouts of sickness, with extreme colic. They require constant adult attention, day and night, and are generally very poor sleepers. Some have very poor weight gain during the first six months and may be identified as 'failing to thrive'.

There is evidence of delayed motor milestones, e.g. independent sitting, crawling and walking. The majority of dyspraxic youngsters fail to go through the crawling stage, preferring to bottom-shuffle before they walk independently, usually between 16 and 18 months of age.

Approximately 50 per cent of the youngsters in my current sample population had some difficulty acquiring language skills. They developed a single-word vocabulary at the age of 3, but articulation was poor and only familiar adults were able to identify all of the speech sounds.

The recent green paper (October 1997) *Excellence for all Children*, presented by the Secretary of State for Education and Employment, David Blunkett, highlights the need for early identification of learning difficulties:

> The best way to tackle educational disadvantage is to get in early. When educational failure becomes entrenched, pupils can move from demoralisation to disruptive behaviour and truancy. But early diagnosis and appropriate intervention improves the prospects of children with special educational needs, and reduces the need for expensive intervention later on. For some children, giving more effective attention to early signs of difficulty can prevent the development of special educational needs…an integrated approach by child health professionals, social services and education staff is needed right from the start, making full use of the children's services planning process. (DfE 1997)

In some instances, despite parents' best efforts to have their children's difficulties recognised, confirmation comes only after entry to educational provision. This could be the pre-school play-group, nursery or reception class.

In 1994, statistics suggested that the majority of youngsters referred for assessment were in Years 4, 5 and 6 of primary education. Examination of my own case load from 1996 to 1998 indicates an increasing awareness of the benefits of early referral and intervention. Many youngsters now receive appropriate intervention programmes delivered at Stage 3 of the Code of Practice and several terms later move back down the stages. Later referral increases the probability of pupils passing from Stage 3 to Stage 5 and the likelihood of greater evidence of emotional and behavioural problems.

Referral for assessment was often the outcome for a child who:

- appeared to be bright and verbally articulate but who was unable to transfer thoughts to paper

- had very poor concentration and could remain on task only for periods up to five minutes

- showed evidence of such extreme behavioural difficulties that his work and that of the rest of the class was suffering.

More recently requests are made when, after discussion with parents, teacher observation suggests that:

- the child, although only 3 years of age, has problems expressing himself verbally and is already choosing to isolate himself within his peer group

- he appears to enjoy outside play but he is constantly tripping and falling over. He avoids the construction table and finds it difficult to concentrate at story-time

- the child's parents are concerned about the limited variety of foods he will eat, his erratic sleeping pattern and problems with toilet training.

These behaviours, which are characteristic of youngsters with developmental dyspraxia, have been discussed in the previous chapter. The purpose of this chapter is to determine whether observational assessment alone can give an accurate diagnosis.

Early development

The starting point of any assessment is to obtain a detailed profile of the child's early developmental history and determine whether there were any significant factors at an earlier age which may have contributed to the present difficulties. Have there been any medical problems? In more than 70 per cent of the cases in my current sample, the developmental profile was as shown in Figure 4.1.

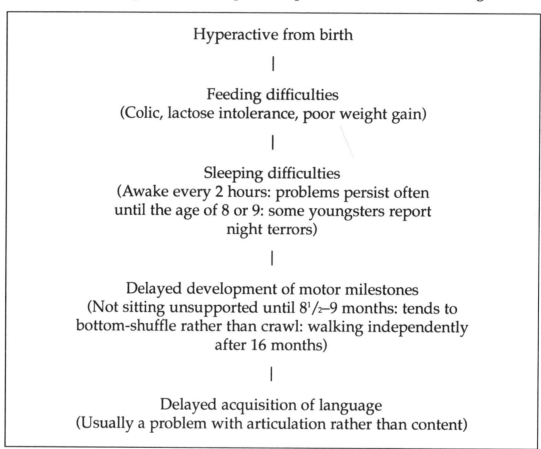

Figure 4.1 Developmental profile

In addition to motor difficulties the child will have perceptual problems and as a consequence will avoid constructional play like Duplo and Lego, jigsaw puzzles and formboards. He finds it difficult to sequence sounds, and will rely heavily on information he can receive visually. Relatively young children watch some adult serial programmes on television and follow the story line: the child with dyspraxia will prefer the colourful cartoons such as Disney or pre-school favourites like Fireman Sam and Postman Pat which tell the story through pictures rather than words. This interest may continue well into full-time schooling and it may appear that the child's social interests are relatively immature.

Although laterality is usually established by the age of 3, the dyspraxic child finds difficulty deciding which hand to use for drawing and writing before the age of 6. Looking at evidence from my own sample population there appears to be a higher incidence of left-handedness in the population, of youngsters identified with dyspraxia: this occurs in the ratio of approximately 1:4, whereas in the general population it would be expected to occur at a rate of 1:8.

It is important to obtain the views of parents and teachers and identify the major areas of concern. Some behaviours may be evident in one setting and not in another.

Attainment tests

The dyspraxic youngster relies heavily on his strengths to overcome his weaknesses. Generally, reading ability follows the normal curve, with 50 per cent of youngsters below average and 50 per cent above. Although reading may be identified as a strength, when the child is asked to speak aloud the delivery can be hesitant, without punctuation and with a misuse of tone and pitch.

To spell accurately the child must be able to sequence the letter sounds appropriately. This presented far greater levels of difficulty for the youngsters in the sample, with only 15 per cent achieving a level commensurate with or above their chronological age.

Standardised assessments of reading and spelling, numeracy attainments and perceptual skills supplement information obtained from neuro-psychological assessment and the motor-skills screening, which are discussed in later chapters. A pro-forma is provided to record this data (Figure 4.2 *see also* Figure A2 in Appendices)

Assessment of handwriting

Assessment of handwriting skills is a factor which contributes to the diagnosis of dyspraxia. Speed of handwriting, pencil grip and muscle tone in the fingers should be recorded and, in addition, information about letter formation. In 90 per cent of the diagnosed cases of dyspraxia in the sample, particular features were evident. The child preferred to print rather than join up letters. The words were a mixture of upper and lower case letters with little or no punctuation. The pupil's lack of perception of space and shape was evident when words were started on one line, perhaps with only the first letter, and finished on the next. There was little evidence of spacing between the words. When the child was asked to repeat the exercise there was no evidence of improved writing skills even when additional time was allowed. Figures 4.3 and 4.4 are examples to illustrate these features.

Perceptual problems also present difficulties when the child is asked to record the answer. Although the conceptual understanding of mathematics may be within the average expected for his age, the ability to translate this understanding and record it manually is impaired. If the child sets out the numbers incorrectly on the page it is unlikely that he will arrive at the correct answer. Figure 4.5 is an example of the difficulty experienced by an 8-year-old child trying to reproduce his worksheet. Figure 4.6 is an example of an accommodation made for a 5-year-old child perceived as having difficulty reproducing his numbers.

Additional Information

Name... **DoB**....................

Reading Age	CA	Date
Spelling Age	CA	Date
Numeracy Attainments	CA	Date
Perceptual Skills	CA	Date

Comments

Figure 4.2 Record sheet

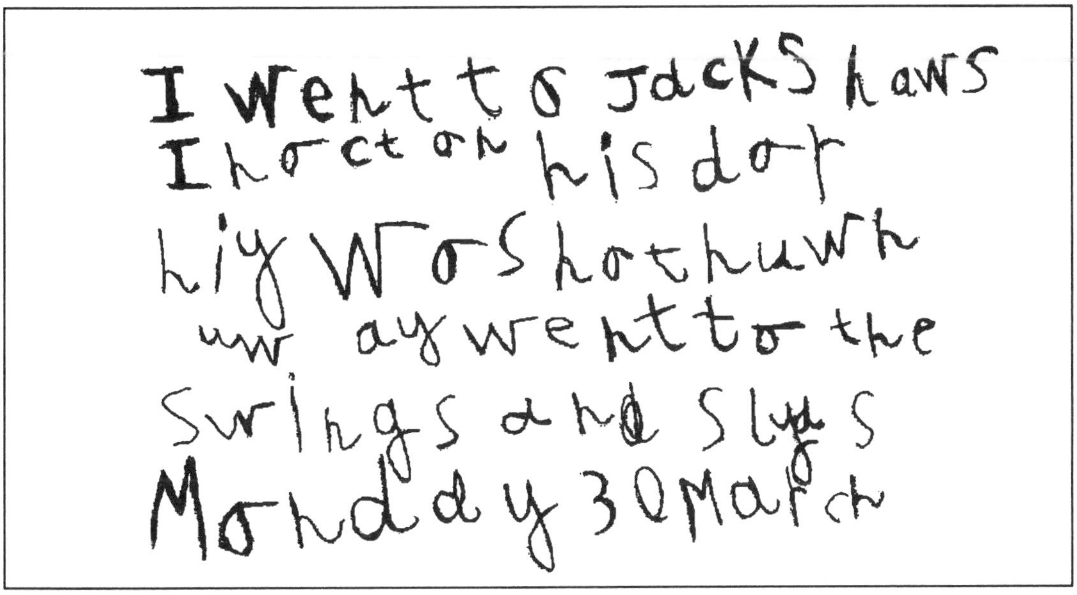

I went to jacks haws
I noct on his dor
liy wros hot huwh
uw ay went to the
Swings and slyds
Monday 30 March

Figure 4.3 Thomas, aged 9

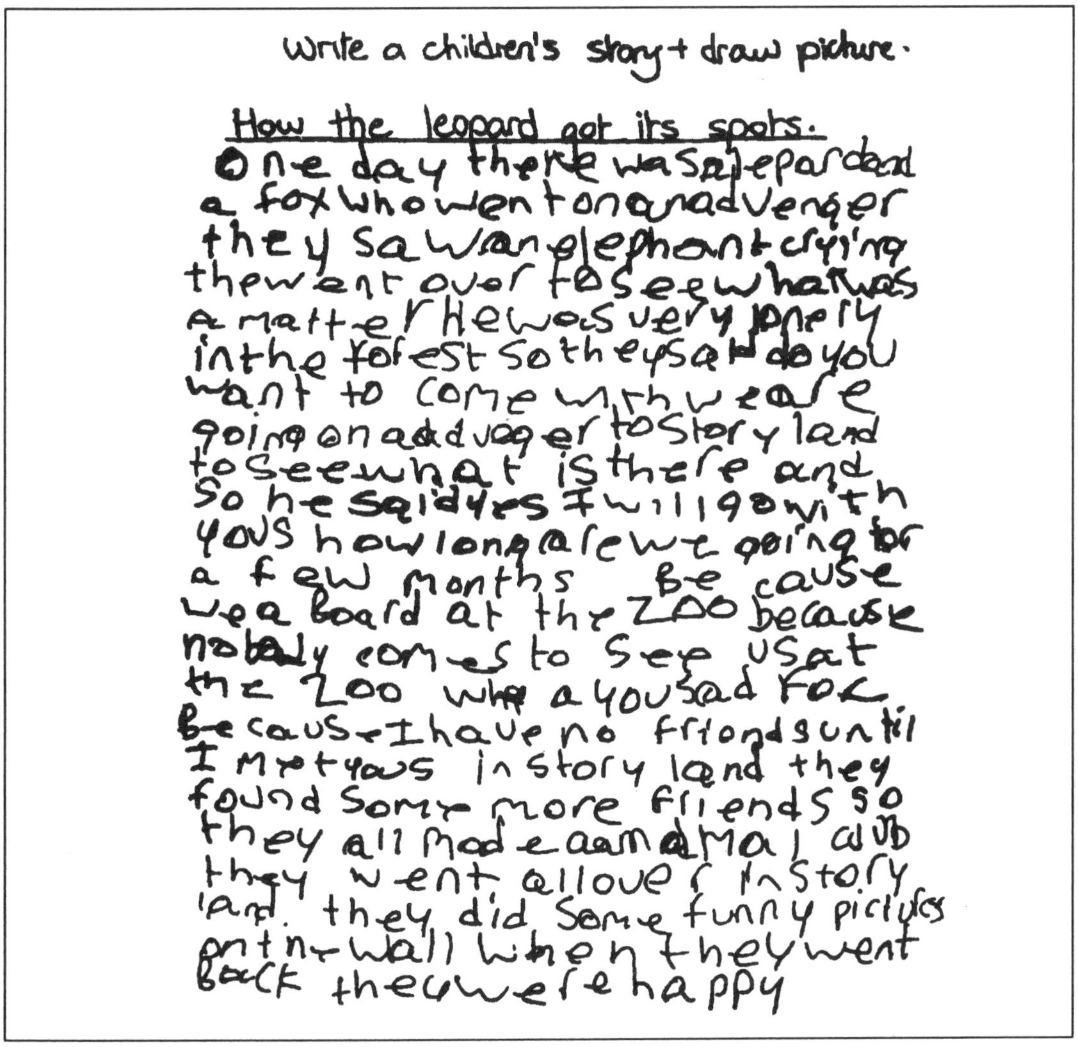

write a children's story + draw picture.

How the leopard got its spots.
One day there was a lepard and
a fox who went on an advenger
they saw an elephant crying
the went over to see what was
a matter he was very lonely
in the forest so they said do you
want to come with we are
going on addveger to story land
to see what is there and
so he said yes I will go with
yous how long are we going for
a few months be cause
we a board at the zoo because
nobady comes to see us at
the zoo what a you said fox
because I have no friends until
I met yous in story land they
found some more friends so
they all made a amamal club
they went allover in story
land. they did some funny pictures
on the wall when they went
back they were happy

Figure 4.4 Sam, aged 11

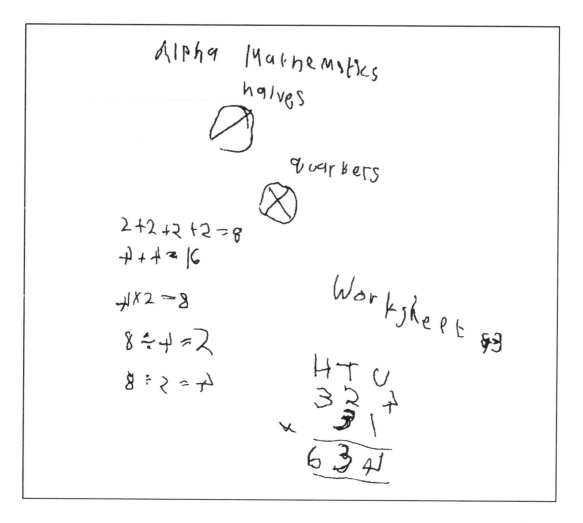

Figure 4.5 Matthew, aged 8

Matthew sets out some multiplication and division sums on the left side of the page The second calculation, 4 × 4, shows an incorrectly angled multiplication sign which reads 4 + 4. When the exercise is marked Matthew will not understand why this is incorrect. He knows 4 × 4 = 16. Why has the teacher marked it with a cross? In the next worksheet again Matthew cannot find a mistake. He placed 4 in the units column, then added 1 + 2 resulting in 3 being placed in the tens column and 3 + 3 makes 6. Matthew had taken much longer to complete the work than other members of his class. It had taken an hour and a great amount of effort to produce it. He was beginning to wonder whether it was worth the bother; most of it was wrong anyway.

Ben was given a maths work-book, appropriate for his age and ability. He was required to insert the correct numbers into the carriages of the train. It is evident from the first row he is misplacing the numbers and is consequently having difficulty achieving the correct answer (Figure 4.6).

In the next example Ben has been given a series of 'stick-on' numbers which have been appropriately placed. Wherever possible, teachers should address the recording difficulties these youngsters have and accommodate them wherever possible (Figure 4.7).

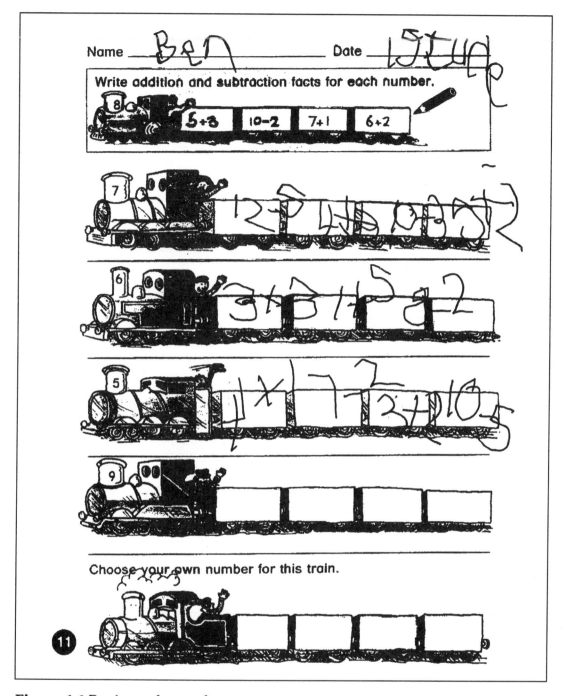

Figure 4.6 Ben's maths work

Cognitive assessment

Where pre-school children have been given the opportunity of a multi-disciplinary assessment, the outcome will be dependent on the particular tests used. It is usual, when assessing a young child, to use a developmental checklist, e.g. the Griffiths Mental Development Scales. Such assessments consider the following areas of development:

- gross and fine motor skills

Figure 4.7 Ben's maths work with teacher intervention

- personal/social development

- hearing and speech

- eye and hand co-ordination and performance.

The dyspraxic youngster will be expected to present an uneven profile of development, thus identifying specific strengths as well as weaknesses. With this assessment, given the developmental pattern expected, the child would show some delays in his gross and fine motor skills. He will have difficulties co-ordinating a knife and fork and may have additional toileting problems; therefore, social skills may be depressed. In 50 per cent of the cases of youngsters assessed there are significant speech problems; again it is the third area of assessment which shows developmental delay. Eye and hand co-ordination assesses features like hand-preference, reproducing lines in imitation, using scissors and copying shapes such as circles and squares. The dyspraxic child again will be identified as failing. The assessment of performance requires the child to complete successfully inset boards within a given time and reproduce the pattern on a template using blocks: a problem for the dyspraxic child. From the age of 2 a further category is introduced – 'practical reasoning'. Here, the requirement is to compare insets for size and identify 'which one is bigger?' Counting to ten is a requirement, as is the repetition of four numbers in sequence. Auditory sequencing is a particular problem for these youngsters.

The outcome of the assessment, instead of identifying particular strengths, will indicate that there are generalised learning difficulties. This is not an accurate reflection of the child's true ability. Where early developmental characteristics would suggest a diagnosis of developmental dyspraxia, a more accurate profile can be achieved using the Wechsler Pre-school and Primary Scale of Intelligence (WPPSI).

For children of primary school age, the Wechsler Intelligence Scale for Children (WISC) gives a comprehensive profile of the child's verbal and non-verbal ability. It enables the clinician to assess the intellectual ability of children aged from 6 years to 16 years 11 months. David Wechsler himself sounded a note of caution when he stated in 1979: 'Intellectual ability is only one aspect of intelligence. Those who are responsible for interpreting the results of intelligence testing must be careful to distinguish between test scores or IQs on one hand and intelligence on the other.' The purpose of the Wechsler assessments is to obtain a broad sample from an individual's full array of cognitive abilities to determine areas of particular strength or weakness. This assessment of neuropsychological function, i.e. the pattern of behaviours which gives information as to how the brain is operating, is confirmed by Kaplan *et al.* in their 1991 report that the qualitative interpretation of the individual performance in the sub-tests supports the notion that the Wechsler Intelligence Scales can be neuropsychological instruments.

The WISC III UK comprises 13 sub-tests which are divided into assessments of verbal and non-verbal ability.

Summary of sub-tests of the WISC III UK

Verbal scores	**Performance scores (Non-verbal)**
Information	Picture completion
Similarities	Coding
Arithmetic	Picture arrangement
Vocabulary	Block design
Comprehension	Object assembly
(Digit span)	(Symbol search)
	(Mazes)

The sub-tests identified in brackets are supplementary, but provide important additional information if they are completed.

Format and purpose of each sub-test

Information

The child is asked to respond verbally to a series of questions which assess his general knowledge. They reflect how well information about the environment is absorbed. As the child progresses through primary and on into secondary education, he is expected to absorb more factual data from books. The pupil with reading difficulties may have problems with this test.

Similarities

The child is presented with two words such as 'chair' and 'table' and asked to say why they are the same. This reflects the child's understanding of language. The child is encouraged to give as much detail as possible in his response.

Arithmetic

This test relates to the child's general intellectual ability and he is required to respond orally to questions of mental arithmetic. Some youngsters perform much better giving verbal responses than when required to write down the answer.

Vocabulary

The child is asked to give the definitions of a series of single words and is encouraged to give as much information as possible. He often inserts the word into a sentence to convey the meaning.

Comprehension

The child is presented with a series of questions beginning: 'What should you do if...?' The responses give an indication of the child's social code. This assessment differs from reading comprehension tests where the child is asked questions which relate to the passage in which the answer can be found.

Digit span

The child is asked to repeat a series of numbers of increasing length forwards and backwards. The scaled score is based on the combined raw scores for digits forwards and digits backwards which may involve different cognitive processes, especially in certain clinical groups. For example: a study by Rudel and Denckla (1974) found that children with developmental disorders involving right-hemisphere deficits had impaired performance. The performance of dyspraxic youngsters highlights significant weaknesses in repeating the digits backwards. This assessment measures short-term ability to retain auditory sequential information. This test requires concentration and can present difficulties for children with attention deficits.

Picture completion

A series of coloured pictures is presented to the child and he is asked to identify which part is missing. This sub-test assesses the child's ability to concentrate and analyse data presented visually to him.

Coding

Younger children are required to draw a symbol inside a series of simple shapes. Older children (8+) copy symbols under a series of numbers. Youngsters with a poor short-term visual memory or significant visual motor problems experience particular difficulty with this sub-test because they are required to concentrate and co-ordinate eye and hand movements at speed.

Picture arrangement

A set of cards, each a picture, is mixed up and presented to the child. He is required to rearrange them into the sequence which correctly relates the story. This assesses the child's visual sequencing ability.

Block design

The child is given initially four cubes and then, as the designs become more complicated, nine cubes. A two-dimensional pattern is placed in front of the child, who is then required to reproduce it using the cubes. This assesses the child's visual perceptual skills.

Object assembly

A set of jigsaw pieces is presented to the child who is required to assemble them in a recognisable form. The tasks become increasingly complex. This measures the child's ability to organise visually presented material into a whole from its component parts.

Symbol search

A series of paired groups of symbols is positioned on the left side of the page. The child scans the row to determine whether the symbols are present farther along. This requires concentration and the ability to co-ordinate eye movement to scan the page at speed.

Mazes

The child is given a starting point and, using a pencil, works his way through without crossing any of the lines. Good hand–eye co-ordination is needed.

The profile of scores achieved in the sub-tests of the WISC III UK can vary from one child to another. Some youngsters achieve such very low scores in some areas that it is unhelpful to calculate their overall verbal and performance intelligence quotient. What must be considered is whether there is a wide discrepancy between sub-test scores. Scaled scores achieved by dyspraxic youngsters vary according to age (see Chapter 5), but some tests appear to present particular difficulties in more than 90 per cent of dyspraxic youngsters: they are arithmetic, coding, and block design. Figures 4.8 and 4.9 represent two profiles.

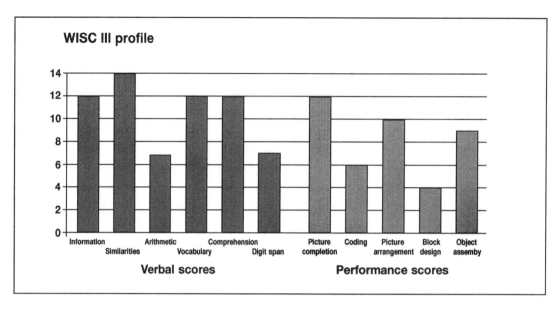

Figure 4.8 Sophie, aged 8 years 3 months

Interpretation of Figure 4.8

The scaled scores range from 1 to 19, where 10 is the average. Scores between 9 and 11 are in the average range. In the sub-tests administered, Sophie has achieved average scores in two, above average in five and below average in four. The assessment shows that in seven out of 11 sub-tests, Sophie's ability is average to above average. If the scores are converted into an intelligence quotient, Sophie has a verbal score of 103 and a performance score of 86 which suggests that her ability is average to low average. To ensure that Sophie has access to a curriculum which is stimulating, her strengths must be recognised and her specific visual-perceptual and visual-motor difficulties identified.

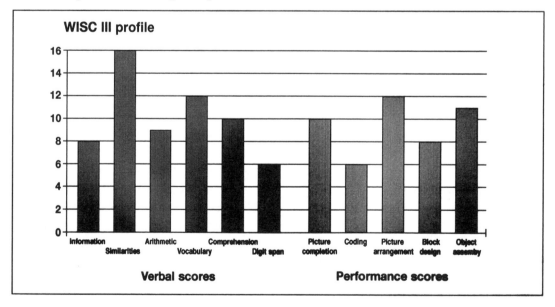

Figure 4.9 Paul, aged 10 years 2 months

Interpretation of Figure 4.9

In the sub-tests administered, Paul has achieved average scores in three, above average in four, and below average in four. Like Sophie, Paul's ability is average to above average in seven out of 11 sub-tests. Paul's verbal IQ is 101 and his performance IQ is 104. Contrary to some definitions of the criteria for a diagnosis of dyspraxia, Paul's performance score is higher than his verbal score. However, like Sophie, Paul has visual-perceptual and visual-motor problems but, in contrast, his visual sequencing and ability to create a picture from its components are good. The assessment also highlighted some difficulties with Paul's short-term auditory memory.

The cognitive assessments of Paul and Sophie showed that although they presented similar patterns of behaviour there were operational differences in the way they processed information.

Youngsters who present behaviours within the autistic spectrum have a different cognitive profile. With dyspraxia, picture arrangement is high in comparison with block design. Where children are given a diagnosis of autism, their perceptual skills are usually competent and they achieve a relatively high score in the block design sub-test. They find picture arrangement problematic.

When children have attentional problems they do less well on timed activities. They can be relatively competent in the block design sub-test if they are encouraged to remain on task. If the directions for administering the assessment are adhered to, these youngsters usually lose interest and perform badly.

Motor skills screening

The neuropsychological assessment of cognitive function does not in itself provide sufficient information to diagnose dyspraxia, as profiles vary markedly between individuals. Other factors which must be considered are:

- early developmental history
- curriculum attainments
- handwriting
- language development
- social/life skills.

The final part of the assessment is to evaluate the child's motor skills. As outlined in Chapter 2, motor patterns and the responses of specific muscle groups to testing give additional information about the way the brain is functioning. The child's performance in each of the sub-tests must be accurately recorded.

The purpose of the motor-skills screening is to identify major deficits and observe whether they follow a pattern. For example, the child may exhibit predominantly left-sided difficulties. This would suggest that the region of concern is the right hemisphere. (The right hemisphere controls the left side of the body and vice versa.) This may confirm details from previous assessments if the child appears to have poor perceptual skills (right-hemisphere activity) in comparison with age-appropriate language development.

The tests most frequently used to assess motor skills are:

• The Bruininks-Oseretsky Test of Motor Proficiency

• Movement Assessment Battery for Children.

These assessments are comprehensive, but can take in excess of an hour to administer. After working extensively with both, I compiled the Motor-Skills Screening which selects some activities from each and contains additional items from the Fog test, which screens for neurological difficulties. The motor-skills screening enables the assessor in approximately 20 minutes to identify youngsters aged 7+ who exhibit motor difficulties. The results from this screening, in addition to the cognitive assessment and the developmental history of the child, would confirm the diagnosis of dyspraxia.

Table 4.1 Motor skills screening

Motor Skills Screening		
Name... Date............................. Age...........................		
Walking	**Behaviour**	**Date**
1. Walking on toes forwards and backwards		
2. Walking on heels forwards and backwards		
3. Walking on insides of feet		
4. Walking on outsides of feet		
5. Recognising fingers touched when obscured from view. Right hand then left		
6. Finger sequencing – right then left		
7. Wrist rotation		
8. Balancing on each foot		
9. Touching end of nose with index finger of each hand (eyes closed)		
10. Jumping: feet together		

This pro-forma enables the assessor to record the behaviours observed during the assessment. It is important that all indications are detailed so that an effective remediation programme can be produced. Look for all associated mirror-movements and other physical signs such as tremors or tongue thrusting. Using the motor-skills screening the behaviours in Figure 4.10 would indicate a motor difficulty.

Activity

1. Walking on toes

Behaviour

Arms move outwards and hands bend at the wrist away from the body

Activity

2. Walking on heels

Behaviour

Arms held upwards from the elbow, hands bend upwards towards the body

Activity

3. Walking on insides of feet

Behaviour

Arms extended behind, hands bend turning away from the body

Figure 4.10 Associated movements (continued overleaf)

Activity

4.   Walking on outsides of feet

Behaviour

Arms bend outwards and wrists turn in

Activity

5.   Obscure one of the child's hands. The examiner touches two of the child's hidden fingers simultaneously. Ask the child to point out (with the other hand) those touched
Record 5 times with each hand

Behaviour

The child is consistently unable to identify the correct fingers

Activity

6.   Ask the child to sequence each finger against the thumb of the same hand, slowly at first, then more quickly. Test each hand separately, then try hands together

Behaviour

Look for associated movements with the relaxed hand. Usually the child mirrors the activity

Figure 4.10 Associated movements (continued)

Activity

7. Demonstrate and ask the child to rotate both wrists simultaneously with the thumbs moving towards and then away from each other

Behaviour

See whether the child can rotate his wrists without his elbows moving outwards

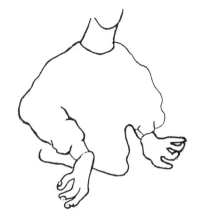

Activity

8. Ask the child to balance on each foot

Behaviour

The child should be able to achieve 10+ seconds on each foot

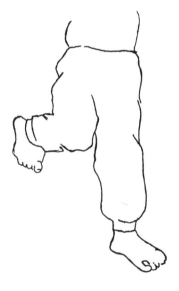

Activity

9. Demonstrate by standing in front of the child. Make a wide arc first with the right hand and then the left, and touch the end of your nose with the index finger of each. Make sure that eyes are closed

Behaviour

Child will probably distract the examiner by coughing at the last minute or will touch his nose with the whole of his hand

Figure 4.10 Associated movements (continued)

Activity

10. Ask the child to jump repeatedly with feet together

Behaviour
Problems will be observed in establishing the jumping routine. Elbows held tightly into waist, arms upwards and fists clenched

Figure 4.10 Associated movements (end of continued figure)

The assessments described in this chapter are also appropriate for youngsters in secondary education. Although the results in the cognitive profile follow a similar pattern, motor difficulties may become less evident.

Between the ages of 7 and 11, dyspraxic children develop strategies for survival. They have been excluded from their peer group and they strive desperately to belong. Some accept their isolation but develop school phobia. They complain of frequent headaches and stomach pains which rarely occur during holiday periods. Alternatively, they may be easily led and be directed to misbehaviour by the group leaders in the class. They accept that any attention, even if it is negative, is better than total exclusion.

Concentration is a major problem for dyspraxic youngsters, particularly during their primary school years. With access to a greater variety of curricular subjects in secondary education it is probable that in some subjects their attention will be improved. However, in later school years the dyspraxic child exhibits more extensive behavioural difficulties and is much more likely to suffer from depression.

Dyspraxic children continue to be extremely emotional and motor stereotypes such as hand-flapping persist when they become anxious or excited. The symptoms continue even when the children move on to further education. They do not 'grow out of it', and can benefit from intervention programmes even if they are not diagnosed until well into their teens.

5 Research evidence

This chapter examines data collected between 1988 and 1998 and determines the relationships between the assessment information and the youngsters' cognitive abilities, educational attainments and behaviour.

The sections consider:

• profiles of pupils using the Wechsler Pre-school and Primary Scale of Intelligence Revised (WPPSI-R UK) and the Wechsler Intelligence Scale for Children III UK (WISC-III UK)

• a study of eight pupils aged between 5 years 3 months and 6 years 8 months in an infants school

• a study of seven secondary pupils aged between 11 years 3 months and 13 years 9 months in a comprehensive school

• the case study of Thomas, aged 5 years 6 months.

Pupil profiles using the Wechsler Intelligence Scales

The Wechsler Scales enable the assessor to measure cognitive abilities of children from the age of 3 to adulthood. There is continuing debate about the reliability of instruments which measure those abilities in children under school age (3–5), because assessment using a developmental checklist, for example, can reflect the child's access to external factors rather than assess his 'potential'. A child who has not had access to a bike will not be able to pedal; a child who has not been encouraged to examine shapes and complete inset puzzles will not excel initially at fitting jigsaw pieces together. Knowledge of colours is dependent on the child having them named to him.

As the tasks in developmental assessments become more complex they align more closely with those found in standardised intelligence tests like the WPPSI. This comparison can be made if we consider the eye–hand co-ordination task of the Griffiths Mental Developmental Scales (Year III) and the geometric design section of the WPPSI. Both require the child to draw horizontal and vertical lines and reproduce a cross and a circle.

Although abilities such as spatial awareness, perceptual skills and language development are emerging by the age of 3 and can be measured successfully using psychometric assessments, dyspraxic children are severely disadvantaged. As outlined in Chapter 3 where developmental profiles were discussed at length, many emerging skills which could be expected to be present by the age of 3 do not develop until 5 or 6. This is confirmed by the results achieved by dyspraxic youngsters in psychometric tests. The WISC profiles alter with the age of the child. However, it is the magnitude of the deficit in significant sub-tests which alters, rather than the child's general ability profile. Adult profiles are discussed in Chapter 9.

The data collected since 1988 now comprises a total of 435 completed WPPSI-R, WISC-RS and WISC III assessments. They were categorised as follows:

- 57 WPPSI (41 male, 16 female), age range 3.2 years to 7.3 years

- 139 WISC-RS (126 male, 13 female), age range 7.7 years to 15.3 years

- 239 WISC-III (211 male, 28 female), age range 6.2 years to 16.10 years.

Note: The ratio of males to females in the WISC-III sample is heavily biased because of the inclusion of results from the 69 juveniles (all male) assessed at Deerbolt Young Offenders Institution: see Chapter 6.

Figure 5.1 shows combined average scaled scores achieved in each sub-test for the total sample population. Names of the sub-tests are derived from the WISC-III but the geometric design (WPPSI) is scored with the coding sub-test. The scores range between 1 and 19, the average being 9–11.

Averages for each sub-test were:

Verbal scores		Performance scores	
Information	9.86	Picture completion	9.2
Similarities	10.5	Coding	5.2
Arithmetic	6.2	Picture arrangement	10.4
Vocabulary	9.6	Block design	5.6
Comprehension	9.8	Object assembly	9.8
Digit span	7.3		

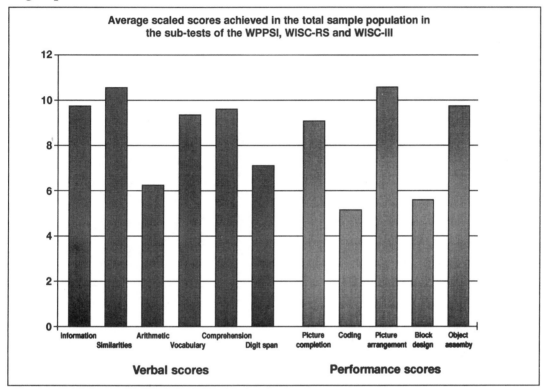

Figure 5.1 Average scaled scores achieved in the total sample population in the sub-tests of the WPPSI, WISC-RS and WISC-III

If the arithmetic and digit span sub-tests are excluded, the average of summed verbal scores = 9.94. If the coding and block design sub-tests are excluded, the average of summed performance scores = 9.77. The average of arithmetic, digit span, coding and block design sub-test scores = 6.07.

There are some differences, depending on age, in achievement in the coding, picture completion and object assembly sub-tests. This will be discussed later in this chapter.

However, what emerges from analysis of the results is that the neuro-psychological assessment does identify specific weaknesses, in the majority of cases, in four areas. Therefore we should not consider the discrepancy model of the performance IQ being lower than the verbal IQ as a diagnosis of dyspraxia. What we can say is that if the scaled scores in the sub-tests of arithmetic, coding, block design and digit span are significantly depressed in relation to the scores in the other sub-tests, these are indications that the child is dyspraxic.

If the magnitude of the weakness is greater in block design and coding than in arithmetic and digit span sub-tests, obviously the performance IQ will be lower.

However, there are many examples of the converse occurring, thus showing a depressed verbal IQ. It is the individual sub-test profile which is significant, not the overall IQ.

The analysis of sub-test scores of completed WPPSI assessments shows a similar pattern, but verbal scores on average are higher than performance. This is based on a sample of 57 pupils: 41 boys and 16 girls.

Figure 5.2 shows the average scaled scores achieved in each sub-test. Although arithmetic, geometric design (coding equivalent) and block design are again the most significantly depressed scores, the verbal scores are on average higher and the performance scores lower than the full population sample. The perceptual and motor planning difficulties are more evident. Averages for each sub-test were:

Verbal scores		**Performance scores**	
Information	10.5	Picture completion	9.4
Similarities	9.3	Geometric design	4.6
Arithmetic	8.2	Mazes	7.9
Vocabulary	10.5	Block design	5.2
Comprehension	10.9	Object assembly	8.7

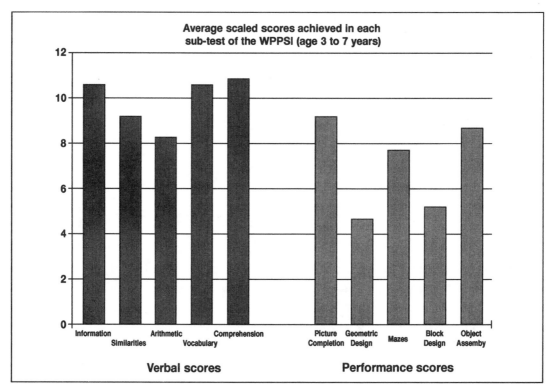

Figure 5.2 Average scaled scores achieved in each sub-test of the WPPSI (age 3–7 years)

If the arithmetic sub-test is excluded, the average of summed verbal scores = 10.3. If the geometric design and block design sub-tests are excluded, the average of summed performance scores = 8.7. Averages of arithmetic, geometric design and block design sub-test scores = 6.0.

There can be many explanations as to why the performance scores are more depressed in the younger child. It is probable that the motor component is more significant at this level, so that any test which involves eye–hand co-ordination and perceptual skills presents major problems for the child.

Figure 5.3 shows the average scaled scores achieved in each sub-test by pupils assessed using the WISC-RS and WISC-III. The sample comprises 378 pupils from the total of 435. As expected, because the sample size is nearly 87 per cent of the total, the results follow a similar pattern to those in the whole population.

Averages for each sub-test were:

Verbal scores		Performance scores	
Information	9.78	Picture completion	9.4
Similarities	10.2	Coding	5.6
Arithmetic	6.34	Picture arrangement	10.3
Vocabulary	9.5	Block design	5.2
Comprehension	9.7	Object assembly	10.0
Digit span	7.3		

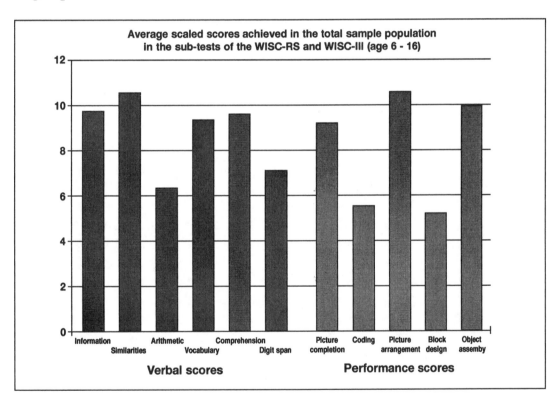

Figure 5.3 Average scaled scores achieved in the total sample population in the sub-tests of the WISC-RS and WISC-III (age 6–16 years)

If the arithmetic and digit span sub-tests are excluded, the average of summed scores = 9.79. If the coding and block design sub-tests are excluded, the average of summed performance scores = 9.9. The average of arithmetic, digit span, coding and block design sub-test scores = 5.71.

When the results for pupils under the age of 8 years are analysed, the scaled scores are higher in the coding sub-test but lower in picture completion and object assembly.

In this sample there were 39 males and 8 females. The average scores achieved were:

Coding	7.8
Picture completion	8.2
Object assembly	8.7

The nature of the coding task changes when the child reaches the age of 8 and it is possible that the assessments are measuring slightly different capabilities.

Limited concentration is more evident with younger pupils and this could affect the scores in picture completion. If the child is unable to identify the missing feature quickly, he loses interest and wants to move on to the next card.

If the youngster is familiar with an object he is more likely to reproduce its shape. Greater knowledge of the environment could account for the improved object assembly scores with older pupils.

The majority of youngsters were referred for assessment because concerns had been raised by parents or teachers about their school attainments and/or behaviour. The ratio of boys to girls differs in each age band. In the pre-school and infants group (3 to 7 years) the ratio is approximately 3:1. When the children move into the junior classes and on to secondary education the ratio is much more heavily skewed towards the boys: approximately 8:1. The number of female adults with dyspraxia in further education is higher than males.

If we analyse specific reasons for referral in the early years (up to age 7), parents express concerns that their children have been slow to achieve some developmental milestones and are becoming isolated within their peer group. Problems with concentration, language development, poor co-ordination and delayed acquisition of social skills such as toileting and feeding are identified as major difficulties at this age, and the ratio of 3:1 is probably an accurate reflection of the incidence of dyspraxia. After the age of 7 there is a greater need for boys to develop good motor skills to achieve acceptance within the peer group. Despite equal opportunities policies, observation still indicates boys are more likely to engage in team games such as football, while girls prefer to spend time in smaller groups. Soon there are further displays of behavioural difficulties – the outlet of increasing frustration. Children who present behavioural problems in the classroom are quickly identified. The problems transfer to secondary education where truancy may become a major problem (Chapter 6). Hence the ratio of 8:1 for this age group does not suggest that the dyspraxic proportion has changed but merely that boys are more likely to be identified.

So how can we explain differences in the referral rates of males and females after the age of 16? We may assume that a greater proportion of dyspraxic males are so disaffected with 'the system' that they do not consider further courses of study. This is discussed in more detail in Chapter 9.

Controlled intervention study involving pupils aged between 5 years 3 months and 6 years 8 months

Background information

The head teacher and staff at a local infants school were becoming increasingly concerned about the number of pupils entering the reception class who had significant problems with concentration and organisation of work, and appeared to exhibit fine and gross motor co-ordination difficulties. Some of the children had older brothers and sisters who had presented similar profiles at the same age, many of whom continued to experience subsequent learning difficulties.

In September 1993 one of the teaching members of staff, who was aware of the increasing incidence in the diagnosis of dyspraxia, embarked on a project to identify pupils who had deficits in attention with additional motor and perceptual difficulties, and provide them with daily access to activities designed to remediate their problems.

Pupil selection

The class teachers of the pupils aged between 5 and 7 were asked to identify children in their group who displayed any of the following:

- language difficulties
- immature drawing skills – inability to draw recognisable shapes or pictures
- poor pencil control
- unco-ordinated appearance when running
- limited concentration
- problems remembering instructions
- difficulty working with other pupils
- a mismatch between general understanding and the ability to record or convey information
- high sensitivity.

Parents of the children identified were contacted and given information about the purpose of the intervention. All agreed that if selected their child could participate in the programme.

Initially, ten pupils, (four girls and six boys) were identified. I completed a more detailed screening using the Wechsler Pre-school and Primary Scale of Intelligence and the Motor Assessment Battery for Children. One pupil was absent from school on the day of my visit and another had generalised rather than specific learning difficulties. Therefore the final sample comprised two girls and six boys, each showing varying degrees of dyspraxia.

At the outset, two samples of handwritten work were collected from each pupil. One was a piece of 'free' writing and the other a section from the child's arithmetic book.

Intervention

Children selected worked together as a group and each had access to activities to extend their immature motor skills. The purpose of the exercises was to reinforce the development of neural pathways in the brain which in time would improve the child's cognitive ability and eye–hand co-ordination.

The teaching and auxiliary staff were involved with the programme, which took 20 minutes every day to complete. After the baseline behaviour was established for each child, targets were set individually for every activity and progress was recorded daily and reassessed at the end of each week.

Intervention began in the last week of September 1993 and continued until the December holiday. The next term was a time for consolidation of newly acquired skills. The exercises recommenced in April 1994 and continued until June 1994.

Activities

There was some variation in ability between the pupils in the group and this was reflected in the activities. The programme is detailed on below.

A number of adults were involved in monitoring the pupils as they moved from one activity to another so the instructions had to be specific to ensure continuity from one day to the next.

Skipping rope

A skipping rope 3 metres in length is secured at one end (tied to a handle or wall bar). The child is positioned far enough away so that when he is holding the free end the centre of the rope just touches the floor.

Making a large arc, the rope is turned clockwise 30 times with the right hand and then anti-clockwise with the left.

Record how many times the movement breaks down before 30 turns are achieved.

Measured line

It is important that the distance remains constant so that improvements in behaviour can be recorded accurately.

Mark a line 2 cm wide and 7 metres long.

a) The child walks along heel to toe, each foot in turn.

b) He covers the same distance, hopping first on the right foot then the left.

c) He jumps, feet together, along the line.

Observe carefully during these exercises the position of the child's arms and hands. The purpose of the activity is to restrict the associated movements so, if the other limbs are waving around the body involuntarily, give the child something to hold, heavy enough to bring his hands down by his side. Then reduce gradually the weight until the arms and hands become naturally relaxed on each side of the body.

If only one hand/arm is affected use weights only on that side.

Measured crawl

It is important that the child is able to use arms and legs independently. This is a difficult task for youngsters to master if they have not gone through the crawling stage as babies. After demonstration, use a variety of heights and textures to crawl over.

Bean bags – measure distance and target.

Bean bags have an advantage over tennis balls in that they do not bounce and the session is not spent chasing them.

The child should be positioned away from the target so that he can achieve a 4/10 success: 2 metres is the usual starting distance when aiming at a target half a metre square.

As the child becomes more skilful, increase the distance. Assess the success in ten tries for:

a) both hands

b) right hand

c) left hand.

Assess associated movements: if the child is unable to stand still while throwing he could place his feet under the lower frame of a bench: if the left hand is waving while the right is throwing use weights to bring the arm down.

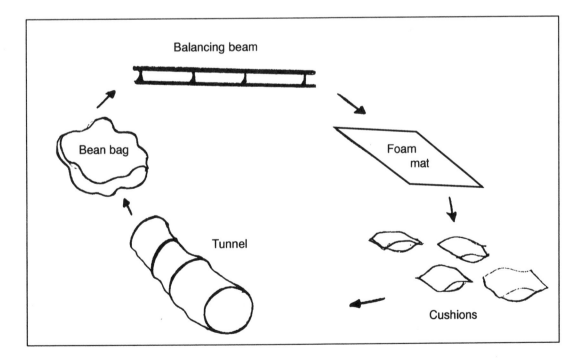

Figure 5.4 Course layout

Record Sheet   Date...............

ACTIVITY	Baseline behaviour	PROGRAMME DURATION										TARGETS	ACHIEVED Y/N
		3/5	4/5	5/5	6/5	9/5	10/5	11/5	12/5	13/5	16/5		
Measured line, jumping feet together (time taken in seconds)	Absent 29.4.94 Not tested	✓	✓	✓	4	✓	✓	✓	✓	6	✓	8	N
Jumping, feet together, over turning skipping rope (nos in seconds)		✓	✓	✓	6	✓	✓	✓	✓	24	✓	20	Y
Clapping 1, 2, 3, 4 (nos in 30 seconds)		✓	✓	✓	10	✓	✓	✓	✓	12	✓	15	N
Large ball, single bounce and catch (nos in 30 seconds)		✓	✓	✓	8	✓	✓	✓	✓	8	✓	10	N
Small ball, single bounce and catch (nos in 30 seconds)		✓	✓	✓	6	✓	✓	✓	✓	16	✓	15	Y
Skateboard, low-kneel, both hands working together (4 metres)		✓	✓	✓	13	✓	✓	✓	✓	18	✓	15	Y
Long-sitting, 5 objects either side 10 times (6 to cross mid-line)		✓	✓	✓	3	✓	✓	✓	✓	7	✓	10	N

Figure 5.5 Activity record sheet

Large ball play

As before, ensure the child stands a measured distance from the target and record success in 10 tries for:

a) both hands

b) right hand

c) left hand.

Check for associated movements.

Skateboard

Use a measured line between 7 and 10 metres in length. Ask the child to propel himself, using only his arms, forwards and backwards along the measured line. The position should be:

a) long-sitting, facing forwards with legs out in front
b) low-kneeling, on both heels and balancing on the board.

Each child was given access to the activities described. Targets were adjusted weekly as skills were achieved. The record chart was marked each day the child accessed the programme and progress was measured every Friday.

Figure 5.5 shows a completed activity chart dated April 1994. The programme has been extended to reflect the pupil's developing skills.

The sequence of activities, and how to determine those most suitable for individual children, is detailed in Chapters 7 and 8.

In June the pupils were re-assessed and their achievements discussed with parents. After the intervention, seven of the youngsters in the study had developed motor skills which were well within the average range expected for pupils of their age. The pupils, parents and teachers were asked to comment on the effectiveness of the programmes. Samples of pupils' work illustrate some of the changes (Figures 5.6 to 5.11).

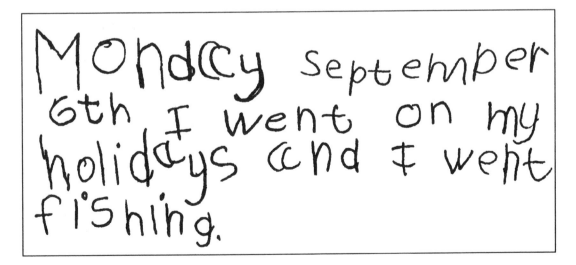

Figure 5.6 Writing sample from Pupil X (September 1993)

Monday November 22hd
I Was diging up the snow
with my brother. (and) We
Had a snow fight. With him.
I slipped On the path
coming to School.

Figure 5.7 Writing sample from Pupil X (November 1993)

Monday   september   6tn
I   Went   snopping   get to   new shoes and I
bought   jeans tney are grey.

Figure 5.8 Writing sample from Pupil Y (September 1993)

Friday 16th January 1994
Helen Went to her school to do
some exerases. I Went to see
my   Dads Friend. He Was
Just going   to get some
petrol. We Went
straight back home. Mum
thought I and Dad got lost.

Figure 5.9 Writing sample from Pupil Y (January 1994)

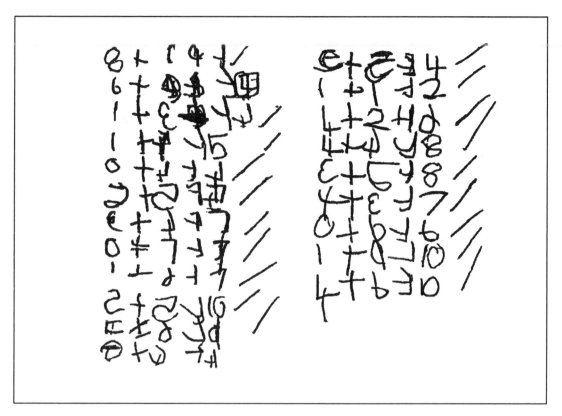

Figure 5.10 Writing sample from Pupil Z (September 1993)

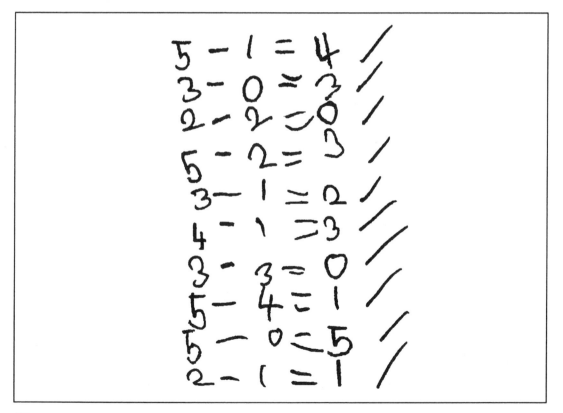

Figure 5.11 Writing sample from Pupil Z (November 1993)

Pupil responses

The programme was viewed as very enjoyable and all selected pupils were keen to take part.

Pupils not on the programme asked to be included and were encouraged to join in whenever possible.

The children were aware of significant improvements in their written work even at the end of the first term.

Parents' responses

All parents reported that the exercises were accepted by their children as part of the school routine and they had been willing to complete them.

One did not feel that her child required access to the programme but still agreed to let him take part.

Another parent wished her elder child had been able to take part. She felt the younger child's co-ordination had improved greatly and her work and attitude towards it were much better.

Two said they were 'over the moon' at the improvement in their children's schoolwork and reading.

Other comments suggested parents wished to continue with further programmes to ensure progress was maintained; one parent was grateful her child had been identified at such a relatively early stage, and thought further assessment of his difficulties would be invaluable.

Observations from the teacher responsible for the intervention

- Ensure time-tabling allows the programme to be completed daily. If, for example, assembly is held on three mornings each week then 9.00 to 9.30 might not be a good choice of time.

- Be prepared to compromise – one or two sessions might need to be completed out of doors.

- Avoid taking the children out during class teaching sessions.

- Ensure that the same person re-assesses the child at the end of the week for consistency of recording.

Generally, the teachers reported improved behaviour and said the pupils selected became much less demanding in the classroom. One asked: 'Is that because of the programme itself or because spending time on the activities gave these children the extra attention they seem to need?' Although the pupils extended their ability to remain on-task, completed legible written work within the time allowed and improved their relationships with peers, it is impossible to predict how these behaviours would appear now had they not had access to the programme.

Controlled intervention study involving pupils of secondary school age

Background information

The parents of a dyspraxic child due to transfer to secondary education contacted the receiving school to discuss the provision arrangement for him. The Special Educational Needs Co-ordinator (SENCO) was anxious that the staff should be fully informed about the new pupil's difficulties and arranged for a lecture about dyspraxia to be given to teachers and parents. That meeting was attended by members of the senior staff who were committed to identifying other pupils in school who, although undiagnosed, might have been dyspraxic.

Form tutors, teachers of English, PE, and those who provided support for children with learning difficulties were subsequently asked to identify pupils who showed any of the characteristics of dyspraxia, which included:

- excitability – frequent mood swings

- inattention and behavioural difficulties

- difficulties with relationships in peer groups

- work never finished on time

- mismatch between intellectual ability and written work

- inability to remember instructions

- lack of co-ordination in PE.

Pupil selection

The tutors selected 13 pupils (12 boys and 1 girl) whose ages ranged from 11 years 3 months to 13 years 9 months, and I arranged to assess them individually. I used the Wechsler Intelligence Scale for Children and the motor-skills screening to provide more specific information, and on the basis of these results, seven pupils from the original group (six boys and one girl) were offered access to the activities.

The parents of the pupils were involved from the outset and asked to comment on the behaviours they observed at home. Samples of handwriting were selected from each pupil at the start of the programme.

Intervention

The gymnasium or hall was made available and the 20-minute session time-tabled for the lunch break. Five members of the teaching staff agreed to supervise the project. The SENCO was present each day with at least one other member of staff. The first block of activities began during the last week in January 1995 and ended in the first week in March 1995. At the outset we had no idea what to expect as this was the first project with secondary age pupils.

As outlined in the previous chapter, children who are dyspraxic become increasingly disaffected and present more behavioural difficulties as they mature. Many of these problems arise outside the classroom and are the result of criticism from other pupils. Initially, the most noticeable factor was the increasingly positive attitude towards themselves shown by the youngsters in the group. Bad weather in January and February often inhibits the enjoyment of outdoor activities at lunch-time and it was a positive move to allow these children to remain inside the school. In addition they had permission to be at the front of the queue for meals to allow sufficient time to complete the exercise programme. The profile of the pupils involved was raised immediately and in contrast to the youngsters singled out to receive remedial help, in reading for example, these children were envied. By the end of the first week requests were coming from other pupils wanting to join in. The SENCO quickly used this to advantage and allowed an additional group of volunteers to become involved with the daily recording. At the end of the third week I visited the school to observe the lunch-time session.

Exercises were completed with enthusiasm but even more impressive was the encouragement given by the 'helpers'. Shouts of 'Brilliant!' and 'That was five seconds faster than yesterday' were audible. Staff supervision was reduced to one teacher. After the exercise routine was established the pupils organised the programmes themselves. Enjoyment was evident but the purpose of the intervention was to improve not only the attainments but also the self-esteem and in some cases the behaviour of those involved.

During the period from the beginning of March to the third week in May activities were suspended to allow for the consolidation of skills. Activities were then restarted and continued until the beginning of July.

Activities

The exercises are similar to those previously described for use with younger children. They continue to be appropriate for youngsters of secondary school age who are significantly neurologically immature. They are extended depending on the progress of the individual and targets are regularly reviewed. An example of one activity chart is shown in Figure 5.12.

Evaluation

Changes in pupils' attainments and behaviour were measured by:

- comparing handwriting samples before and after intervention
- interviews with the seven pupils involved, and assessment of their personal constructs (changes in the way the pupils perceived themselves in relation to others in school and at home)
- interviews with classmates and those involved in supporting the control group
- comments from teaching staff
- comments from parents.

Record Sheet   Date ....   Name ....

ACTIVITY														Targets	Achieved Y/N
1. Walking on heel to toe and back on line															
2. Jumping, feet together, there and back on line															
3. Hopping half way on line and back	right														
	left														
4. Measured crawl															
5. Skipping rope	right														
	left														
6. Bean bag, aiming with both hands at target															
7. Large ball aiming with both hands at target															
8. Bean bag at target	right														
	left														
9. Large ball at target	right														
	left														
10. Tennis ball in bucket	right														
	left														
11. Skateboard, long-sitting on line: there and back															
12. Skateboard, long-kneel on line: there and back															
13. Skateboard, tummy on line: there and back															

Figure 5.12 Record sheet

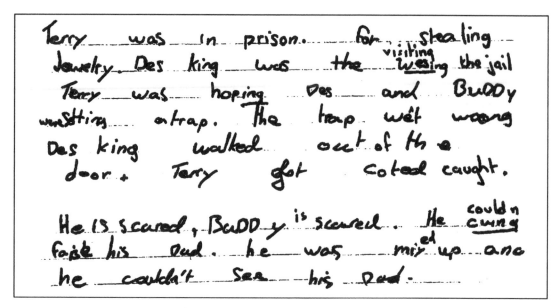

Figure 5.13 Child X (September 1994)

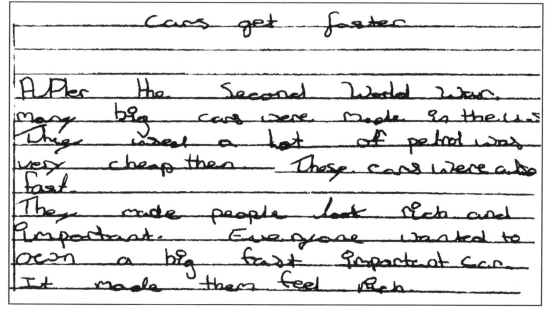

Figure 5.14 Child X (June 1995)

Handwriting

In September 1994 each pupil was asked to submit a selection of hand-written pieces, covering a variety of subjects. Further examples of 'free' writing were collected the following March and June. Figures 5.13–5.18 represent the improvements between September and June shown by three pupils from the group. Letter formation and speed of writing had changed significantly. The youngsters were asked whether they could offer any explanations for improvements. Although all said handwriting required less effort, they believed the most important factor was their motivation. They felt that not only teachers but also fellow pupils had achieved a greater understanding of their difficulties as a direct result of the intervention, and they had been given far greater encouragement in the classroom. They reported that written work had always presented difficulties and it had been easier to employ a range of carefully-acquired strategies to complete the minimum or avoid it altogether. Now their attempts had gained positive recognition they were keen to produce more.

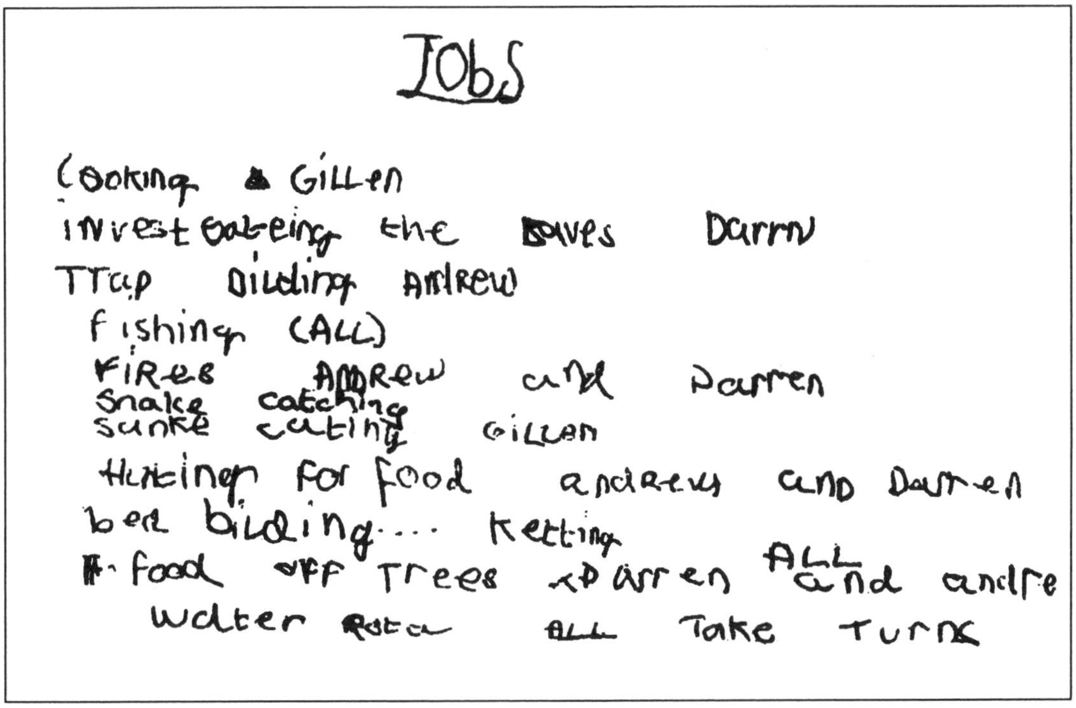

Figure 5.15 Child Y (September 1994)

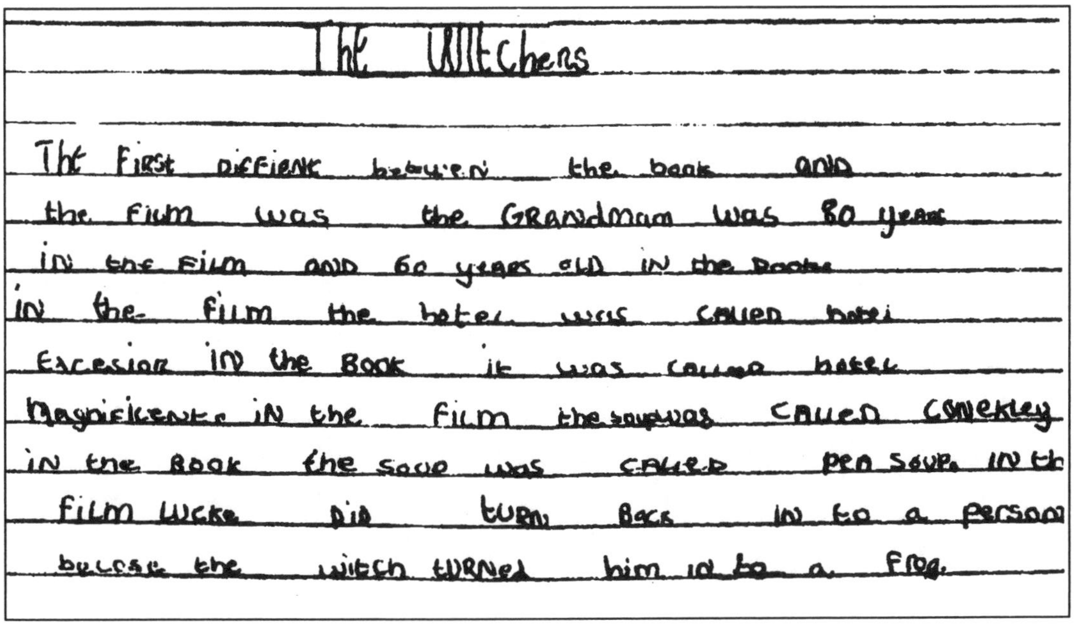

Figure 5.16 Child Y (July 1995)

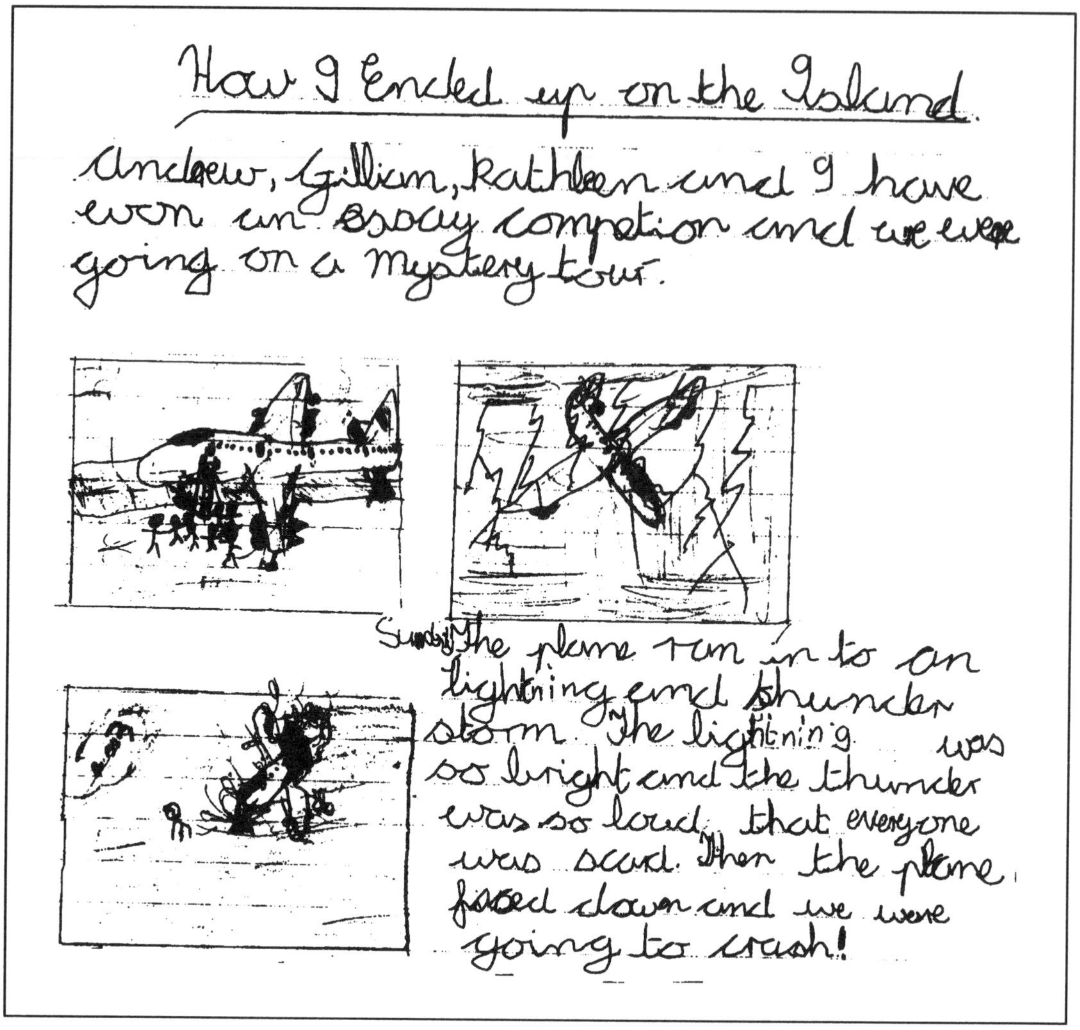

Figure 5.17 Child Z (September 1994)

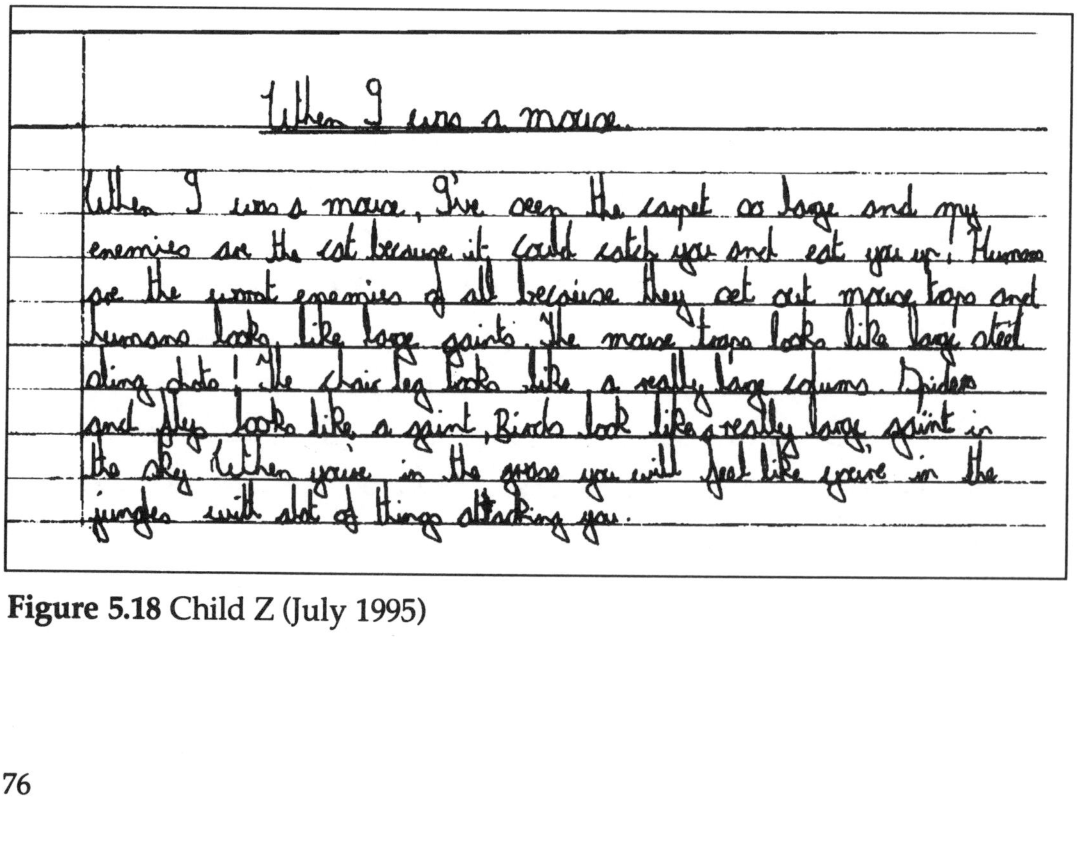
When I was a mouse.

When I was a mouse, I've seen the carpet so large and my enemies are the cat because it could catch you and eat you up! Humans are the worst enemies of all because they set out mouse traps and humans looks like large giants. The mouse traps looks like large steel sliding shuts! The chair leg looks like a really large colums. Spiders and flys looks like a giant, Birds look like a really large giant in the sky When you're in the grass you will feel like you're in the jungles with alot of things attacking you.

Figure 5.18 Child Z (July 1995)

Interviews with pupils completing the exercise programme

All pupils reported that they had developed better relationships within their class groups. They had developed special relationships with one or two pupils and described them as friends they had never had.

The least positive statement about having to work on the exercise programme was: 'I didn't mind doing it'. The most enthusiastic pupil said: 'It's been great. I loved the skateboard, I'm really good at it now'.

Some of the pupils felt the quality of school life had improved. One said: 'I haven't had any headaches for ages' and this was attributed to feeling less pressure in lessons where large amounts of handwritten recording were expected.

The following is a selection of additional pupil comments:

Skipping has helped me to move my wrists. My writing is now much better.

It has certainly helped with my writing but spelling is still very hard.

This school is loads better than my last one. I didn't have any friends at the beginning of the year. Now I have lots.

Having your friends in to mark the charts is a good idea. I have one best friend and it would be difficult if she was by herself every lunch-time.

I usually have nothing to do at lunch-time. Doing the exercises has stopped me wasting my time.

I have tried very hard because my friends A and B kept shouting: 'Come on, come on, beat the time!'.

I have shown my Dad my new writing and he says it's good.

I've been every day and reached all of my targets. I prefer to work by myself and I'm best at hitting the targets with the bean bag.

I know my writing has improved but I would still like it to be better. The teacher says I can go to classes with her at lunch-time, and I will.

Because I can write more now the teachers expect me to do more homework. I still liked the exercises.

It's great having help from the older ones because when they pass you in the corridor they speak. That's good because it makes my friends a bit jealous.

Interviews with classmates

Two female Year 8 pupils gave the following overview of their involvement:

Q: Why did you become involved?

A: We wanted to help because there wasn't anything else as interesting to do at lunch-time. We knew that the exercises were to help with co-ordination. Some of the things had to be demonstrated and we were really surprised that they found it so difficult. Even things like just turning a skipping rope. The programme didn't take much getting used to and the record sheets were easy to understand. It is a shame that all the pupils in the school can't understand the problems that some children have just trying to write things down.

Q: Has working on the project helped you?

A: Yes, it makes you feel really good when you see someone getting better because you have taught them. There has been a really good atmosphere and we've made friends with people in our class we didn't really know. It's as good as getting something right yourself. In fact I think it feels better because it's not just you but the other person who feels good about themselves as well.

We have both enjoyed it and we would be interested in doing it again next year.

Q: What changes did you see in the pupil you were helping?

A: Well, he just smiles a lot more. He's much more friendly and he seems much more relaxed. At first he was a bit embarrassed but he loves the attention really. We were also helping X and he has improved not just with his exercises. Before, he could be quite insulting with his comments when you walked past. Now he's really friendly and calls you by your first name. He's worked very hard with the activities and he seems just to be happier in school.

Two male pupils helping with the project answered the same questions.

Q: Why did you become involved?

A: We were told that some work would be going on at lunch-time to help people who had co-ordination difficulties. We didn't join in at first because we didn't really know much about it. Then we saw them racing up and down on skateboards and playing football and we thought we would like to join in. We were shown how to fill in the record forms and we were given people to work with. The atmosphere was good and we spent a lot of time laughing. We really enjoyed it.

Q: Has working on the project helped you?

A: It has made me very interested in seeing how X is doing in class. I know the exercises are supposed to help him do his work and I'm always checking to see what marks he's got. Because he's a friend of mine now I sometimes go over and help him with his work if he needs it. It's good to see him getting good marks when I've helped. We've all become better friends and this club is a really good idea for that. Mind you, we could do with a few more helpers and we need better equipment.

Q: What changes did you see in the pupil you were helping?

A: Well, you could never read X's writing before: now you can. We thought he didn't try very hard but we know now that he just couldn't make the words properly. X used to keep himself to himself and never talked to anyone. Now it seems much easier for him to get into a group and I like him. The rest of the class accept him now and choose to work with him. It must be better to be part of a group than always by yourself. I just think we should have the club every day. It could help a load more people with bad handwriting.

Youngsters invited to join the group and record the progress of their classmates completing the activities were as enthusiastic as those directly involved in the exercises. The comment repeated over and over was that many pupils enter formal education and have no understanding of the difficulties experienced by children with special needs. All the 'helpers' felt that raising all the pupils' awareness would foster better peer group relationships and create a more positive school environment.

Comments from teaching staff

The subject teachers involved with the seven youngsters in the study were given questionnaires and asked whether they had observed any difference or improvements in the pupils, in the following areas:

- social skills/relating to others in the group

- handwriting/presentation

- organisational skills

- attitude to school/work (is it more positive?)

- language skills

- concentration/on-task behaviour.

In total, 49 questionnaires were returned and the number of reported positive improvements are ranked in Table 5.1:

Table 5.1 Teachers' comments

Areas of recorded change	Responses (max. 49)	% of pupils showing improvement
attitude	38	77.5
concentration/behaviour	32	65.3
social relationships	28	57.1
handwriting	27	55.1
organisational skills	24	48.9
language skills	12	24.6

Teacher comments reflected the changes highlighted by the pupils. The area of greatest improvement, which was much less significant in the studies with younger children, was the marked change in attitude to schoolwork. Pupils in the study had become highly motivated not only to complete written work but also to participate in class discussions. This generated a more positive attitude towards the pupil, who in turn attempted to become more involved. As a direct consequence, concentration improved, off-task behaviour was less evident and new and positive relationships developed between the pupils and other members of the class.

Comments from parents

Parents of the pupils involved were asked to complete a questionnaire following the intervention. Responses to many of the questions were very similar:

Q: Has your child talked about the exercises he has been doing in school?

A: Yes, but says very little.
Rarely mentions them but this is usual on all school matters.
Usually talks vaguely about school.
Loves the skateboard and constantly talks about the exercises.

Q: Why does your child think he has been chosen to be part of the programme?

A: To improve his handwriting.
To improve co-ordination.

Q: How does your child feel about being involved? Is he positive in his attitude towards the activities?

A: Enjoys them and is pleased to have been selected.
Quite happy.
X knows that they are going to help with schoolwork.

Q: As a parent have you noticed any change in behaviour at home? Is he talking more or less positively about school?

A: No noticeable change at home but X is talking a great deal about the activities in school.
Behaviour has improved at home but very little is said about school.
X has started to talk about other aspects of school life now.

Q: Do you think there are any benefits for your child having access to the programme?

A: His overall balance, co-ordination, confidence and general ability have improved over the last few months.
It has made X feel more confident about himself
There have been great improvements in X's handwriting.

Q: Are there any other comments you would like to make about the project?

A: The greatest benefit has been to improve X's social skills so X is now able to mix more easily with other children.
X is reluctant to try anything new, especially if it involves physical activity.
We know it has done him good and he hasn't minded the exercises.
Anything which will help X with his schoolwork will be of benefit.

The parents all describe children who are reluctant to discuss aspects of school life. Dyspraxic youngsters have great difficulty forming secure relationships and in secondary education this is frequently because they are rejected by their peer group. One of the major benefits of the activity programme was the raised awareness of these pupils' problems within the class group.

Acceptance replaced rejection and attitudes towards school immediately became more positive. What was more important was that these children felt more positive about themselves.

Improvement in the pupils' behaviour, concentration and presentation of written work observed in the infants and secondary school studies largely reflects the commitment of the staff involved. Their positive support and encouragement enabled the youngsters to develop confidence in their own achievements. Pupils acknowledged the requirement of staff to offer their own time to run the project and this deepened the personal relationship between themselves and the teachers.

My research indicates that with parental support the most successful interventions have been school-based because of the raised awareness of the child's difficulty with other pupils and with all involved members of staff.

In the case of individual pupils following school-based programmes without access to teacher or support staff time, parents have found the programmes much easier to implement themselves on the school premises. Arrangements have been made for the parent and child to arrive 20 minutes before the start of school or spend time at the end of the day completing the activities in the hall or gymnasium. This gives added structure to the programme and although the parents are recording progress, the staff in school are aware of the work being done.

Thomas – a case study

Thomas was referred for assessment when he was 6. He had transferred to a primary school in the county at 5 years 6 months, and was admitted into the reception class.

Thomas had found it very difficult to relate appropriately to the other pupils. He had speech and language difficulties and he often attempted to make contact using physical gestures. He was viewed by the children as rough and at times aggressive. His class teacher was most concerned about his very limited concentration and poor fine motor skills. After a term in his new school, parents and staff believed that a detailed assessment of his behaviour was necessary to provide a baseline for an individual education programme.

A meeting with parents revealed that there had been difficulties from birth. He was premature and his mother had gone into labour at 35 weeks. There were signs of foetal distress during the second stage and Thomas was born by emergency caesarean section. His mother reported: 'He cried constantly during the first six months'. A variety of milk-based and substitute products had been tried with little success. Weight gain had been poor and at 8 months he was admitted to hospital for observation because of his failure to thrive.

Largely the crying ceased at 10 months but he always appeared to be insecure. Mother said that until starting nursery she had to take him with her even when going to the toilet.

Thomas was able to sit independently at 9 months and began to 'bottom-shuffle' at 13 months. He could pull himself to a standing position at 18 months and walked independently at 22 or 23 months.

There had been some concerns at the 18-month check because Thomas was able to drink only from a feeder cup and was making no attempt to use a spoon appropriately. He was making some babbling sounds but was unable to say any recognisable words. Referral was made to the speech therapy service and he was assessed at 2 years 6 months.

Between the ages of 2 and 3 Thomas had uncontrolled tantrums, screaming and kicking and sometimes banging his head on the floor. When Thomas was 3 years 2 months his sister Helen arrived. At the same time, Dad was made redundant and could only find work abroad. The next six months Mum said were the worst time of her life. Thomas, who could never be described as a good sleeper, was waking even more frequently (six or seven times during the night). He was aggressive towards his younger sister and he would become very easily distressed about nothing. One example was when he had been given a chocolate bar to eat and when the wrapper was opened it had broken into two pieces. Thomas's response was one of 'hysteria' which continued for almost an hour.

At the age of 3 years 6 months Thomas was placed in a pre-school language unit every morning and attended weekly sessions at the Department of Child and Family Psychiatry. Sibling rivalry and the absence for long periods of a father who had previously been very involved with his son were, perhaps understandably, thought to have been the explanation for Thomas's difficulties.

Although there was a significant improvement in Thomas's speech during the next 12 months there was little change in his behaviour. Mum, by then, found Thomas so difficult that she felt she could no longer manage on her own. Dad gave up his job and returned home. It had been expected that this would effect a change in Thomas's behaviour. None was observed. The problems remained unresolved and 12 months later Dad found new employment and the family moved. Thomas was referred to me a term later.

Thomas had a very immature pencil grip and he found it very difficult to co-ordinate movement in his hand. Colouring and copying skills were approximately two years delayed and he had very limited perception of objects in space. He ran with an awkward gait, with his hands moving wildly in the air. Gross motor skills were similarly delayed. Thomas was unable to write his name unaided and his copy-writing was indecipherable, but his understanding of mathematical concepts was age-appropriate. He could add 11 + 7 and verbally give the right answer. He could not write it down. Assessment using the WPPSI confirmed that his general knowledge and comprehension skills were also age-appropriate although some of his words were indistinct.

Thomas's developmental and cognitive profiles confirmed that he was dyspraxic. His working day was broken down into shorter periods and the amount of manual recording required from him was reduced by 50 per cent. For Thomas it was his parents' greater understanding of his difficulties which brought about the most significant changes. Instead of giving him a string of instructions he was asked to do one thing at a time. This meant he could actually remember what he was doing. Work at school was now completed so he no longer spent playtime finishing off. He began an exercise programme with two other pupils with similar although less severe difficulties. The three boys started to develop a close friendship, and they called for each other at weekends.

Thomas continued to have problems with concentration, but because he was allowed to move to another activity after 10 minutes in a 60-minute session he was on-task for between 45 and 50 minutes. If, instead, he had had access to only two activities, each of 20 minutes duration, he would have achieved a maximum of 20 minutes on-task during the hour session.

There are increasing numbers of youngsters who are now being diagnosed as dyspraxic. While there are many behaviours which are consistent among the majority, each child must have an individual programme of work which emphasises his strengths and gives him sufficient confidence and raised self-esteem to attempt to progress in areas he finds difficult.

6 Behavioural problems: neurological? psychological?

My original research, which considered the relationship between identified neurological immaturities and the evidence of significant behavioural difficulties, began in 1988. The youngsters in that sample, aged between 9 and 16 years, were allocated day or residential provision outside mainstream education because of their emotional and behavioural difficulties. Of the 107 pupils 77 per cent showed symptoms of neurological immaturity.

When this data was published in my first manual, Sheilagh Matheson, the producer of the BBC2 programme 'Head, Shoulders, Knees and Toes' which was screened in January 1997, asked whether pupils in this population which had failed in the mainstream system were likely to move on to criminal behaviour? Was the incidence of this specific learning difficulty similarly elevated in the population of young offenders? She believed that such information would be valuable and as part of the documentary programme arranged for me to have access to the juveniles at Deerbolt Young Offenders Institution, Barnard Castle, County Durham.

Deerbolt study

I visited the young offenders' institution on a number of occasions between July and November 1996. The Governor, Peter Atkinson, allowed me access to the juveniles, and information about the development of Deerbolt was supplied by Dave Douglas, Principal Officer, and Terry Bateman, Senior Officer. In the Education Department the co-ordinator Chris Holroyd and the Senior Teacher Jane Marden gave detailed information about help that was available.

Deerbolt opened as a borstal in 1973 for youths aged between 16 and 21. It was then reopened as a Youth Custody Centre following the Criminal Justice Act and accommodated inmates aged between 15 and 17. It is now a Young Offenders Institution and houses inmates aged between 15 and 22. It has accommodation for more than 420 young offenders.

Juveniles are youngsters under the age of 18 and at the time of my involvement this population at Deerbolt totalled 140. There were 160 inmates serving juvenile sentences. The length of stay ranged from two weeks to four and a half years. Those under school leaving age had access to educational provision for six hours each day, from 9.00 am until 12 noon and 2.00 p.m. until 5.00 p.m.

Selection of sample population

In total I screened 69 youngsters selected randomly from the list of 140 possible inmates. Assessment involved:

- a personal interview
- completion of a neuropsychological assessment
- a motor-skills screening
- assessment of reading and handwriting skills.

Letters were sent to the parents of inmates requesting permission for my involvement. There was only one refusal. The youths were asked whether they wanted to co-operate and agreement was given by all.

Background information

Time spent with each inmate varied considerably and was dependent upon their willingness to communicate. Some of the youths were awaiting sentencing, others experiencing a relatively short stay for a minor offence and still others involved in much more serious crimes. Many of the personal histories of those interviewed showed evidence of instability in the home and educational environment. Some merely exhibited specific learning difficulties which had perhaps not been recognised while they were still at school. Research evidence suggests that there is a high correlation between conditions such as dyspraxia, dyslexia, attention deficit and hyperactivity and some behaviours in the autistic spectrum. The evidence from my assessment did indeed confirm high levels of comorbidity between dyslexia and dyspraxia (approximately 45 per cent).

The majority of youngsters cited school failure and peer group pressure as major factors in their offending behaviour.

Steven's story

Steven said that his early school days had been happy. He remembered with fondness particular teachers and the friends that he had made in the infant school. He felt that as the work became more difficult he was made to look foolish in front of other members of the class. He believed that he was being treated differently by the teachers and other pupils. Nevertheless he had managed to survive until the end of primary school but felt that his inability to play football and other games skilfully excluded him from the group of boys with whom he would have liked to have been involved. On transfer to secondary school he found it was much easier to disguise his learning difficulties and discovered that insolence and verbal abuse towards teachers and peers achieved the desired outcome. He was removed from the classroom and allowed to spend the rest of the day in a room by himself.

By the age of 13, he had such a bad school record that he was given a number of fixed-term exclusions. In many ways this delighted him further because it meant that he did not have to go through the motions of attempting to do work and finding distractions to remove himself from it. He discovered that it was less stressful either staying at home or spending time with gangs of older youths, some of whom had left school and were unable to gain employment: at least they accepted him. He was the youngest member of the 'gang' and he was constantly being required to confirm his allegiance by doing as he was told.

By the age of 15, he had decided that he should no longer attend school and truanted every day. A variety of strategies had been employed to facilitate his return. None was successful.

By the age of 16, he had been convicted of a string of offences including taking cars without the owners' consent, and petty theft from large shops. It was his conviction for an aggravated burglary that resulted in his imprisonment in Deerbolt.

On assessment Steven performed all of the tasks required to the best of his ability. He enjoyed being out of his cell and talking about himself. Although Steven had significant reading, handwriting and spelling problems with additional motor delays and perceptual difficulties, he achieved many average scores in the sub-tests of the Wechsler assessment.

Steven was asked about his future. He did not appear to have a great deal of hope. Any friends that he had had from his school days had long since gone. His mother had told him to leave home on numerous occasions prior to his custodial sentence. He held out no hope of returning home. He was due for release within two months but talked at length about the security he had found at Deerbolt. He was aware that he had lost his freedom and hence many of his privileges. He did not feel that there was a lot on offer outside. He thought he would not be able to afford any clothing. He did not know what sort of accommodation he would be offered and he just smiled and did not answer when I suggested that there might be the prospect of some training or job opportunities. His first statement was to attach some blame to his criminal record for his circumstances, but then he said, 'I can't get a job, I can't do anything, I can't even read properly.'

Assessment

Case histories varied, as did the long-term memories of the juveniles interviewed. It was very difficult to obtain specific details in relation to information about early development as parents were not part of the assessment process. Although the nature of the crimes in the sample group differed, there were many consistent behaviours in those who were subsequently identified as having dyspraxia. Some juveniles had acted impulsively and were led on by group pressure. Some said they had just been unable to get away quickly!

I interviewed 69 young offenders but two assessments were incomplete. Consequently the sample population was 67 from a possible total of 140. After spending some time discussing educational history and the reasons for their detention at Deerbolt each juvenile was asked to complete a hand-written exercise. This involved copying a passage from *The Iron Man* by Ted Hughes. The passage and two samples of handwriting are shown in Figure 6.1.

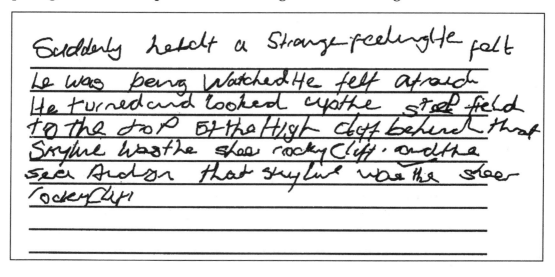

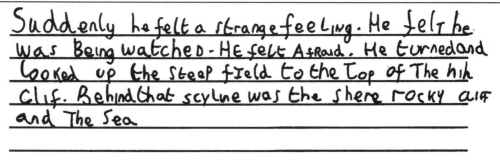

Figure 6.1 Handwriting samples: John and Peter

A motor-skills screening determined whether there was evidence of neurological immaturity. Laterality was also assessed. The WISC-III and WAIS were used to assess verbal and non-verbal skills, and reading ability was determined using the Wechsler Objective Reading Dimensions (WORD).

The results of this screening are as follows:

• 13 juveniles presented with generalised learning difficulties (19 per cent).

• 41 juveniles showed symptoms ranging from mild to severe dyspraxia (61 per cent).

• 19 of the same juveniles also exhibited symptoms of dyslexia. This indicated that the comorbidity of dyspraxia and dyslexia in this sample population was 46 per cent.

• 34 juveniles had a reading ability of 9 years or less (52 per cent).

The psychometric profile of the juvenile offenders showed greater evidence of problems in verbal as well as non-verbal ability. This takes into account the comorbidity identified in the sample population. The average values for each sub-test of the Wechsler assessment were:

Verbal scores		**Performance scores**	
Information	8.9	Picture completion	9.32
Similarities	9.3	Coding	5.7
Arithmetic	5.1	Picture arrangement	9.6
Vocabulary	9.2	Block design	6.3
Comprehension	9.6	Object assembly	9.8
Digit span	8.4		

Intervention

At present there is little scope for high levels of specialist input to provide individual programmes of learning for those identified with specific rather than generalised learning difficulties. Even if that were possible, there are questions as to whether outside support would be acceptable to the inmates. I had the opportunity to discuss with some juveniles their suggestions about programmes to overcome their neurological immaturities and learning difficulties. The responses were really an extension of opinions given by the secondary school pupils.

The juveniles, some of whom had had help in primary school on an individual or small-group basis to address identified learning difficulties, felt that this method of intervention was acceptable for younger pupils. They stressed how their differences, in secondary education, had made them an object of verbal abuse and criticism and stated quite emphatically that to receive individual support either within the classroom or on a withdrawal basis would have made life even more difficult for them.

The suggestion that they should be singled out for remedial help within the Young Offenders Institution was totally unacceptable. The juveniles themselves provided the solution. Additional funding for specialist teachers is unlikely and from the information given by the juveniles it would not be accepted anyway. Their solution was to establish a system where they were helping one another. Without prior knowledge they were really describing the

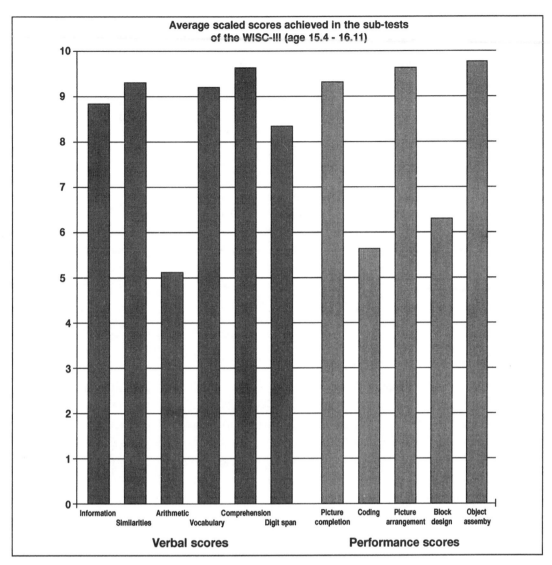

Figure 6.2 Average scaled scores achieved in sub-tests of the WISC-III (age 15.4 – 16.11)

programme which had produced a successful outcome in the secondary environment. The youngsters there were supported by their peers who took upon themselves the responsibility to ensure the progress of their partner. When the possibility of individual programmes for improving reading, perceptual ability and motor skills was suggested they became quite enthusiastic about the possibility of its implementation through peers. The positives of course were not just promises of improvement in the areas mentioned but greater opportunity for social interaction with other youths.

At this point of the interview it had ceased to be a question and answer session. The juveniles were enthusiastically brainstorming ways of helping themselves. If this system could be put in place it would reduce the requirement for high spending and ensure that those in the programme accepted responsibility for improving themselves. It is so easy to assume failure from the outset when there is no requirement for commitment on the part of the recipient.

The Home Office is currently considering strategies which could improve the outcomes for identified young offenders. Procedures are being developed to identify these disaffected pupils within the educational environment before they enter the criminal justice system. These suggestions for improvement have been made by the client group that government policies and programmes are trying to assist. We should listen to them and examine in detail the strategies they suggest.

Early identification will reduce the numbers of youngsters who have become school failures and feel that life has nothing of value to offer them. If we can provide opportunities for those already in the criminal justice system, not only to improve their skills base, but also to improve their perceptions of themselves, then we would be breaking into the current cycle of failure. It should also be possible to offer similar programmes of intervention to juveniles who have not been given custodial sentences but who are already identified as young offenders.

Conclusion

Many studies have provided evidence which highlights the high incidence of specific and generalised learning difficulties within the young offenders and prison population. We have to ask ourselves why this is the case. The Governor of Deerbolt, Peter Atkinson, said about my research, 'Whilst there is no one theory which can account for all of the reasons for young offenders ending up here, it is an important one and it must be followed through.'

We have to ask ourselves why there is such a disproportionate number of offenders with learning difficulties. Developmental dyspraxia can be identified from an early age. Neurological immaturities are present and, whilst appropriate intervention can have a great effect, they are programmed virtually from birth. In Chapter 2 there was discussion about the nutritional aspects of the condition. It is probable that the nutritional factors are relatively high in youngsters within the prison population. The socio-economic groupings of committed youngsters have been examined and they are likely to come from backgrounds where there have been high levels of material deprivation. There are higher rates of premature birth, poor nutrition and, in some cases, inadequate health care. This study did not set out to be specific in the identification of pre- and post-natal factors but it is important that much more research is done into this field, so that the environment for youngsters who may be categorised as 'at risk' because of poor nutrition can access a good diet in their early years to minimise the effects of poor neural transmission.

7 Intervention in the 'early years'

Early intervention is of great benefit to the child. By the age of 3, many symptoms of dyspraxia are apparent. There will be some evidence of delayed acquisition of motor skills, perceptual problems and possibly language difficulties. Chapter 3 outlined specific targets for achievement, and the aim now is to look at programmes to ameliorate the difficulties experienced by dyspraxic children. Skills are usually acquired in a particular sequence, so if we establish a baseline for the child's ability in all areas of development, we can specify the next target. For example, the child requires a good pincer grasp to be able to complete inset boards competently, therefore appropriate activities to develop the skill should be devised. The following programmes identify sequentially the developmental targets and suggest methods of teaching the skills.

Social skills

Dressing: This can be a nightmare which continues well into secondary education if a routine is not established at an early age. Children must be given sufficient time to complete the task. When the process is so lengthy, the temptation for parents is to take over and dress the child themselves.

If the child has not achieved competency by school age, allowances must be made if there is a requirement to change for PE.

Encourage the child to hold his arms and legs in the correct position for the removal and putting on of jumper and trousers.

As this is achieved let the child pull off his own socks. Start with the sock halfway off the foot and then allow the child to remove it. Gradually reduce assistance until he can manage unaided.

Similarly, teach the child to put on his socks, beginning by pulling the leg of the sock just past the ankle. Move it farther down the foot until he can eventually manage himself.

Trousers (remember to choose those with an elasticated waist) can be mastered if at first the child is required only to pull them up from his knees. Progress to ankles and then teach the child how to place legs in separately. By giving the child the easy part of the task to learn first, he will be encouraged to keep trying. This technique can be adopted for all articles of clothing.

Try to choose shoes with Velcro fasteners if you expect the child to have increasing success at this age. Fastening laces or buckles is a difficult skill to master and can be taught at a later stage in development.

Feeding: Manipulating just a spoon to the mouth may require a great deal of practice. Very young dyspraxic children find it almost impossible to co-ordinate two feeding implements. Children with dyspraxia have motor-planning difficulties: they have problems co-ordinating lip and mouth movements to chew food appropriately. Many will resist textured food

Ensure that the child is presented with appropriately textured food. If there are problems with swallowing, gradually introduce small pieces into the pureed preparation. Sometimes it is better to go from pureed food straight to 'ordinary food': then the child is not concerned about 'finding lumps'. Up to the age of 3 encourage the child to feed with just a spoon or fork. Ensure that there is sufficient food on the plate so the child is not trying to co-ordinate his movements to stab one pea. Cut food to the correct size for eating and, during the early stages, place your hand on top of the child's to steady the movement from the plate to the mouth. As the child becomes more competent, move your hand to his elbow reducing the level

because swallowing presents similar difficulties.

of help required. The child will become confident only if he has had success while trying to acquire the new skill. If the task has been too difficult from the outset he will become easily frustrated and refuse even to pick up a fork or spoon.

Drinking: Changing from a bottle to a handled cup and then a beaker presents great difficulties. Allow sufficient time for swallowing between each mouthful.

Follow the same routine as for feeding. Give the child a two-handled cup and steady the base while the child brings it to his mouth. Again, reduce your assistance gradually and move slowly to a one-handled cup and then a beaker. The consumption of food continues to present difficulties for the dyspraxic child, often into secondary education. If these skills can be taught at an early stage a great deal of embarrassment will be avoided.

Sleeping: Often patterns established during the first 6–12 months, which may have been the result of severe colic or milk intolerance, are extremely difficult to change. Some children wake during the night and can be distressed. They require reassurance and may insist an adult remains with them until they go back to sleep.

The child may be having 8–10 hours sleep each day but this may be split into many cat-naps. Discourage sleeping during the day if possible and this may enable some of the brief periods of sleeping to merge. Once the child starts to settle for 5+ hours reduce further sleeping outside this time and ensure that he is active during the day so he is more likely to be tired at bedtime. Some children continue to be very restless even when they are able to sleep for longer periods and parents report that this unsettled behaviour can become a part of the dyspraxic child's routine.

Relationships with other children: Language plays an important part in communicating with others. The dyspraxic child may be severely disadvantaged if he has problems with articulation.

Encourage the child to become involved in games which develop co-operative play. It is important that an adult is present to organise the activity. The dyspraxic child imitates others at play and copies rather than co-operates. Defined activities are much easier for him to understand: for example, to play on a see-saw requires the two children to work co-operatively. Turn taking is a problem and it is important that they are encouraged to wait until the toys are available rather than physically remove the object from another child.

Toilet training: Many dyspraxic youngsters have problems with diet and this can adversely affect their bowel control. Ensure that the diet contains adequate fruit, vegetables and cereal. Some youngsters show intolerance to wheat products so rice-based cereals may be preferable. The child, apart from understanding when it is appropriate to use the toilet, has to learn to remove his clothes appropriately and replace them.

Once the child recognises the physical symptons which indicate the need to use the toilet, try to make it as easy as possible to achieve success. Choose clothes with elasticated waists so trousers can be removed easily. The child must feel secure while using the toilet and steps must be taken to compensate for the problems with balance experienced by dyspraxic youngsters. It is helpful to place a small box next to the toilet for the child to rest his feet. If the legs are left swinging the child will spend more time establishing a secure seating position than using the toilet appropriately.

Behaviour: The dyspraxic child can become easily frustrated but it is important to decide how much of his difficult behaviour directly relates to the condition.

Sometimes the 'label' can be used as an excuse for a whole range of difficulties: behaviour, to name but one. If the child is unable to complete a task or cannot comprehend the instructions given, then we may excuse the inappropriate behaviour which is a direct consequence of his frustration. If the child merely wants his own way or responds aggressively towards another pupil, this is not acceptable and strategies to encourage appropriate behaviour should be employed. Parents know when their child is likely to become provoked. Try to avoid the escalation of any situation which will result in distress. If a task is too difficult, distract him with an alternative. Give clear instructions so that the child knows exactly what is expected. Always be consistent in your own behaviour: if the child's behaviour is unacceptable, always reaffirm the consequences.

Language development: A speech therapist may already be involved and will provide specific programmes to follow. Single words may be indistinct and slow to

If there are general concerns about language development, involve the child in games and exercises which use and strengthen the facial muscles. Make faces and ask the child to copy. Blowing bubbles is always popular and it encourages the movement of the lips. When the child begins to make sounds, use them to devise

develop. Language development is usually delayed, not disordered. | single words. If he can say 'b' choose words which begin with 'b' – ball, bag, bat – and reinforce the word with the real object at first, then move to pictures. As concentration is a problem, the child is more likely to retain his interest in the discussion if a real toy is present. The young child finds it difficult to process large amounts of verbal information, so keep instructions short and limit sentences to as few words as possible like: 'Point to the ball'. Repeat sentences in the same form and encourage the child to listen to and repeat nursery rhymes.

Motor skills

During the early stages of development, it is the execution of motor-skills which encourages the development of the neural pathways in the brain. Access to motor-skills programmes is fundamental in the remediation of dyspraxia. This is paramount, irrespective of the age of the child. Dyspraxic children find it extremely difficult to execute tasks which involve co-ordination of arms and legs and, whereas the majority of youngsters acquire naturally a level of ability in such activities, the dyspraxic child only does so with practice.

Some parents have said to me: 'He couldn't possibly be dyspraxic: he plays football for the school team'. The child has practised a particular skill to a level which is more than competent. However, with dyspraxic youngsters these skills do not generalise to other areas and in the case of the good footballers they had very poor co-ordination of their upper limb movements. Because these skills are not acquired naturally each has to be taught sequentially to the child. Co-ordinated arm and leg movements for swimming should be taught separately. Children with dyspraxia can master the skills, but they require regular structured programmes.

This can be compared with some children who experience difficulties with reading. They may recognise letter sounds but are unable to prefix them to blends. For example, the word ending could be 'at'. With different initial letters the word could be read as:

- mat
- sat
- cat
- bat
- hat.

The child who is unable to generalise the sound 'at' cannot merely prefix the different letters but has to learn five separate words.

If the child cannot generalise newly-acquired movements, each activity has to be broken down into its components and taught sequentially. This is the purpose of directing the child to specific motor activities.

At the pre-school stage (under 3), many parents believe that they are unsupported in working through their child's difficulties. As with older pupils, the rate of progress is much faster when the intervention programme is carried out with the support of other children and familiar adults. This can be the case for the younger child if he has access to structured movement activities outside the home but within the local community. The dyspraxic child will benefit most from the structured sessions because, given the freedom to choose the activity, he would choose one which did not involve much co-ordination of motor skills. Play-groups are important to encourage development of the child's inter-personal skills but in addition the dyspraxic child should have the facility to learn to climb and co-ordinate movements on pieces of large apparatus.

The Tumble Tots programme is one I have studied and would recommend to parents concerned about a child experiencing difficulties with the acquisition of motor skills. Classes are organised for children up to the age of 7.

The idea for establishing such provision originated when Bill Cosgrave, an Olympic gymnastics coach, began working with youngsters in schools in 1979. He believes that physical skills have to be learned; they are not inherited. He has devised programmes which teach the components of basic motor skills in an enjoyable and child-centred environment.

The schemes are well structured and run by trained, qualified members of staff. Although the programmes are designed to benefit all children under 7, the organisation has recognised the importance of extending the provision to include youngsters with special educational needs. The leaders' handbook makes particular reference to youngsters with perceptual motor difficulties and highlights the organisation's awareness of the condition. It suggests that symptoms exist in varying degrees and are compounded by frustration, low self-esteem, lack of patience and repeated failures. The following directions are given to instructors:

- Children will respond to tasks which are appropriate for their level of ability.

- Effort and success must be recognised and praise should be constant.

- Tasks requiring balance, rhythm and co-ordination are most useful. Both gross and fine motor skills will require breaking down into the most simple stages of progression.

- Spatial and perceptual difficulties are evident and these may be signs of poor motor organisation.

- Ball handling skills will be difficult to achieve and careful attention to the correct sequencing is essential for progress.

Motor-skills programmes encourage children to develop their abilities progressively. Parents are involved from the outset to ensure that there is the opportunity to practise newly acquired and emerging skills at home. This is an integral part of the programme as children with motor difficulties need more time to learn to co-ordinate movements.

The Tumble Tots programme incorporates specific activities which relate to the baseline assessment which was introduced in September 1998 for all pupils in the reception class. The record of achievement from Tumble Tots provides additional information for the receiving school.

Class structure

Sessions are divided so that time can be given to the child working individually with large apparatus and part can be spent in the group working co-operatively, manipulating a large parachute or responding with appropriate gestures to nursery rhymes. Examples of some of the equipment and its function can be seen in Figure 7.1:

1 Meccano walking

Apparatus which develops balance and gross motor co-ordination skills. It has a 10 cm walking surface, 7.5 cm off the ground, allowing a wide range of shapes to be presented. Children are encouraged to walk along the beams, arms outstretched.

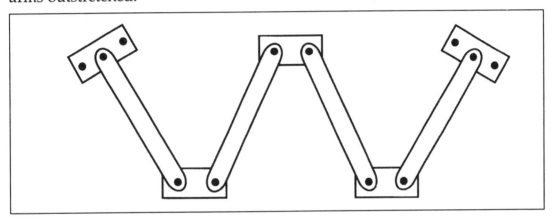

Figure 7.1(a) Meccano walking

2 Wobble boards

This apparatus helps the child to determine the centre of gravity in his body. It develops the ability to maintain balance forward, backward and left to right. A variety of boards offer different surface angles.

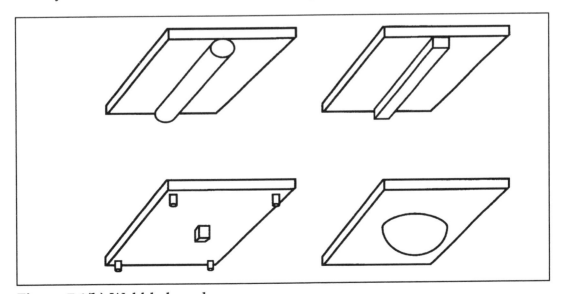

Figure 7.1(b) Wobble boards

3 Box tunnel

The tunnel is designed for the early toddler and incorporates two different heights. The child is encouraged to improve his crawling ability and move his limbs in a co-ordinated manner.

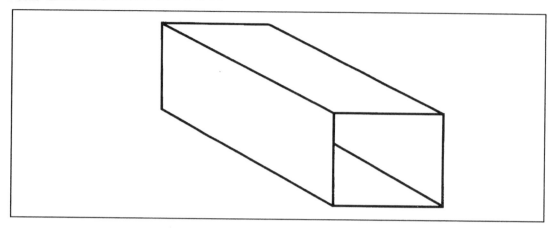

Figure 7.1(c) Box tunnel

4 Spring ball

Appropriate for the development of good eye-hand and eye-foot co-ordination for all ages. A small sponge ball is placed at point B, and pressure applied at point A with hand or foot launches the ball into the air.

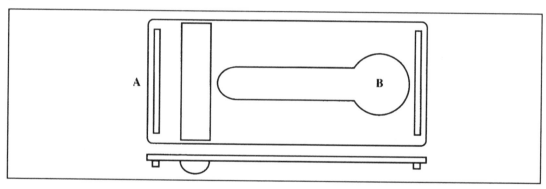

Figure 7.1(d) Spring ball

5 Bird beam

A long wooden beam for low balance and locomotor activities. Comprises an interchangeable 10 cm and 5 cm walking surface.

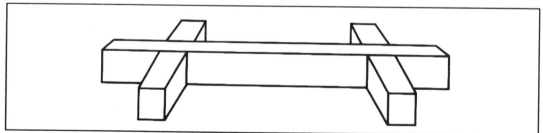

Figure 7.1(e) Bird beam

6 Stepping stones

The child is encouraged to place one foot on each step and the activity is designed to develop eye–foot co-ordination. Body awareness of right and left is also extended.

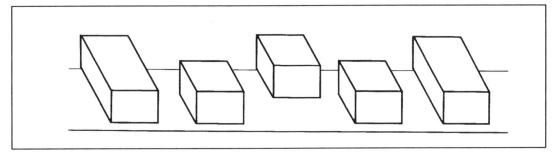

Figure 7.1(f) Stepping stones

7 Monkey walk

Advanced climbing and locomotor apparatus for children aged 2+. It allows an extended range of challenging skills to be offered, from inclined to suspended movement. The pieces may be used independently or combined to form a total system designed to meet the individual needs of developing children.

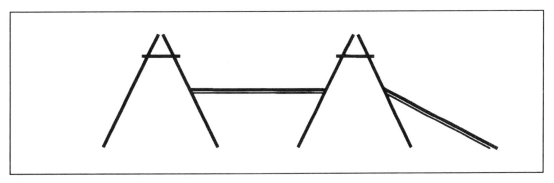

Figure 7.1(g) Monkey walk

8 Penguin line

The child places one foot on each side of the central fixture marked A. The apparatus is ideal for developing the correct angle of foot placement for the early toddler.

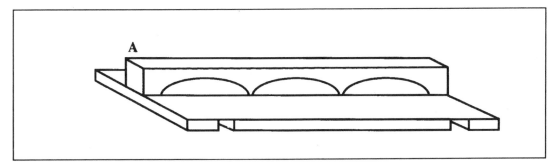

Figure 7.1(h) Penguin line

Tumble Tots classes are available for children of pre-school age. Between the ages of 5 and 7 youngsters are able to attend Gym Bobs, which is an extension of the earlier motor programme.

The purpose of any motor-skills programme, whether completed with an external agency or at home, is to break the task down into manageable steps which can be taught sequentially to the child. Listed below are activities designed to improve gross and fine motor skills prior to nursery admission. Equipment marked * is listed in Appendix C which gives the name and address of the supplier.

Gross motor movement

Observe the child and see how well he is able to co-ordinate his hands when walking and running. If his hands are waving above waist height give him something to carry and repeat the activity. A large foam ball* is light and easy to hold, so measure a distance approximately four metres and place a container/basket at one end. Ask the child to walk the distance and place the ball in the basket. Then repeat the activity with the child running. Keep practising ten times daily until the child is able to walk and run, keeping his hands down without holding the ball.

Throwing a large and then a small ball towards a target will develop gross motor and perceptual skills. Bean bags* or spider balls* are less mobile and may be more appropriate for children who are having difficulty directing their shots.

Encourage the child to crawl; this can be achieved by using a play tunnel* or by making an obstacle course with furniture where the child can crawl under the seat of a chair. He may find it difficult to move arms and legs in opposition to one another so allow the child to follow your demonstration. (Extend right arm, move left leg, extend left arm, move right leg.)

Climbing skills may be very immature: at the age of 3 the child may not be able to place his feet, individually, on each step. Demonstrate using hands and feet, lifting initially the right hand and foot up to the next stair and then the left. When the child is confident climbing on all fours, concentrate on using just the appropriate leg movements. An extension exercise is to encourage the child to make large 'giant' steps, initially on the floor, then using the stepping stones* apparatus described in Figure 7.1.

Jumping, feet together, follows and the child may be unable to propel himself from the floor. Break the task into its components and encourage him initially to jump from a small step. When the child begins to master the action, which requires the ability to balance while the knees are bent, he will develop the posture required to jump. A small trampoline* with a safety handle provides motivation for the child to master the skills and requires less physical effort than jumping unaided on the floor. The next stage is to encourage the child to jump feet together from a low step with hands held.

Dyspraxic youngsters have an under-developed sense of balance and have problems finding their positions in space. Encourage the child to stand on one foot and then the other, counting how many seconds balance is maintained. The child will need to steady himself, holding initially on to a chair with one hand.

The child may find it helpful to rest the lifted foot on a small tennis ball to give additional security. This helps to develop balancing skills before the child is able to do so independently. As confidence improves, increase the size of the ball.

As the child becomes more familiar with the activity let him hold a bean bag* or soft toy in each hand. With improving confidence he will be able to balance without touching anything. If the child is able to achieve five or more seconds on each foot by the age of 4 this is an acceptable standard. Competence in balancing must be achieved before the child is encouraged to hop.

Continue to develop the child's skills by encouraging him to balance on a variety of textures, e.g. sand, foam mat or cushions. There are a number of commercially available products which are designed to develop balancing skills. The foot wobble board* has an uneven base and the aim is to persuade a small coloured ball to loop its way along a groove in the surface. The balance board* resembles a small see-saw and follows a similar principle. The purpose is to move a small ball from left to right along the surface tracks. The balance disc* is circular and coloured feet are drawn on the surface to ensure the correct balance position.

By the age of 3, the majority of youngsters will be able to pedal a trike. This is not the case with dyspraxic children. They find it difficult enough co-ordinating the pedals without trying to steer as well. Unfortunately the trike has the pedals usually on the front wheel, which requires far greater effort to execute the turning movement. It is much easier when the child is 4–5 and can sit astride a bike with stabilisers. The pedals are directly below the line of the body and the larger wheels require less force to make the turning arc. The dyspraxic child may find it impossible to master the skills required to ride the smaller trike so it may be less distressing if he uses a 'sit-astride trike'* and waits until he is tall enough for the larger model. (The sit-astride trike does not have any pedals and the child propels himself using his feet. It is similar in design to the trikes other children the same age would be using.)

Fine motor skills

From an early age, the dyspraxic child avoids tasks which require good manipulative skills. This is unfortunate because the configuring of smaller pieces into larger shapes (Lego and Meccano) and the completion of jigsaws and inset puzzles are the foundation for the development of good perceptual skills. As it is the motor component of the task which is discouraging, it is important to offer alternatives to the usual 'play' equipment of young children. The larger plastic pieces such as Mega Bloks* and Waffle* make construction tasks much easier. In addition, give the child inset boards with large handles* attached to the pieces. This enables him to develop knowledge about shapes without relying on a good pincer grasp to complete the activity.

Ability to co-ordinate eye–hand movement is another emerging skill which needs to be extended. Although it would be expected that by the age of 3 a child should be threading beads and buttons, the dyspraxic child is often not able to manipulate the materials adequately and becomes very frustrated if asked to do so. There are far more interesting threading activities available which do not involve such small pieces of equipment. Suggestions would be 'Threading fruit'*, 'Threading butterfly'* and the 'Lacing shoe'.* The magnetic fish game is always popular with young children and there is a delightful extension of this called 'Foam fishing'* using large fish which can be played in the bath. Any activity should be regarded as fun to complete or the child will be reluctant to participate.

Another activity which improves perceptual skills and develops eye–hand co-ordination is the moulding of clay* and dough* into recognisable shapes. This encourages the development of tactile skills which are often immature in dyspraxic children. Roll shapes like snakes so the child experiences the texture of the material in his hands. Shape cutters provide good templates for directed activities.

The programmes developed for the pre-school child are extended into the nursery environment where the child should be given as many opportunities as possible to improve his skills.

Activities in the nursery

Observing the dyspraxic child in the nursery gives parents and staff the opportunity to record the activities generally enjoyed and those which are avoided. His ability to concentrate, his language skills and relationships with other children are important details of baseline behaviour.

Because the dyspraxic youngster has difficulty understanding the concept of time, the day requires some structure. A method of indicating to the child what is going to happen next should be established. He needs access to a visually-structured environment as verbal instructions are difficult to process. When giving information, always use clear language and remember that dyspraxic pupils have problems separating relevant information from background noise. An example of the type of instruction which might be used at the end of the session is: 'Tidy-up time'. The child should be established in a routine where he knows the procedure when that announcement is made. It is more relevant than saying: 'Now I would like you all to stop what you are doing and clear the tables ready for story-time'. In the example three words convey the same meaning as 20.

The dyspraxic child may find it very difficult to settle down and may be observed moving quickly between activities. Water play and sand are relatively secure and will usually not present any difficulties. The construction table will be visited infrequently, often to knock down rather than build up designs. The drawing table will be avoided, although when pushed he will make a few scribbled marks on the paper. Depending on the nature of the activities, outdoor play can present an excellent means of extending gross motor skills.

Nursery environment

- Use black line drawings on card to identify areas of activity (see Appendix A). Attach the card next to the water play, home corner, computer etc. and keep a separate set of cards for use with the child.

- Ensure that the child knows what is expected of him: demonstrate the activity first.

- Provide structure for the child so that he knows, for example, that the session begins when he removes his coat, is halfway through at snack time and ends with a story or nursery rhymes.

- Ensure that when seated, the chair is the appropriate height for the table.

- Offer the child access to a variety of activities as concentration may be limited to a few minutes.

Extension activities

Gross motor activities

Motor activities can be structured to produce particular movements, for example, when copying the appropriate actions in nursery rhymes. The dyspraxic child takes longer to process information and will perform the actions after the other children. Make sure that an adult is available to help the child to sequence his motor movements in time, and with repetition he will master the task. If support is not in place at the outset he will be aware quickly that he cannot achieve the desired response and will become distressed.

Climbing, running and playing on large play equipment should be encouraged. Access to specific pieces of equipment like play cubes* and tunnels* develops movement skills by-passed frequently in the early years. Balance beams* and wobble boards*, as described previously, extend the child's skills. Parents may encourage their child to attend out-of-school gymnastics sessions.

Colourful cut-out designs of hands and feet (available in two sizes) ensure that the child's position is appropriate. They can be incorporated into a crawling activity if the child is having difficulty placing his hands and feet. Where children have a tendency to walk on their toes, they can be encouraged to place the whole of their foot on the coloured shape.

Fine motor skills

Begin by encouraging the child to make shapes* and patterns in the sand or spray foam using his fingers.

Develop the child's understanding of textures using a 'feelie bag' and tactile touch cards.*

Make shapes from clay,* sand and play dough.* Start using animal or shape cutters.* Give the child access to screw toys to develop fine prehension and wrist movements. Appropriate activities would be Geo nuts and bolts* .

Encourage the child to develop 'cutting' skills, perhaps in the life area with plastic fruit* or bread* where the slices are attached by Velcro.

As described in the pre-school programme, the dyspraxic child will have difficulty threading beads, so access to large pieces of equipment like the lacing shoe* or the butterfly* will enable him to master the skill.

The dyspraxic child needs encouragement to develop pre-writing skills and the activities should be broken into small steps. Direct the child to the painting corner and begin with fingers and hands. When the child is able to hold the brush appropriately, encourage him to make large arcs and circles on the paper. After developing circular motion allow the child to copy vertical and horizontal lines.

When the child is ready to use crayons and pencils he may find the 'chubbi stumps' difficult to manipulate and prefer to use felt-tips or ordinary pencils. If pencil grip continues to be weak, allow the child to use those which are triangular* in shape.

Closing scissors can be extremely frustrating and a suggestion would be to use Stirex* scissors which are manipulated by squeezing the whole hand. The child may then have success with self-opening scissors* which accommodate youngsters with a weak grip. If the whole idea is too difficult it is possible to obtain double-handed training scissors.*

Perceptual skills

As the child develops his fine motor skills, he will be able to complete a range of tasks which extend his perceptual ability. A specially-designed weaving loom* develops good manipulative skills and the child has the incentive to produce a sample which can be converted into a scarf or table mat.

Reproducing shapes either by drawing or building should be extended. Access to large apparatus Waffle* and Mega Bloks* should be offered instead of the more usual nursery equipment like Lego. Templates* can be used but the dyspraxic child who has problems crossing the mid-line of his body may copy around the right side with his right hand and change to his left hand to finish it off. When hand-dominance is established, demonstrate to the child how the shape can be drawn using one hand.

The dyspraxic child has problems co-ordinating both hands and forgets to secure the paper with one hand while drawing with the other. Use Blu-Tack or paper clips to keep the paper in place.

Problems with manipulative skills will discourage the child from attempting jigsaws and formboards. There are many age-appropriate inset boards* available which have large handles attached to the pieces. The sequential sorting box* has replacement lids which offer a variety of five geometric shapes to match with inserts. The lids become more complex and are designed to extend perceptual skills.

Encourage the child to work on sequencing tasks, which may be to order three pictures to make sense of a story or to arrange shapes ▲ ▲ ▲ in order of size. Magnetic boards* and Fuzzy-felt* shapes overcome the problems of drawing. Formogram games* provide a series of plastic templates with printed designs which can be made from triangles, squares, circles and rectangles. Suggestions are made for matching games which develop visual perception and logical thinking. Placeashape* is an extension activity where the templates are more complex.

A three-dimensional game called 'Near and Far'* has been produced to develop a child's understanding of size and perspective. Judging distances is a problem for dyspraxic youngsters. The game requires the child to place familiar objects, e.g. people, in front of a house. It familiarises children with the terms *far, in front of, behind, right* and *left*, while developing perceptual skills.

Language development and social skills

A child with verbal dyspraxia may have good understanding but limited communication skills. With encouragement and direction from the class leader, nursery children readily accept other pupils with speech difficulties. Without teacher involvement the child will become anxious and frustrated if he cannot communicate his ideas. Follow the child's gestures and use the symbol cards to change activity.

The dyspraxic child may prefer to be on his own, so he should be encouraged initially to work alongside and then with another pupil. This environment will have to be created because the other pupils may find his excitable behaviour difficult to accept.

Poor attentional skills are characteristic and a personal target may be set for the child to spend five minutes initially on each activity. This should be extended as appropriate.

The dyspraxic child finds imaginative play difficult to comprehend, but with the help of an adult can learn to relate. Dressing up and playing different roles involves the child with other pupils.

Information conveyed verbally can be very confusing and story-time may present problems. The child is unable to concentrate and sit still for periods in excess of a few minutes and arrangements should be made to accommodate this difficulty. Perhaps he could be allowed to turn the pages and point to the pictures. He may be required to join the group for only the last five minutes, gradually extending the time as his concentration improves.

Additional information

The child must enjoy going to nursery and incentives are necessary to encourage him to attempt tasks he finds difficult. A personal chart* in the nursery and at home is a record of his achievements. Stars and stickers are visible rewards and are a recognition of his effort.

The following is an example of a possible chart. Child X has been attending nursery during the morning sessions for six weeks. He loves using the computer and playing outdoors in the sand pit but has difficulty relating to other pupils and refuses to enter the story corner at the end of the session. In addition his fine motor skills are immature but he is able to scribble with crayons on a piece of paper.

Target behaviour for X

Long-term goals:

1. To work co-operatively with another pupil for five minutes

2. To sit appropriately through story-time, for 15 minutes

3. To copy unaided a ●, ■ and ▲ using a pencil.

The programme must develop X's skills to achieve the long-term goals and offer rewards to encourage him to perform the specified activities.

Symbols on the chart (Figure 7.2) refer to these activities, which in detail are:

On arrival at nursery X will be allowed to use the computer by himself for ten minutes

Still sitting at the computer, X will play co-operatively with another child

X will sit for three minutes at the snack table

X can play in the sand or water until story time

X will sit next to the teacher and hold the story book for two minutes and then be allowed to return to the computer

The child can mark the chart himself each day to record his progress (Figure 7.2). The co-operative play may change and the time spent in story-time can be extended until X's behaviour is appropriate by comparison with the rest of the group. It is not necessary continually to monitor five activities; choose the number appropriate for the child.

Always break the task down into smaller steps to enable the child to achieve success. Use zips and Velcro fasteners instead of buttons and laces if possible. If problems persist when the child is trying to co-ordinate a knife and fork use angled cutlery* until he is able to effect more accurate control.

Activities for children in the reception class

On transfer to reception the child will be aware of the change in the classroom environment. The curriculum is more formal and there is less opportunity for the child to improve his gross motor skills. Outside play is available only at the prescribed time. Organised games and access to specialised equipment is usually restricted to PE lessons, although some schools provide fixed outdoor climbing frames and have permanent markings on the playground for games such as hop-scotch. The dyspraxic child will be able to avoid activities essential for development if he is not directed towards them.

Figure 7.2 Target sheet for nursery children

Integration of the child within his peer group should be established as soon as possible because this is the most significant factor in ensuring future progress and happiness in school. Children who experience rejection from an early stage in school often become isolated, have low self-esteem and exhibit extreme behavioural difficulties before reaching the end of their primary education. Relationships within the classroom may have to be engineered until the other children are able to understand the difficulties experienced by the dyspraxic child. Many teachers express concerns about identifying the problems with some pupils and discussing them with the whole group. Children are very observant and know when another pupil is finding some of the work difficult. By saying nothing, the less able child will become the victim of comment and criticism. A more positive ethos is achieved when the whole class is involved in offering support, as highlighted in the previous chapter.

It is important that parents and staff are involved in planning activities for the child to ensure that approaches are consistent at home and in school.

Classroom environment

- Provide structure to the day and establish routines for entering and leaving the classroom.
- Position the child centrally in the classroom where he cannot touch wall displays or equipment either in cupboards or on tables.
- Allow the child sufficient time to change into outdoor clothing.
- Ensure that eye contact is made with the child before giving instructions.
- Keep verbal information succinct when directing an activity and use visual cues whenever possible.
- Be prepared to modify the task: if there is a motor skill component allow extra time.
- Classroom furniture should be sturdy and secure – dyspraxic children have poor stability.

Extension activities

Gross motor skills

The structured programmes offered by specialist outside agencies are ideal for the child at this stage. Activities are developed by qualified instructors and the child will have access to equipment designed to improve balance, co-ordination and perceptual skills. Parents can continue the recommended exercises during the week as the dyspraxic child requires more practice to acquire the skill. Many youngsters do not have access to outside specialists and parents can implement their own programmes in conjunction with the school. Whether the activities are to be carried out in school, at home or with other specialist tutors the programme should include:

- balancing on each foot, extending activity to different surfaces and wobble boards*
- walking heel to toe along a small beam or painted line
- jumping, feet together – a trampoline will make the task more enjoyable
- hopping a distance of up to 4 metres
- climbing ladders and steps – hand and feet moving in opposition
- crawling on all fours – an activity tunnel* provides greater incentive
- kicking a ball towards a 1 metre target placed 4 metres from the child
- running a measured distance of 10+ metres.

Observe the child's hand movements during these activities. The purpose is not only to acquire the skills to be able to hop, jump etc. but to separate out his associated hand movements. If arms and hands are flailing around, give the child an object to hold. A large sponge ball held with both hands prevents involuntary hand movements and enables the child to achieve better posture and master the skill. Keep practising the activity in this manner until the associated movements cease and then proceed without holding the ball. To achieve the balancing skills the child should complete the activities with his arms outstretched. It may help to hold a bean bag* in each hand.

A programme to develop co-ordinated upper body movement should include:

- throwing and catching a large ball a distance of 3 metres
- target practice – large ball aimed with both hands at a 50 cm target 3 metres away
- wheelbarrow game – hold the legs of the child, initially at the knees then ankles, as he develops the skills of walking forwards on his hands
- hedgehog balls*, which are very stimulating and can be used for massage and finger exercises.

Fine motor skills

By the time the child enters the reception class he will be expected to have developed many pre-writing skills. This depends on the child's ability to interpret what he is seeing and have sufficiently mature fine motor co-ordination to reproduce it. Some of the activities suggested for nursery-age children may be appropriate for pupils of school age. When the child is able to hold a crayon or pencil and can use scissors, even with some residual difficulty, it is important that attention is focused on the development of his handwriting.

The ability to write legibly is a skill which must be taught as it is not simply acquired. The majority of dyspraxic children who, even by the age of 13 or 14, still cannot produce anything on paper which can be interpreted readily, have developed a poor handwriting style. At the outset this was based on incorrect letter formation and a limited conceptual awareness of page layout. As the child progresses through the education system he is required manually to record increasing quantities of information. The quality of that recording can be viewed as a reflection of the child's ability. Dyspraxic children can easily be judged as failing if handwriting is a factor in the assessment. The child will benefit greatly from adopting the correct style in the beginning. Such children are very good at developing their own unsatisfactory compensatory system.

Provide the child with a writing implement which is comfortable to use. Dyspraxic children often have a weak grip and consequently over-compensate by holding the pencil too tightly. The result will be a broken point or a torn page.

A triangular pencil or triangular grip will help the child establish the correct finger positions. Grips with animal shapes* attached are very popular with younger children and are available from the Early Learning Centre. Parents may find it helpful to encourage the child to use the same aids at home.

Encourage the child to colour simple pictures and shapes. Felt-tipped pens require less pressure and produce more colourful results than pencils or crayons. Develop left–right orientation and mark the starting point on the page. Pre-writing skills worksheets* provide a series of graded exercises which encourage left-to-right tracking skills and basic letter patterns. To complement this programme the child would benefit from the Rol 'n' Write* scheme which involves a steel ball slowly tracing the letter in the correct sequence. In addition the child can follow the groove with his finger. The exercise develops fine motor control and improves fluency of letter formation.

The dyspraxic child finds it almost impossible to record sequentially on a blank page. Draw lines and mark the left side of the page with a dot. Allow the youngster to explore the shape of letters before attempting to copy them. When an understanding of the letter shape is achieved the child should be shown how to produce the appropriate size. Typically, dyspraxic children will produce script which is a mixture of upper and lower case letters of varying heights with no spaces between the words. They continue to be unaware of the rules of writing unless these are repeatedly pointed out to them. N.E.S. Arnold has produced a selection of 26 templates which incorporate a series of graded letter grooves. As the letter size decreases the children acquire more controlled handwriting skills and are able to form the correct, appropriately sized shapes.

Handwriting is a major part of the classroom curriculum and there are many activities which encourage the development of the fine motor skills required to produce correctly formed letters. Flexibility of the wrist can be improved if the child is encouraged to make continuous large circular patterns with a paint brush. Attach the paper to an easel as the skill can be mastered more quickly on an almost vertical rather than a flat surface. The Ayres Collection has developed a series of wooden panels with cut-out tracks which become increasingly complex. The target is to pull the bead along the pre-determined track.

Writing pattern boards* are designed to improve the skills of youngsters with limited motor control. Paper is inserted between two boards and a pencil is used to trace the outline shapes cut into the upper surface. The shapes progress from vertical and horizontal lines to zig-zags and curves.

As the child becomes more confident with the pencil control he will enjoy completing simple dot-to-dot pictures* .

Using scissors continues to present difficulties even when they are modified. The child will find it helpful if a border approximately 1 cm wide is created around the picture. It is much easier to cut between lines than to try to manoeuvre scissors along the edge of the picture.

Perceptual skills

Parents and teachers will observe the perceptual problems experienced by the child in his drawings and collage. If the child is given the materials to reproduce a picture he will be unable to place the parts in the correct sequence on the page. In the example (Figure 7.3) the child was given five shaped pieces and asked to place them appropriately to represent the rocket. She could not fit the parts together to reproduce the whole.

The reception class teacher working with Amy has provided some suggestions for shape pictures and they are included in Appendix A (Figure A.12). A magnetic board* with a selection of shapes is an alternative method of developing the skill.

Encourage the child to build three-dimensional models and play games guessing which pieces are farthest away. Multi-link* activities are designed to give practical experience to develop an understanding of shape, measurement and number. They offer a visual representation of the concepts involved in early number skills.

Figure 7.3 Rocket by Amy – age 5

The child may continue to find it difficult to cross his mid-line so activities should be developed to encourage him to do so. An example would be to ask the child to sit on the floor with his legs stretched out in front of him. Place ten objects, five on either side of his thighs. Place a different coloured sticker or picture on the back of each hand to discriminate between left and right. The instructions would be: 'Pick up the ball with your right hand; the red sticker is on the back'.

Large-piece jigsaw puzzles would be appropriate although at first the child may be reluctant to try them. There are also many computer programs which develop the child's perceptual skills and concept of shape. Assess whether the child favours a mouse or joy-stick to control the movement of the arrow.

Always try to minimise the level of difficulty when there is a motor skill component involved in any activity.

Language development

By the age of five, the dyspraxic child will have acquired the skills necessary to communicate verbally in sentences of 5+ syllables. He will continue to use gestures to convey meaning and this will involve him in higher levels of motor activity. The teacher should make allowances for this behaviour and not perceive it as the child being deliberately disruptive.

Information conveyed verbally takes longer to process and the dyspraxic child will rarely respond immediately to requests. Repeat instructions and remind all of the pupils what is required. The child must be included as part of the class group and not continually singled out for negative attention.

Good listening skills are a prerequisite for language development and all pupils can benefit from programmes which encourage their development. Ask the children to sit quietly with their eyes closed and arrange for a series of sounds to be made in different parts of the room. When the child has learned to focus on the direction of the sound he will be able to listen and respond more appropriately to the voice of the teacher.

ROMPA have produced a series of sound and picture matching sets to develop such skills. They are suitable for nursery and reception class pupils. The sounds include: whistling, laughing, sneezing, eating, brushing teeth and chopping vegetables. A second tape offers animal sounds with additional recordings of the rain, wind and sea.

Language development is dependent on the ability to sequence information and reproduce it verbally. Some of the commercial programmes designed to develop such skills are available from the Ayres Collection. The titles include 'Visual sequencing cards'*, 'Visual auditory sequencing on tape' and 'Sequential thinking cards'*. In addition there is a series of picture cards and the child is asked: 'What's wrong?' This generates discussion about the event, but the activity must be completed with an adult.

Additional information

The child should be given personal targets to achieve in areas of greatest concern. Reduce the distractions in the classroom and give constant reminders to encourage the child to remain on task. Offer the appropriate praise whether it is verbal, giving the child a sticker, or recording progress on a chart. Always find something positive to say during the session; children at this age work not for themselves but for the approval of the teacher or another adult.

Arrange activities so that the child is able to work with a small group within the class. Find some means of attaching the paper or book to the desk to stop it moving while the child is trying to draw or write. The classroom environment must be adapted to suit the child as he may find it impossible to adapt to it.

Activities for children in Years 1 and 2

After leaving the reception class, the learning environment is even more structured and child and teacher are under pressure to achieve specified levels in curricular attainments. There is less opportunity for the child to become involved in programmes to develop gross motor skills during the school day. By the age of 6, a child will usually have had the opportunity to experience a variety of activities which would extend his ability to co-ordinate motor movement. As stated earlier, the dyspraxic child cannot acquire these skills naturally. He must be offered a programme which breaks down the skills into smaller steps and teaches them in a sequential manner. The exercise programme detailed in Chapter 8 is suitable for youngsters from the age of 6 who have motor learning difficulties. The entry point on the programme is dependent on the ability of the child, not his age, and is therefore suitable for any child or young adult with perceptual-motor problems.

Classroom environment

- Seating should allow the child to rest both feet flat on the floor.

- The desk should be at elbow height with the facility to use a sloping surface for reading and additional activities.

- The child should be placed so he is able to view the teacher directly without turning his body.

- Make prepared recording sheets available to reduce the quantity of handwriting required.

- Use lined paper with spaces sufficiently wide to accommodate the child's handwriting.

- Attach the paper to the desk to avoid the unnecessary distress of having to hold it in position with one hand while trying to draw or write with the other.

- Reinforce verbal instructions by repeating them several times.

- A distraction-free environment with low noise levels enables the child to focus. This is not easy in an 'early years' environment.

- Allow extra time for the completion of a task.

Extension activities

Gross motor skills

Design either an individual programme or involve a small group of pupils selecting activities from the programme outlined in the next chapter. Completing a baseline assessment and the selection of targets is also discussed in Chapter 8.

Children can be encouraged to develop gross motor skills in the playground. Markings for hop-scotch and other games offer such opportunities.

Fine motor skills

The child will be starting to master the reproduction of letter shapes. He will continue to have difficulty placing the letter or numeral in the correct position on the page. Prepared sheets with columns already drawn which require the child to write only the answer reduce the stress of setting out the work. Aids for ensuring the correct pencil grip may continue to be necessary. Physical pressure required to produce handwritten material can be exhausting for the dyspraxic child. Some youngsters also exhibit a mild tremor which becomes more noticeable when they become anxious or tired. Computer-assisted learning can reduce pressure to produce written material but it should not be viewed as a substitute for handwriting.

Perceptual skills

Difficulties may persist with the child's awareness of connecting shapes. He can reproduce drawings of people and objects but they are misrepresented. Figures 7.4 and 7.5 are illustrations. Although Ian has included all the components of the house and the cat, they are incorrectly positioned when he has re-assembled the parts into the whole. The house has four windows, a door, a roof and smoke coming from the chimney. Ian is able to produce the squares and rectangles appropriately. The cat presented more complex problems. Many of the shapes are irregular and while the face is centralised in the body, the ears and whiskers are external. The Frostig visual-perceptual programme* offers a variety of materials which develop these skills in young children.

When the dyspraxic child is required to understand new concepts he should have access to multi-sensory methods of instruction. The Multi-link* materials encourage the child to develop number skills using blocks and coloured templates. This scheme is extended to MathSafari* which offers challenging activities to explore aspects of mathematics including shape, space, position and rotational symmetry. Pupils learn at their own pace by manipulating pieces of Multi-link in order to problem-solve.

Language development

By the age of 6 or 7 the dyspraxic child may have compensated for his early delayed language skills. He may have an extensive vocabulary but not learned

Figure 7.4 House by Ian (age 6)

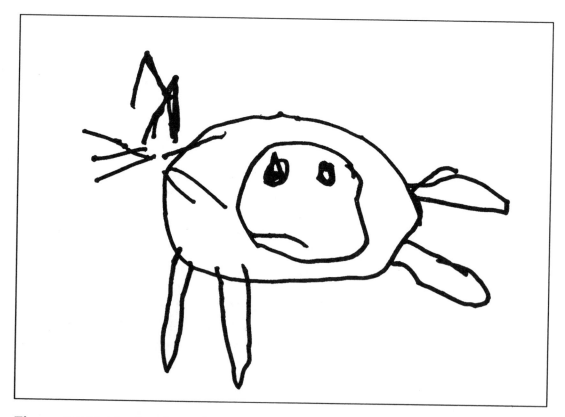

Figure 7.5 Cat by Ian (age 6)

the social rules of conversation. He does not wait for the person speaking to finish, he makes his ideas known as they occur to him. In addition his voice may be loud with poor tone. The teacher needs to be aware of the potential difficulties which may arise if other members of the class pass adverse comments every time he speaks. More time will have to be spent encouraging the child to respond appropriately in class either when asked a direct question or taking his turn as part of the larger group. Allowances should be made for his uncontrollable enthusiasm but firm clear instructions should reinforce the expected behaviour.

Many dyspraxic children are able to read well but if asked to read aloud their presentation is hesitant. Spelling may present some problems but having to record information in writing is their greatest cause of anxiety. Their speed of processing information is reduced and sequencing tasks such as story-writing may prove to be extremely difficult. It would help the child if he could be given sentences or paragraphs to sequence instead of having to write the entire story on paper. Give the child the opportunity to record his work on tape and give oral presentations.

Figures 7.6 and 7.7 are examples of Ian's handwriting before and after intervention. The intervention programme lasted two terms. The exercises are outlined in Chapter 8.

Additional information

The dyspraxic child can appear to be excitable and highly emotional. This is usually linked to the frustration experienced when he is unable to complete tasks to his satisfaction. It is important for the child to have personal targets set for him so he does not see himself in competition with the rest of his peer group. Set targets which are achievable in the short term, perhaps over a period of one or two weeks, so he can observe his progress. Always find something to praise every day to break the cycle of failure he may already have experienced.

Simplify tasks and reduce the added anxiety to a minimum. On days when PE is part of the timetable let the child wear clothing which can be removed easily.

Always allow extra time for the child to finish the task or reduce the quantity of work required. A child who is told he has to stay behind in class to complete unfinished work soon becomes disaffected, especially when he is trying as hard as he can.

The last instruction given to a class should be the one the child is expected to follow. This is important when the class is divided into groups which are allocated different activities. Remember: following a series of verbal instructions is always problematic for the pupil with dyspraxia.

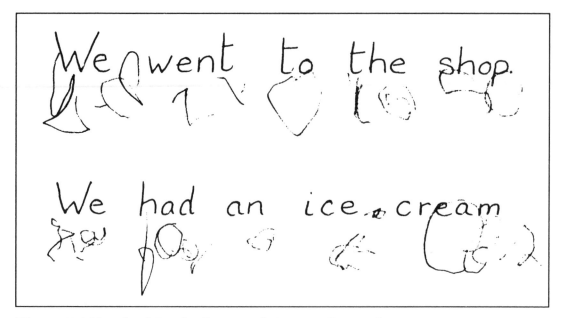

Figure 7.6 Handwriting by Ian, aged 6 years, 3 months

Figure 7.7 Handwriting by Ian, aged 6 years, 10 months

8 Intervention with primary and secondary age pupils

The most effective interventions with children aged 6 and over have involved access to structured exercise programmes. The purpose of this chapter is to explain each activity in detail and identify targets which indicate the child's mastery of that particular skill. It may be several weeks before the child is able to achieve the specified target but he would be set individual targets in the preceding weeks. For example: if the child is able to balance independently on his right foot for two seconds the final target could be to achieve 10+ seconds. The first week's target might be four seconds, extending it as he develops his skills. When the recommended target is achieved the child should move on to the next activity.

Activities should be selected from the programme which build on emerging skills. Do not choose an activity in which the child at the outset is unable to achieve any degree of success. Select one from earlier in the programme where the child is halfway to meeting the target. Between 15 and 20 minutes should be spent each day working on the exercise programme. Younger pupils usually follow up to a maximum of eight activities while older primary-age and secondary pupils are able to complete between 10 and 15.

The activities are organised into different sections:

- finger, hand and arm movements
- hand–eye co-ordination
- foot–eye co-ordination
- balance
- whole-body co-ordination
- sound and movement.

To determine the appropriate access point into the programme, a baseline of current skill level must be completed. The pro-forma can be found in Appendix A, Figure A.4.

Make an assessment of laterality and record details. A young child with co-ordination difficulties will have problems with balance. When a ball is placed in front of the child he would be expected to kick with the 'dominant' foot. When there are difficulties balancing to kick, the child is more likely to rest on the dominant foot and kick with the other. A more accurate assessment, therefore, would be to ask the child to hop.

Ask the child to fold his arms. The dominant arm is the one closest to the chest. Ask the child to throw a ball and record which hand is used. Many youngsters will have a dominant left hand but write with the right.

To assess eye-dominance, give the child a tube and ask him to look through it at a fixed object. The telescope will be held in front of the dominant eye.

The majority of children with specific learning difficulties do not establish laterality until they are 7 or 8 years old. Many continue to use both sides equally.

When completing the baseline motor assessment, record the movement patterns observed:

Activity	Indicators
Crawling	The child should move opposing hands and feet. The sequence should follow: right hand, left leg, left hand, right leg. The dyspraxic youngster may extend arms and pull both knees simultaneously.
	Some children 'crawl' on their knees without placing their feet on the floor.
Balance	Ask the child to balance on each foot separately: 5 years and under for 5+ seconds, 6 years and over for 10+ seconds. Note the level of success on each foot: record arm movement.
Parallel lines	Mark two parallel lines, 20 cm apart and 5 metres long. Determine whether the child can walk heel to toe between the lines without falling over: record arm movements.
	Ask the child to walk on his toes between the lines: record whether arms or hands show associated movements.
	Repeat the above activity on heels.

The child should stand with feet together between the parallel lines. Ask him to move sideways and observe whether arms and hands show associated movements.

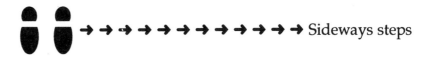 Sideways steps

Running | The child should run on his toes with arms held at waist height. The dyspraxic child usually runs on the soles of the feet with greater pressure on the leading foot (note the difference in sound when each foot is placed).

Jumping | Assess whether the child can jump on the spot with feet together and jump a series of five steps forwards. The dyspraxic child has difficulty leaving the ground and then is unable to land feet together.

Hopping | The child is requested to hop five times on each foot. Observe associated hand movements and possible tongue thrusts.

Rope turning | Attach the rope to a fixed object. The child should be placed so that the rope, when held, just touches the ground. Ask the child to turn the rope with each hand, without assistance, clockwise and then anti-clockwise. Determine whether the child can turn the rope appropriately and observe any movements in the unused hand.

Clapping | Make three consecutive beats with hands or on a tambourine (III, III) and repeat. Ask the child to copy the sounds. If the child is competent remembering a five beat sequence he has achieved the required level.

Finger sequencing | The child is asked to move the fingers of each hand separately; after an adult has demonstrated. Observe associated movements and record which fingers are difficult to move independently.

The baseline motor assessment will highlight strengths and weaknesses. Select some activities in which he may develop skills quickly and some which are more difficult. Provide the child with an individual programme and encourage him to record his own progress.

Intervention programmes

<table>
<tr><th colspan="2">Section 1: finger, hand and arm movements</th></tr>
<tr><th>Activity</th><th>Target</th></tr>
<tr>
<td>1 The child may have difficulty using each finger independently. Moving the index finger may result in the others having to extend simultaneously. Use finger puppets, either the type which fit over the finger or draw faces directly onto the fleshy tip. Initially encourage the child to use only the index finger of one hand and extend the programme until the fingers of one hand are able to move independently. Farmyard animals and nursery rhyme characters make the exercise more enjoyable.

Observe
Associated mirror movement with uninvolved fingers on the same and opposite hand. It will help the child to master the skill if initially he is able to rest all of his fingers, except the one required to move, on the edge of the table. Holding a small ball in the opposing hand will also reduce unnecessary movement.</td>
<td>To move each finger independently of any other.</td>
</tr>
<tr>
<td>2 Use 2 finger puppets (index and second finger) to co-ordinate two fingers in opposition to the rest of the hand.

Observe
Whether the right-hand fingers move without associated movements in the left and vice versa. If associated movements are in evidence, encourage the child to hold a small ball in his uninvolved hand or place his hand flat on the table surface.</td>
<td>To move two fingers simultaneously on each hand in a co-ordinated manner without associated movements in the other.</td>
</tr>
<tr>
<td>3 Use whole-hand puppet to co-ordinate three fingers appropriately.

Comments
This skill will be mastered easily if activities 1 and 2 have been taught previously.</td>
<td>To manipulate a hand puppet appropriately.</td>
</tr>
</table>

	Activity	Target
4	The child should first place his right hand and then his left on five sequential white notes on a keyboard. The notes should be numbered 1–5. **Comments** Develop the child's ability to play the notes forward with confidence before attempting them in reverse. A computer keyboard can be used if finger strength is weak.	To play the notes in sequence 1–5, then in reverse with each hand in 5 seconds.
5	The child should place each hand separately on the keyboard as before on notes numbered 1–5. **Comments** Say the numbers slowly to give the child time to process the information.	An adult will direct the child. Play separate notes not in sequence e.g. 3–5–2–1–4 without hesitation. Child to achieve 5/5 success.
6	Two chime bars placed in front of the child 5 cm apart. Child to use striker in each hand alternately. First right hand then the left. **Comments** Improves flexibility in up, down and sideways movements of the wrist. Eliminate associated movements and tongue thrust if evident. Have him hold a soft ball in opposing hand to reduce unnecessary movement.	Chime bars 20 cm apart. Child to strike each in turn 10/10 times in ten seconds.
7	Ask the child to strike each bar of the xylophone forwards and backwards in sequence. **Comments** Observe child for tongue thrusts and, if opposing hand is clenched, have him hold a small ball in his palm.	To strike each note appropriately.
8	Extension of activity 7. Remove alternate bars from the xylophone and ask the child to strike the remaining bars in sequence, forwards and backwards.	To strike each note appropriately.

Activity	Target
Comments Observe tongue thrusts and elimate associated movements in opposing hand.	
9 Give the child a small marble and ask him to manipulate it slowly between the thumb and index finger of each hand. **Comments** The child requires visual feedback so try to extend the activity when the child has mastered the skill to manoeuvre the marble with his eyes closed.	To manipulate the marble for 30 seconds with the thumb and index finger of each hand.
10 Ask the child to repeat the activity described in 9, manipulating the marble between the thumb and successive fingers on each hand. **Comments** Tongue thrusts are common so encourage the child to keep his teeth and lips together.	To manipulate the marble for 20 seconds between the thumb and successive fingers on each hand.
11 Tie a skipping rope 3 metres in length to a secure support. Ask the child to hold the other end initially in his right hand and then in his left. The child should be positioned so that the rope, when held, is a few centimetres from the floor. The child is asked to turn the rope in a wide arc from the shoulder. **Comments** Initially there will be problems when the child tries to achieve regular movement. It is important that the skill is mastered in the first instance with the arm extended. A baton or quoit may be held in his non-turning hand to keep arm down and prevent associated movements.	To turn the rope continuously in a clockwise and then an anti-clockwise manner ten times without associated movements in the opposing arm.
12 Repeat the activity outlined above with the right and then the left hand holding the rope. Hold elbows to the waist and turn the rope from the elbow.	Turn the rope 20 times with each hand.

Activity	Target
Comments The child may use his whole arm to start the rope turning: bring elbows in to the waist quickly.	
13 Repeat the activity, turning the rope from the wrist. Hold elbows to the waist for additional stability. **Comments** In activities 11, 12 and 13 observe associated movements such as tongue thrusts, motion in the opposing arm and whether the child is able to keep his feet still while turning the rope. It is important that these additional movements are eliminated.	Turn the rope 20 times with each hand.

Section 2: hand–eye co-ordination	
Activity	**Target**
1 Ask the child to hold a bean bag in each hand. Begin with both hands touching below the waist. Slowly lift hands along the mid-line of the body until both arms are extended above the head. Separate the hands and bring slowly down towards each side of the body until hands touch again below the waist. See diagram. **Comments** The child may have difficulty executing the action in a fluid manner. He may also move one arm more quickly than the other. Ensure that the actions in both arms are at the same speed. Observe tongue thrusts and discourage.	Repeat movement, co-ordinating both hands simultaneously ten times.
2 Blow a number of large bubbles into an open space. Ask the child to 'pop' them by clapping hands together on each bubble. **Comments** Use the correct fluid as children become very impatient when the bubbles burst before leaving the dispenser. Blow bubbles within reach of the child to reduce the requirement to chase after them. Encourage the child to keep teeth and lips together as tongue thrusts are common.	To burst as many bubbles as possible in two minutes.
3 Repeat activity 2, allowing the child to burst the bubbles with a large-surface bat. Use each hand for half the allocated time.	To burst as many bubbles as possible, one minute for each hand.

	Activity	Target
	Comments This task extends the child's ability to co-ordinate his hands and arms.	
4	Place the child in a low-kneeling position 3 metres away from the target. The most popular target is a set of six skittles placed 10 cm apart in front of the child. Ask the child to roll a tennis ball or equivalent to knock over the skittles. Use the right hand initially and then the left.	5/6 skittles in 2 attempts right hand. 5/6 skittles in 2 attempts, left hand.
	Comments Gradually extend the child's distance from the target until he is able to achieve the same degree of success at 5 metres distance.	5/6 skittles in 2 attempts, first with right then with left hand.
5	Standing feet together, give the child 5 bean bags. Place a basket (waste paper size) 3 metres away. Instruct the child to throw the bean bags one at a time into the basket. Throw 5 times underarm with the right hand then 5 times underarm with the left. Repeat both with over-arm throw.	4/5 successes with right and left hands using underarm and over-arm throw.
	Comments Use the bean bags to reduce the amount of time the youngsters spend chasing after balls which have missed the target. Observe child for tongue thrusts. Hold ball or bean bag in non-throwing hand to reduce associated movements.	
6	The extension activity for older pupils would require placing the target 5 m from the child. Increase the number of attempts with each hand to 10.	8/10 successes with right and left hands using underarm and over-arm throw.
	Comments As the child becomes more competent, encourage him to stand with the opposing foot in front while throwing. For example, if he is throwing with his right arm, his left foot should be placed forward to counter-balance his movement. Again observe any associated movements.	

	Activity	Target
7	Line 5 targets (skittles, plastic bottles, boxes) in a row at 4-metre distance and shoulder height. Give the child five bean bags or small soft balls and ask him to throw with his preferred hand. **Comments** A child of 9+ years will need to establish dominance and improve the skills in his preferred hand. Ensure that the opposing foot is placed in front of the body when child takes aim.	4/5 successes in 2 attempts.
8	Encourage the child to hold a large sponge ball. With two hands at waist height, bounce it once, then catch it using both hands. **Comments** The child must look at the ball because he will have difficulty in judging its speed.	Bounce and catch 10 times in succession.
9	When the child has mastered activity 8, allow him to throw the ball with a single bounce to another pupil or adult. The ball should be returned in the same way. The pupils should be positioned 3 metres apart. **Comments** The child may become very excited waiting for the ball to be returned. Encourage him to stand still by providing a small ring or square in which to stand.	10 complete catches in 40 seconds.
10	The extension activity for older pupils would be to throw the ball with a single bounce into a hoop prior to being caught by another pupil or adult. The ball is returned in the same way. Pupils should stand 4 metres apart. **Comments** Observe and eliminate any associated movements.	10 complete catches in 40 seconds.

Activity	Target
11 Bounce a large ball repeatedly on the floor, first with the right hand then the left. **Comments** The unused hand may be held in a clenched position. Give the child a small ball or baton to hold to extend the fingers. Observe and eliminate associated movements.	10 consecutive bounces with each hand.
12 Place a target 20 cm in diameter, initially 2 then extending to 4 metres distance from the pupil. Throw a large sponge ball placed at chin height towards the target. Use both hands together. **Comments** Place the target at a distance where the child can initially achieve success 4/10 times. When this is raised to 9/10 move the target farther away to a maximum of 4 metres.	9/10 success.
13 For the older pupil, 10+ years, use a wall-mounted or free-standing basketball ring. The youngster should stand 2 metres away and throw 10 times with hands together and 10 times with hands separately. **Comments** If the child is unable to achieve two or more scores in his first attempt, spend more time on activity 12.	To throw the ball through the ring with 6 or more successes in 10 attempts.
14 At this stage in the programme the child should be able to judge more accurately the speed and direction of the throw. Develop throwing and catching skills without bouncing the ball. Position pupil and adult/peer 3 metres apart. They should throw a large sponge ball to one another 10 times.	10/10 is the final target for this activity.

Activity	Target
Comments Ensure that both participants are at a level of ability where success will be achieved on 4/10 throws, otherwise frustration will be evident.	
15 Extend activity 14 using a small sponge ball. The thrower should use his right hand 10 times and then the left hand 10 times. The ball should be caught in both hands. **Comments** Do not embark on this activity until skills 1–14 in this section have been mastered.	4/5 balls caught when thrown with the right hand. 4/5 balls caught when thrown with the left hand.
16 Place 2 obstacles (cones) 1 metre apart. The child should initially stand 2 metres away. Place a small sponge ball at the feet of the child and instruct him to direct it between the posts using a bat or hockey stick. **Comments** The child should hold the stick with both hands, standing sideways to the target. If he is right-side dominant, his left side should be facing the target; the converse if he is left-sided.	8/10
17 Extend activity 16 until the child is able to achieve the same level of success 4 metres from the target. **Comments** Wait until he has achieved successes of 8/10 at 2 metres before moving the target farther away.	8/10
18 Extension activity for older pupils would be to use a short-handled bat and tennis ball. Aim at a target 3 metres away, 20 cm in diameter and at shoulder height. Ball to bounce once prior to strike at target.	8/10

Activity	Target
Comments Ensure the elimination of all associated movements. The child should stand sideways to the target, holding the bat in one hand.	
19 Two children stand 3 metres apart and face each other. They throw the catchball* and points are scored depending on the prong by which the ball is caught. **Comments** This game can involve a number of players and introduces the dyspraxic youngster to working co-operatively in a group.	8/10

Section 3: Foot–eye co-ordination	
Activity	**Target**
1 Mark two parallel lines on the floor, 6 metres long and 20 cm apart. Ask the child to walk heel-to-toe forwards and backwards between the lines. **Comments** If the child is unable to walk appropriately, cut-out shapes of feet can be used as a guide. Initially, place them in a 'normal' walking pattern, then move to a heel/toe position. Shorten the distance to 3 metres forwards and backwards if the child has difficulty completing the task. Examine the position of the hands and arms. The fists may be clenched. If so, give the child an object, e.g. tennis ball or baton, to hold. Heavier objects provide the child with increased stability. Extend the distance and remove the hand-held objects when appropriate until the child achieves the target with hands and arms held in a relaxed manner on either side of the body.	To walk forwards and backwards without stepping outside the parallel lines.
2 Using the parallel lines from activity 1, ask the child to walk on tiptoes forwards and backwards along the distance of 6 metres. **Comments** On tiptoes the child is more likely to move with hands clenched. As described in activity 1, give the child an object to hold in each hand and extend and reduce the tension in the fingers.	To walk forwards and backwards without stepping outside the parallel lines.
3 Again using the parallel lines, ask the child to walk on his heels forwards and back-wards. This activity requires greater physical effort than walking on toes so the measured distance should be reduced to 4 metres.	To walk forwards and backwards a distance of 4 metres without stepping outside the parallel lines.

	Activity	Target
	Comments The child may walk with hands extended upwards. It is important that the hands are brought down and this can be achieved either by placing them in pockets or holding slightly heavier objects than those described in activities 1 and 2. When the child is able to hold his hands in a relaxed position, remove weights.	
4	Using a single line of 6 metres, ask the child to walk along heel-to-toe. **Comments** Child's hands may be clenched, so give him appropriate objects to hold.	To walk along without stepping off.
5	Place a skipping rope on the floor in the shape of a snake. Ask the child to walk heel-to-toe alongside. **Comments** If the child has his fists clenched, give him appropriate objects to hold.	To be able to follow the rope contours.
6	Use the parallel lines and instruct the child to walk sideways along the 6-metre distance, leading with his right foot one way and his left foot the other. **Comments** Observe any associated movements and ensure that they are reduced.	To travel the distance up and down in 20 seconds.
7	Use the parallel lines and place four obstacles across. Mini-hurdles* are ideal: otherwise arrange for obstacles to be 30 cm high. The child is instructed to walk between the lines and 'climb' over the obstacles. **Comments** Initially it may be necessary to place obstacles only 5 cm high so the child achieves success.	To walk the distance up and down in 18 seconds without knocking over the obstacles or standing outside the parallel lines.

	Activity	Target
8	If the 'stepping stones' apparatus is available as described in the previous chapter the child should walk along on his toes, one foot on each step. **Comments** Observe the hand position and extend fingers if clenched.	To move along the apparatus without stepping off.
9	Place two posts/cones 1 metre apart. Place a large sponge ball 3 metres away. From a standing position shoot at the gap, first with the right foot then the left. **Comments** Observe position of arms and hands. Minimise associated movements.	4/5 successes with the right then with the left foot.
10	Extension of activity 9. Increase the distance to 6 metres and shoot at the target, right foot then left. **Comments** Gradually extend the distance from 3 to 6 metres. Establish a baseline where the child can consistently achieve a score of 2/5. It may be necessary to vary the distance for each foot.	4/5 successes with the right then with the left foot.
11	Mark out squares for the game of 'hopscotch' with five 'hops' and five 'jumps'. The child begins on the single square, standing on one foot, and moves on, jumping with both feet. **Comments** Demonstrate the activity and start by using half the grid. If the child has problems with balance give him a large sponge ball to hold with both hands. Keeping the arms and hands into the body improves the child's stability. As he masters the skill, remove the ball.	To move along the grid appropriately.

Activity	Target
12 If there is access to a large surface area and a scooter can be obtained, foot–eye co-ordination may be further extended. This is a very difficult skill to master and the child should concentrate on placing his leading foot on the platform and propelling the scooter with the other leg. **Comments** This activity should be developed at home rather than at school.	To propel the scooter around the circuit.
13 Stampabouts* look like two upturned plastic beakers which are threaded at the top. The strings are kept taut and the child balances one foot on each cup. They are based on the same principle as stilts but require a little less foot–eye co-ordination. A distance of 4 metres would seem appropriate. **Comments** Aids which provide extra interest to the co-ordination activities in this section are not essential but add fun.	To be able to walk on the cups a distance of 4 metres.

Section 4: Balance	
Activity	**Target**
1 Ask the child to balance on each foot separately. Initially allow him to hold the back of a chair or touch the wall lightly. Alternatively, the child can rest his raised foot on a ball of appropriate size. As the child becomes more competent, encourage him to stand without support. Then demonstrate the activity, balancing on one foot and holding a bean bag in each hand with arms outstretched on either side. Ask the child to copy. **Comments** Develop the child's stability before asking him to stand unaided. Begin by setting smaller targets of 3, 5 and 8 seconds. The bean bags reduce the clenched movement in the fist and outstretched arms help improve balance.	To balance unaided for 10 seconds on each foot.
2 Extend activity 1 by asking the child to balance on separate feet standing on a variety of surfaces, e.g. sand, foam cushion, skipping rope. **Comments** Ensure that activity 1 is mastered before attempting different surfaces. Correct tongue thrust if evident.	To balance unaided and on a variety of surfaces for 10 seconds on each foot.
3 A selection of wobble boards, as described in the previous chapter, develops a child's awareness of the centre of gravity in his body. Encourage the child to adjust his weight so it passes through one leg, then the other. **Comments** Some boards have adjustable heights and offer an extension of this activity.	To manoeuvre the board for 20 seconds without falling off.

	Activity	Target
4	The child should develop the skills to enable him to walk along the length of a beam 10 cm wide, taking short steps. The beam should be approximately 2 metres long. **Comments** Encourage the child to extend his arms and hold a tennis ball in each hand if the fists are clenched.	To walk slowly along the beam, arms outstretched, without falling.
5	Extend activity 4 by requiring the child to step over two small obstacles placed across the beam. **Comments** During the first few attempts hold the child's hand while he steps over the obstacles.	To walk the length of the beam in small steps.
6	Reduce the width of the beam to 5 cm (the base of an upturned bench is suitable) and repeat activities 4 and 5. **Comments** Wait until the child is confident balancing on the narrow beam before placing obstacles.	To walk the length of the narrowed beam in small steps without falling.
7	Give the child a short-handled bat with a large surface area. Hold the bat horizontal and balance a bean bag on the top. Ask the child to walk 4 metres balancing the bean bag on the bat. Change hands and walk back over the distance. **Comments** Observe the unused hand. If it is clenched use a tennis ball to extend the fingers. If the unused arm is waving give the child a more substantial weight to carry, such as a baton.	Walk a distance of 4 metres, balancing the bean bag on the bat. Use the right hand first, then the left.

	Activity	Target
8	Extend the activity to balancing a small sponge ball on the surface of the bat. Begin with a walking distance of 2 metres and extend it to 4 as the child masters the skill. **Comments** Check again for associated movements and eliminate them.	Walk a distance of 4 metres with the ball balancing on the bat. Use the right hand then the left.
9	Ask the child to lie face downwards, resting his stomach on a skateboard. Legs should extend together in a straight line beyond the board. Using both hands together the child propels himself the distance of 4 metres. **Comments** The child must apply equal pressure with both hands or the board will deviate from a straight line.	Establish a baseline by timing the activity. Reduce the time by half.
10	Ask the child to sit on the skateboard with legs stretching out in front. Again using both hands, simultaneously propel the board forwards along the 4-metre distance. **Comments** The child should lean forwards slightly to ensure that the centre of gravity is in front of the body.	Time the activity and reduce by half.
11	Ask the child to kneel on the skateboard and rest on his heels. Propel the board forwards using both hands along the 4-metre distance. **Comments** The child should again lean forward slightly to move the centre of gravity to the front of the body.	Reduce baseline time by half.

Activity	Target
12 An extension activity is to develop the child's ability to co-ordinate movement on a small trampoline. The exercise is fun but is not a specific requirement of this programme. **Comments** The child should have the skills necessary to jump from a standing position on the floor before attempting this activity. Observe the child's hands and arms while jumping. If any tension is evident give him a large sponge ball to hold which can be removed as his skills develop.	To achieve 10+ continuous jumps without breaking the pattern of movement.
13 Using a Pedal-go* is another activity which provides enjoyment and improves balance; two platforms are positioned between two sets of wheels. The child propels himself forwards by placing his weight on one leg then the other. **Comments** A popular exercise for pupils of all ages. Keep arms down if they exhibit associated movements.	To move forwards a distance of 4+ metres.

Section 5: Whole-body co-ordination	
Activity	**Target**
1 Appropriately place a sequence of cut-out hands on either side of a 4-metre line. (Right-hand shapes on the right of this line and left-hand shapes on the left.) Circles can be used to position the knees. Demonstrate the 'crawling' movement – right hand, left leg, left hand, right leg and place hands and knees on cut-out shapes. **Comments** The child may have no idea about co-ordinating hands and feet. Demonstrate slowly. Many youngsters crawl on their knees with feet raised in the air. Feet must be placed appropriately on either side of the line.	To co-ordinate arms and legs to crawl a distance of 4 metres.
2 Provide the child with a box tunnel*. The child should crawl on hands and knees along the length of the apparatus. Check that he is able to co-ordinate hands and feet. Demonstrate the required movements. **Comments** Many dyspraxic youngsters never go through the crawling stage and find this activity very difficult. Continue until the child can co-ordinate movements reflexively.	To co-ordinate arms and legs to travel a distance of 4 metres.
3 Place a selection of cut-out hand and foot shapes along a 4-metre line. The child is asked to travel the distance on hands and feet. He may place his hands only over the corresponding shape, and the same with his feet. **Comments** Establish a baseline by timing the child's movement from the start to the end of the line. Encourage him to achieve a faster time on subsequent days.	To travel the 4-metre distance using shapes appropriately.

	Activity	Target
4	Design an obstacle course comprising large bean bags, benches and an assortment of mats. The child is requested to crawl around on hands and knees. Establish a baseline by timing the child's first attempt at completing the course. Encourage him to achieve a faster time each day. **Comments** Ensure that the child is wearing suitable clothing. Smooth surfaced tracksuit bottoms are the most comfortable.	To achieve a faster time each day. Discontinue after 10 days.
5	Ask the child to walk at medium pace around the sides of the gymnasium or playground. Observe the whole body movement. Note the position of the hands and whether the child extends his right arm when placing his left foot forward. **Comments** Co-ordination of arms and legs may not occur naturally and the skills will need to be broken down into their components and taught.	Establish flexible co-ordinated body movement while walking.
6	Arrange a variety of coloured hoops on the floor so that the child can step easily between them. The child chooses his own starting point and is told which colour to move on to. **Comments** The distances between hoops can be increased as the child gains confidence.	To co-ordinate arms and legs appropriately.

	Activity	Target
7	Ask the child to walk on his toes a distance of 4 metres between two parallel lines 20 cm apart. If his hands show associated movements, i.e. bend backwards from the wrist, give him a weighted baton to hold in each. When the child begins to relax his hands and swing them freely at his side remove the weight. **Comments** This is a basic skill and all associated movements must be eliminated.	Walk on tiptoes without associated movements.
8	Ask the child to walk on his heels as in 7. Associated movement will be evident if the hands bend forwards from the wrist. Use a weighted baton to position arms and hands correctly. **Comments** Again ensure that associated movements are eliminated.	Walk on heels without associated movements.
9	An extension of activity 5 is to ask the child to run at medium pace in a large circle. Observe the child's hand and arm movements and determine whether they are co-ordinated with the position of the legs. **Comments** Eliminate associated movement if the child's arms are held higher than waist level.	To co-ordinate arms and legs appropriately while running.
10	To climb successfully the child needs to co-ordinate arm and leg movements. With a younger pupil the climbing frame in nursery or reception class is the ideal apparatus. Older pupils may require access to wall bars in the gymnasium. **Comments** The movement will have to be demonstrated as the dyspraxic child has to be taught how to move his limbs in opposition.	To climb apparatus appropriately co-ordinating all four limbs.

Activity	Target
11 Ask the child to stand with his feet together and arms by his side. On command he should jump with feet apart and arms extended at shoulder height. Repeat the exercise, counting 1, 2 – 1, 2. **Comments** Proceed slowly at first and then accelerate, counting when a rhythm is established.	To co-ordinate arms and legs while completing ten jumps.
12 Ask the child to hop on the spot, first on the right leg then the left. Continue with this activity until he is able to repeat the movement five times without it breaking down. While the child is developing the skill, allow him to steady himself, using the back of a chair. As the skill develops he will discover that better balance is achieved when holding a large sponge ball with both hands. **Comments** Break the activity down into smaller steps and provide weights or balls if associated movement in the arms interferes with the balance.	To hop continuously five times on each foot.
13 Ask the child to skip freely round the hall. **Comments** Hopping must be mastered before the child is able to skip. Break the activity into smaller steps and demonstrate movement. Eliminate any associated movements.	To skip with arms appropriately placed at the side of the body.
14 Hop a distance of 3 metres between parallel lines 20 cm apart, first on the right foot then the left. **Comments** Give the child a large sponge ball to hold with both hands as this prevents his arms waving around and reducing co-ordination. As the skill develops, allow his arms to move freely.	To hop a distance of 3 metres without stepping outside the parallel lines.

Activity	Target
15 As in activity 14 encourage the child to jump, feet together, a distance of 3 metres between two parallel lines 20 cm apart. **Comments** Initially, associated movement in the arms will affect the child's ability to co-ordinate his jumping. Give him a large sponge ball until the skill develops, then allow the arms to move freely.	To jump continuously with feet together a distance of 3 metres.
16 Swimming is an excellent activity to develop co-ordination between the arms and legs. Unfortunately this presents many problems for the dyspraxic child. Do not try to co-ordinate all movement from the outset. Ask the child to hold a float in front while using his feet to propel himself forwards on his stomach. **Comments** When the child is able to propel himself forwards and backwards using his legs, begin to introduce arm movements.	Using a float, to propel himself on his stomach, moving legs only.
17 Encourage the child to lie on his back, holding a float on his stomach. Begin by showing how to co-ordinate leg movements. **Comments** Many dyspraxic children are anxious in water, so slowly introduce new activities.	Using a float, to propel himself on his back the width of the baths, slowly moving his legs.

Section 6: Sound, touch and movement	
Activity	**Target**
1 Place ten assorted shapes into a container or bag. The shapes should be two-dimensional ●, ■, and ▲ of varying sizes. Ask the child to close his eyes, select and identify each in turn. **Comments** The child must be confident in identifying shapes when visible before attempting the the activity.	10/10
2 Place ten commonly used objects into the bag. These may include a spoon, eraser, coin, clothes peg, car, piece of Lego, jigsaw piece, crayon, marble, toothbrush, watch or key. Ask the child to select and identify each in turn. **Comments** This activity will present difficulties for dyspraxic youngsters. Simplify or extend the task depending on the ability of the individual.	10/10
3 Ask the child to sit on the floor with his legs stretched out. Place five objects on each side of his body. Mark the back of his right hand with a red sticker for identification. Ask the child to pick objects with the left and right hand. The purpose of the activity is to encourage the youngster to cross the mid-line of the body, so ensure that the majority of objects requested with the right hand are positioned on the left side of the body. **Comments** When the child is consistently able to identify the right and left hand, remove the sticker.	10/10

	Activity	Target
4	Extend activity 3 by asking the child to touch different body parts, for example, 'touch your left knee with your right hand.' Touch five parts with each hand. **Comments** Allow the child sufficient time to process the request as verbally communicated information may be difficult to sequence.	10/10
5	The dyspraxic child finds rhythms very difficult to sequence. Begin by asking the child to copy a simple pattern of three strikes which is repeated five times. III III III III III The child can clap, hit a tambourine or use castanets. The last provides better hand stimulation. **Comments** Demonstrate the activity and continue with the rhythm while the child joins in.	5/5: the strikes must be in time, and equally spaced.
6	Using a tambourine, the child beats with fingertips, then the palm of the hand. Repeat five times. **Comments** Different combinations can be demonstrated for the child to follow.	To achieve regular beats.
7	Vary the pattern of rhythms and introduce heavy and light taps. The sequence could be: II II II II or III III III HL HL HL HL HLH HLH HLH **Comments** Do not exceed four beats in a repeating pattern, for example: IIII IIII is acceptable IIIII IIIII is too difficult.	5/5: same degree of success as activity 5.

Activity	Target
8 To co-ordinate tapping hands and feet, for example, ask the child to sit and start tapping his feet in a regular rhythm. When this is established, demonstrate two taps followed by two claps, with this sequence repeated five times. **Comments** Extend this activity to introduce more complex patterns involving feet and hands.	5/5

The activity programme is the most significant feature in the remediation of the child's difficulties. Targets should be selected from the areas which show the greatest deficits. Entry into the programme is the activity which best reflects the child's emerging skill; i.e. he is able to achieve some success but has not reached the specified target. Activities may be selected from all the sections or they may be restricted to one or two if they are the only areas of concern. The programme should be of 20 minutes duration maximum and the next activity selected when the child has achieved the target for five consecutive days. The purpose of the programme is to enable the child to acquire the necessary skills and progress through the activities as quickly as possible. The activities are not designed to produce world-class athletes but to increase the neural pathways in the cerebral cortex and improve the child's ability to interpret and process information.

Preparing the activity programme

The baseline motor skills assessment will have identified specific areas of difficulty and indicated whether it is predominantly a left- or right-sided problem. Activities remain the same but greater attention should be focused on the weak side if there are significant differences.

Select activities from the appropriate sections and summarise them on the child's record chart. Decide who will monitor the programme: whether it is a parent or member of staff. Try to offer consistency and ensure that the activities are completed at the same time and in the same place each day. Some parents are given access to the school facilities and take their children to the hall or gym half an hour before school starts, or stay behind at the end of the day. Secondary schools may allow older pupils to monitor the programmes of the younger children, or they may be completely home-based. Whatever the arrangements, access to the activities on at least five days each week is essential.

Intervention for Rebecca (aged 8)

Rebecca was dyspraxic and her class teacher completed the motor assessment. Her profile was as follows:

Laterality	right-eyed, right-handed, left-footed
Crawling	extension of right arm and leg simultaneously, attempted the same with the left and then gave up
Balance	right leg three seconds left leg four seconds
Parallel lines	walked appropriately on soles, toes and heels. When side stepping, raised both arms to a position level with shoulders
Running	on toes but a more pronounced sound when left foot hit the floor
Jumping	competent: Rebecca had practised with her older sister
Hopping	right foot: two hops forward left foot: four hops forward
Rope turning	very competent: Rebecca had practised skipping
Clapping	managed to repeat a five-beat sequence (II III) (II III)
Finger sequencing	good: Rebecca can play the recorder.

The purpose of the intervention programme is to identify skills which are not fully developed and should be broken down into achievable targets. Rebecca had already mastered many skills which dyspraxic children find difficult. It had taken almost two years to learn to skip but she was determined to be the same as everyone else. She had attended weekly recorder classes from the age of six and the daily practice had improved her finger-sequencing ability.

Using the information from the assessment, targets were selected from the intervention programme. Rebecca's foot–eye, balance skills and whole-body co-ordination were identified as entry points.

The first item selected for her activity chart was section 3, activity 6.

Activity	Target
Use the parallel lines and instruct the child to walk sideways along the 6-metre distance, leading with his right foot one way and his left foot the other. **Comments** Observe any associated movements and ensure that they are reduced.	To travel the distance up and down in 20 seconds.

The second item selected was section 4, activity 1.

Activity	Target
Ask the child to balance on each foot separately. Initially allow him to hold the back of a chair or touch the wall lightly. Alternatively, the child can rest his raised foot on a ball of appropriate size. As the child becomes more competent, encourage him to stand without support. Then demonstrate the activity, balancing on one foot and holding a bean bag in each hand with arms outstretched on either side. Ask the child to copy. **Comments** Develop the child's stability before asking him to stand unaided. The bean bags reduce the clenched movement in the fist and out-stretched arms help improve balance.	To balance unaided for ten seconds on each foot.

The third item is section 5, activity 1.

Activity	Target
Appropriately place a sequence of cut-out hands on either side of a 4-metre line (right-hand shapes on the right of this line and left-hand shapes on the left). Circles can be used to position the knees. Demonstrate the 'crawling' movement – right hand, left leg, left hand, right leg and place hands and knees on cut-out shapes. **Comments** The child may have no idea about co-ordinating hands and feet. Demonstrate slowly. Many youngsters crawl on their knees with feet raised in the air. Feet must be placed appropriately on either side of the line.	To co-ordinate arms and legs to crawl a distance of 4 metres.

The daily programme should take between 15 and 20 minutes so additional activities from the sections identified can be added.

Most encouraging results are achieved when the child follows the programme for eight weeks, spends the next six weeks consolidating skills, and then restarts the activities for a further eight weeks. It is important that these activities are not seen to be going on indefinitely. The child needs to develop the skills described in each section but mastery of the task is insufficient. It is the associated movements which must be eliminated. As long as they persist the child will continue to have difficulty not only co-ordinating movements but co-ordinating thoughts and ideas.

Case study

Paul was referred for assessment at the start of his final year in primary school. He presented as a tall, shy, articulate youngster who experienced great difficulty recording his work on paper. Parents and the head teacher were concerned that his poor handwriting and social skills would prevent him being placed in secondary school classes which matched his intellectual ability.

Paul was most enthusiastic when an activity programme was suggested, and he went willingly from his classroom every day to complete his 20-minute exercise session. As his skills improved he became more anxious to extend the programme. His improvement was evident when a comparison was made between a handwriting sample from September 1993 and another in June 1994 (see Figure 8.1).

Paul had been distanced from his peer group for some time and was rarely chosen for team games. However, during the summer term of Paul's last year in the juniors an outside specialist was invited to give basketball coaching to the pupils. Through the activity programme Paul had developed good hand–eye co-ordination and for the first time in his school career he was the best in the class. His name was called out first for a position in the team. Paul gained social acceptance before leaving primary education and continued to achieve success in his secondary school.

Classroom environment for junior age pupils

As the child progresses through the education system he is expected to produce more independent work. Background noise levels are reduced and therefore less problematic for the dyspraxic child. Requests for teacher help are also reduced and this can present difficulties for the dyspraxic child who repeatedly asks questions to remind himself of the task. All the pupils will benefit from having the instructions repeated. All directions should be given using clear precise language. Always try to find ways to make the task of recording less traumatic for the dyspraxic child.

- Allow him to choose writing tools which are comfortable, whether they are pencils, pens or fine felt-tips.

- Encourage him to produce legible handwriting: give him the choice of print or cursive styles, despite the requirements of the National Curriculum.

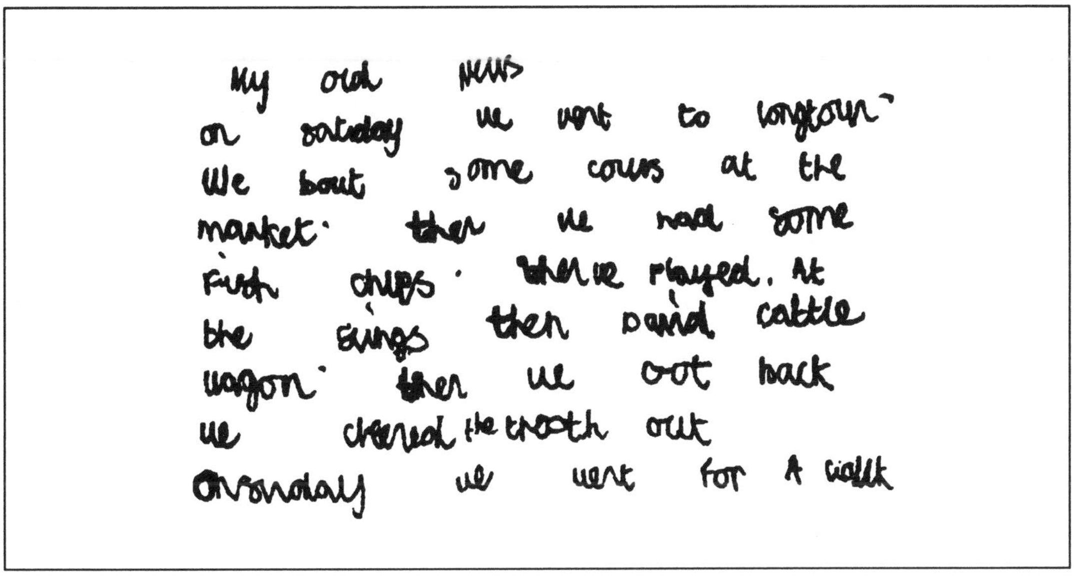

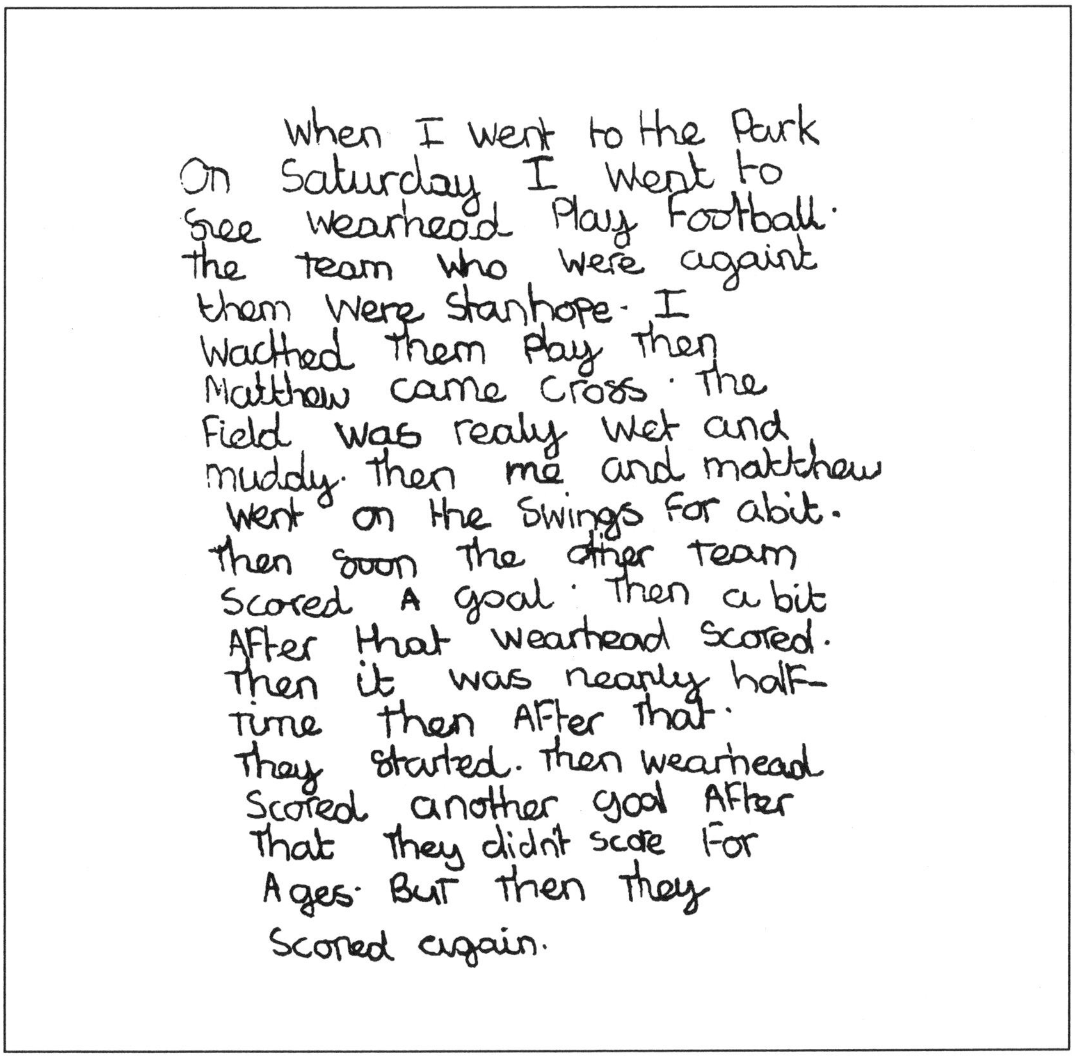

My oun News
on satday ue uent to longtoun
We bout some cours at the
market. then ue had some
Fish chips. then ue played. At
the suings then david cattle
uagon. then ue oot back
ue checked the trooth out
On snday ue uent for A ciollk

When I went to the Park
On Saturday I went to
See wearhead Play Football.
the team who were againt
them Were Stanhope. I
Wacthed Them Play then
Matthew came Cross. The
Field was realy Wet and
muddy. then me and matthew
Went on the Swings For abit.
then soon the other team
Scored A goal. Then a bit
AFter that wearhead scored.
Then it was nearly half-
Time then AFter that.
They started. then wearhead
Scored another goal AFter
That they didnt scoe For
Ages. But then they
Scored again.

Figure 8.1 Paul's handwriting samples: September 1993 and June 1994

- Provide lined paper and give him access to a handled ruler when appropriate.

- Request only the quantity of written work which can be completed in the allocated time. Do not expect the child to spend every playtime and lunch break finishing tasks.

- The child at this age will become frustrated by the untidy appearance of his handwriting and drawings, and will be aware that this may imply that he is of poor ability. So often the child is told what is wrong with his work. It is important that each day the child is given some positive feedback about his achievements. He does not need constant reminders from the teacher that 'this work is untidy'. He already knows.

- Sensitivity should be exercised when correcting work. Mark on the basis of content; it can be extremely discouraging if all the mistakes are underlined.

- Encourage oral presentations as an alternative to some written work.

The classroom environment can be adapted to meet the needs of the dyspraxic child and minimise the anxiety frequently experienced. Figure 8.2 is an example of a 9-year-old pupil's handwritten story.

Daniel is a very articulate youngster who is an avid reader of nature books. Everything about animals and their habits is of great interest to him. During his science lessons he constantly questions how and why things work. His task was to produce an imaginative story. This was something he could really enjoy. He chose as his subject a skeleton. He explored the plight of the little skeleton who wants to 'learn things': he is unable to attend school so night classes are suggested. Daniel spent the entire session completing his handwritten script. He had included a drawing to add interest.

The work, when presented to his class teacher, appeared untidy and was almost impossible to read. This was Daniel's best effort. He had produced a wonderful story which could have been easily disregarded had the class teacher not been aware of his difficulty.

Daniel was invited to read his story aloud and it was processed on the computer by the teacher. Daniel's exercise book still contains his handwritten story with the translation on the facing page.

How different the picture might have been. For so many dyspraxic pupils, handwritten work is judged on form rather than content. Asking the child to rewrite the story does not bring any visible improvements; it merely adds to the child's frustration and further lowers his self-esteem.

An explanation as to why the handwriting of dyspraxic youngsters follows this characteristic pattern was offered by Ellis in 1987. He describes handwriting as a complex perceptual-motor skill which requires visual and kinaesthetic feedback, at least part of the time, to execute the correct movements. A controlled experiment was carried out in which a group of unaffected subjects was placed in circumstances which prevented them monitoring and controlling their handwriting. Visual feedback (sight of the hand and the pen) was eliminated by obscuring the sight of the writing hand and an additional task, either counting or tapping, was included to interfere

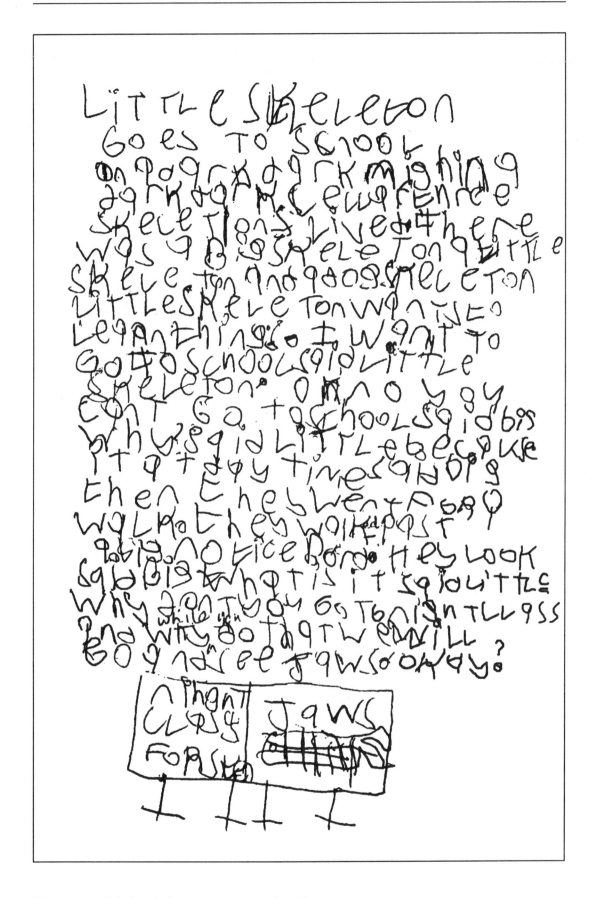

Figure 8.2 Little skeleton goes to school

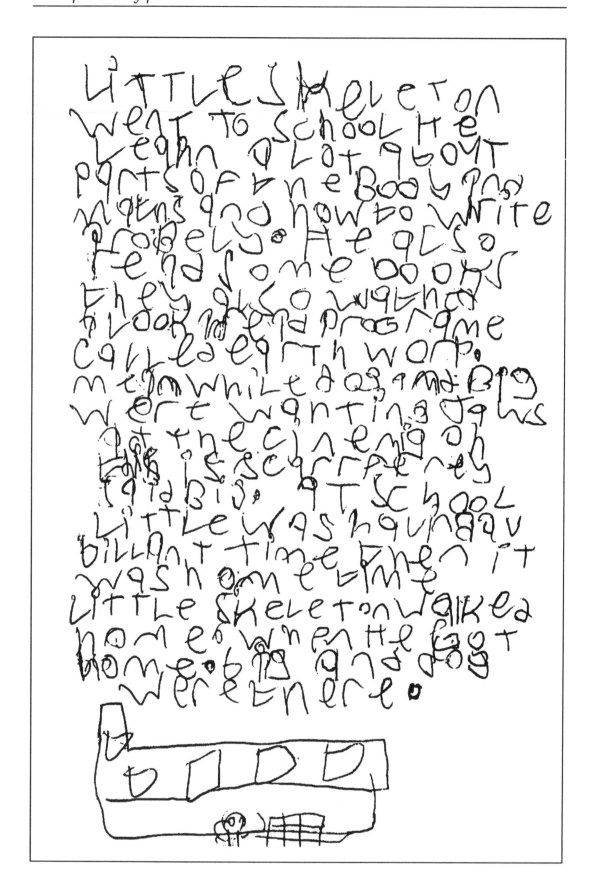

Figure 8.2 (continued)

LITTLE SKELETON GOES TO SCHOOL

On a dark dark night
in a dark dark cellar,
three skeletons lived.
There was a big skeleton, a little skeleton and a dog skeleton.
Little skeleton wanted to learn things.
"I want to go to school," said little skeleton.
"Oh no you can't go to school," said big.
"Why?" said little.
"Because it's at daytime" said big.
Then they went for a walk. They went past a big notice board.
"Hey look" said big.
"What is it?" said little.
"Why don't you go to night classes?" said big "and while you do that, we'll go and see JAWS at the cinema!"
"Okay" said little.
Little skeleton went to school. He learned a lot about parts of the body and maths and how to write properly. He also read some books. They also watched a Look and Read programme called EARTHWARP.
Meanwhile big and dog were watching JAWS at the cinema.
"This is scary" said big.
At school little was having a brilliant time. Then it was hometime.
Little skeleton walked home. When he got home big and dog were there.

Figure 8.2 (continued)

with the writers' ability to attend to kinaesthetic feedback. Research showed that unlike the unaffected subjects, the dyspraxic pupils' writing was no more error-prone with eyes closed than with eyes open. It appears therefore that dyspraxic pupils are permanently unable to use visual feedback to monitor for errors or help correct them. In addition, when the dyspraxic child has his forefinger moved, with eyes closed, to form a letter shape, he experiences great difficulty using kinaesthetic information to identify letters.

Figures 8.3 and 8.4 show the handwriting samples of two 10-year-old pupils. Example A was 'free' writing while B was completed with eyes closed. Pupil 1 was dyspraxic; pupil 2 the control.

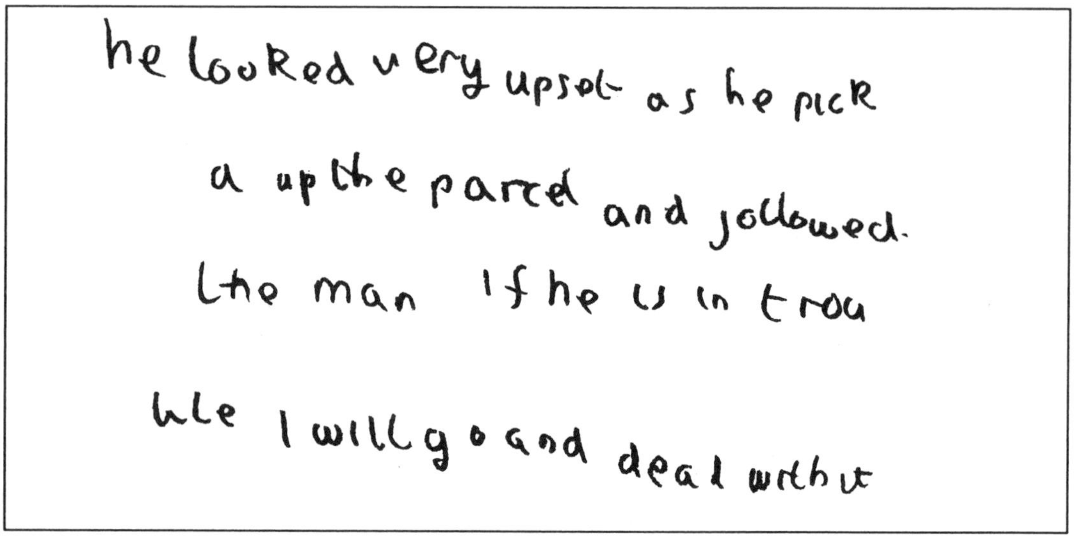

Figure 8.3 Handwriting of Pupil 1, sample A

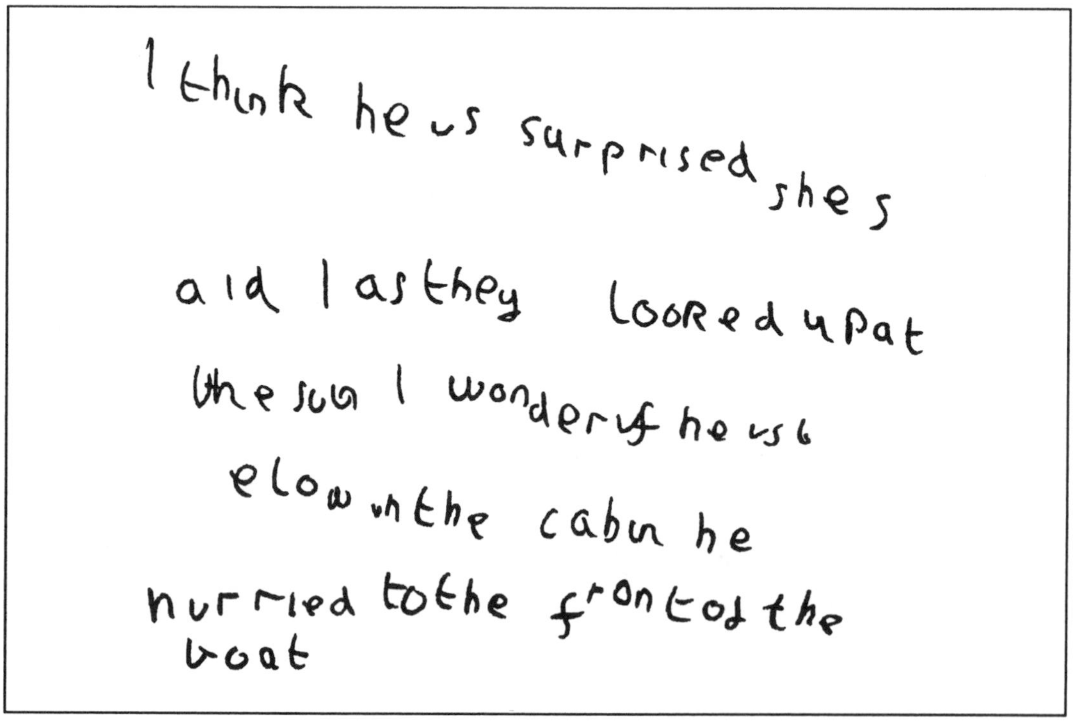

Figure 8.3 Handwriting of Pupil 1, sample B

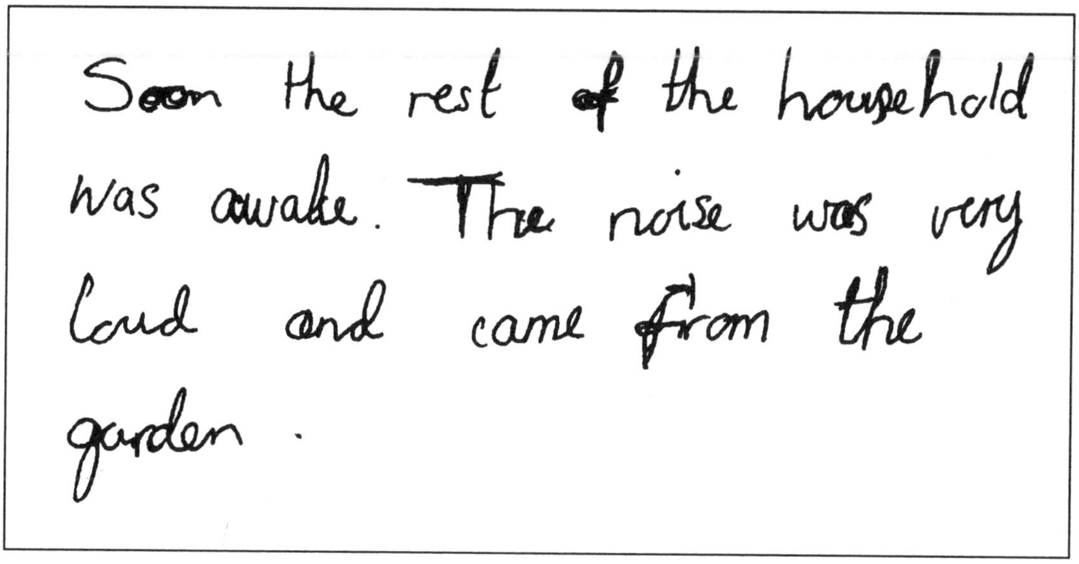

Soon the rest of the household was awake. The noise was very loud and came from the garden .

Figure 8.4 Handwriting of Pupil 2, sample A

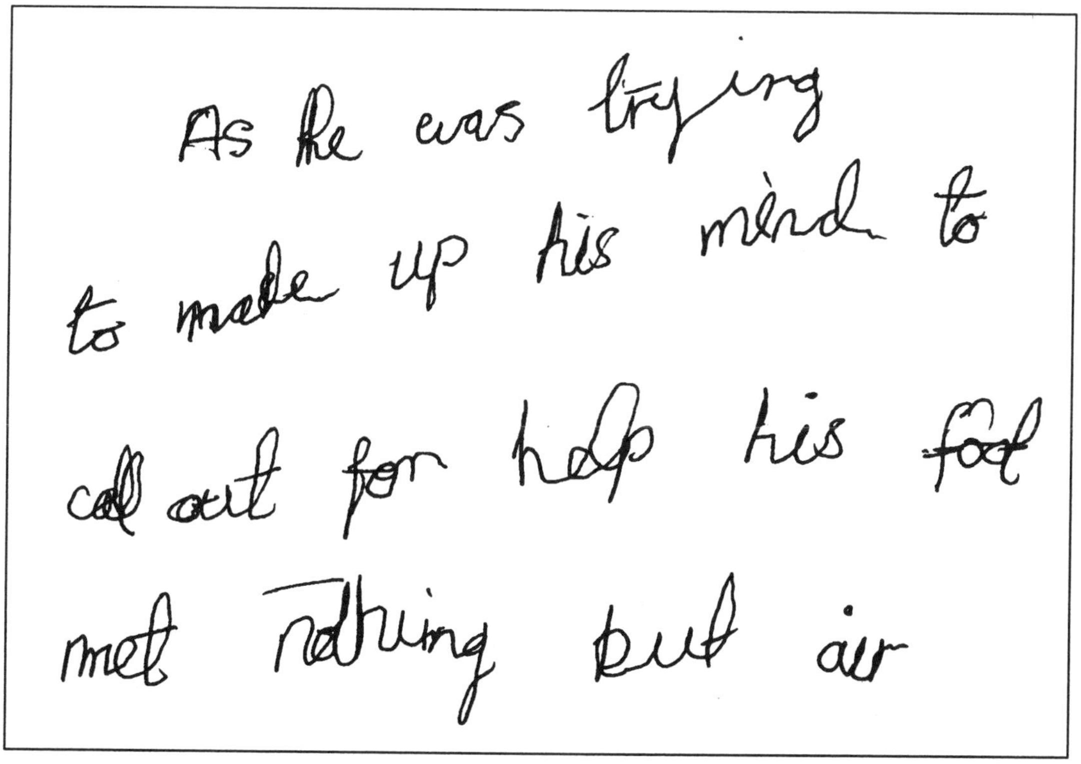

As he was trying to make up his mind to call out for help his foot met nothing but air

Figure 8.4 Handwriting of Pupil 2, sample B

Writing patterns exhibited by the majority of dyspraxic youngsters are termed dysgraphic. Writing begins as a linguistic process and ends as one which is perceptual-motor. It is unsurprising, therefore, that dyspraxic youngsters, many of whom have problems developing early language skills and who subsequently exhibit perceptual-motor difficulties, find handwriting an almost impossible skill to master.

By the age of 8 or 9 the child will be well aware of tasks he finds difficult and will have developed an extensive repertoire of avoidance tactics. They will range from forgetting books, writing materials and the PE kit to the appearance of physical symptoms such as headaches and sickness on particular mornings. In addition, the child's unco-ordinated movements are dismissed as careless behaviour. If left untreated a pattern will emerge of:

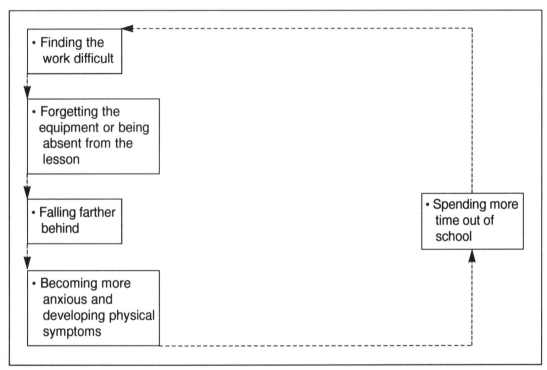

It is the responsibility of the class teacher to provide differentiated programmes of work to meet the needs of the individual. No child wants to fail, so it is important that he feels capable of achieving something which is valued by his teacher. Pupils of primary age are not usually self-motivated to work hard; they do so to obtain praise from their parents and teachers.

Perceptual skills

Access to the Frostig programme will offer extension activities for 9- to 11-year-old pupils. In addition the child will acquire perceptual skills more easily if he has a good understanding of two-dimensional shapes. Clear templates of the patterns which aid development are provided in Appendix A.

Present the child with the sheet comprising two large squares of 16 dots joined by horizontal and vertical lines (Figures 8.5 and A.6).

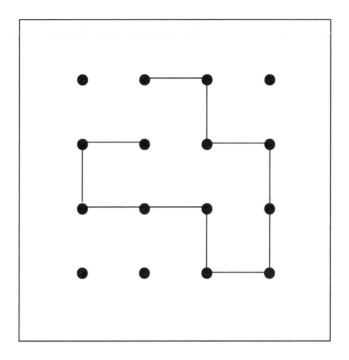

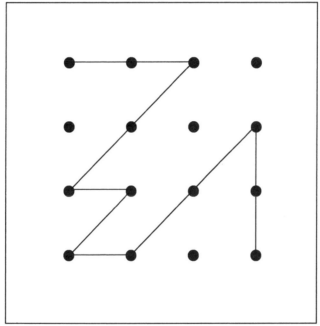

Figure 8.5

The child then copies the shapes (on to the recording sheet at Figure A.5). These should become more complex as his skills develop.

When the child is competent in completing the large shapes, provide him with the prepared template of 12 smaller dot shapes (Figure A.8) and his own unused recording sheet (Figure A.7). Provide the template for five consecutive days. The child is timed and encouraged to improve on the time of the previous day. Ensure that the template is presented with the same starting figure in the top left corner. When the child is able to copy the shapes in 60 seconds, rotate the template and start the programme again. When the skills are mastered, the activity can be extended by presenting the child with patterns which follow a diagonal line (Figure A.9). The transition to this activity may present some problems initially, so begin with only three boxes instead of 12.

Language development

This becomes less of a problem as the child gets older. If reading aloud to the class group is required, check whether the child feels sufficiently confident to do so. The sequencing of ideas in story-writing may cause some concerns, so discuss with the child how the events develop and provide a story planner for him. This might be achieved best by producing a series of three line drawings depicting the beginning, middle and end. This idea may benefit many other pupils in the class.

Additional information

If the child has not been able to access some parts of the curriculum during earlier school years because of his limited perceptual skills, he should be given the opportunity to rediscover basic concepts in subject areas like mathematics. N.E.S. Arnold has produced a range of materials designed for such pupils in the top end of primary and the lower end of secondary education. The concepts are delivered through practical activities and use the Multi-link blocks. The basics are taught through the number skills plus programme, and handbooks are provided which relate specifically to levels 1–3 of the National Curriculum.

Extension programmes are:

- Rediscovering fractions;
- Shape and space;
- Towards algebra through structures.

In all areas of the curriculum, set targets where the child is judged against his own efforts and not by comparison with the rest of the class. Raise the child's position in the group by giving him a post of responsibility, whether it is to collect finished work from all pupils or to be allowed to tidy the chairs at lunch-time. The responsible task may enable the teacher to involve the child in working with another pupil if he has relationship difficulties with class members.

Try to predict situations which may cause anxiety and offer alternatives. If teams are to be selected, the teacher should divide the class. It is always a humiliating experience to be the one left at the end. If the system in operation at lunch-time requires children to carry trays of food to their tables, arrange the seating so the dyspraxic child has the shortest distance to travel. Reduce the number of opportunities to single out dyspraxic pupils for negative attention, by either staff or peers.

School environment for pupils of secondary age

Transferring to secondary education can present anxieties for many pupils but perhaps more so for the dyspraxic child. As highlighted in previous chapters, visual perceptual tasks require a greater processing time. Finding the correct room and following a timetable to attend the specific lesson is a skill which takes longer to acquire. At the outset the child needs to develop a close relationship with a personal tutor who is aware of his needs. Getting lost is an excuse for many youngsters to avoid the lesson; this may not be the case for the dyspraxic child. In secondary school where there are many different subject teachers it may not be possible for them to have the same awareness of the child's problem as the personal tutor. There is increasing likelihood that a supply teacher who has no knowledge of the child will be covering the class. It is for these reasons that the child has to be able to confide in a concerned member of staff who can present his case to the teacher who is annoyed that X is late for the lesson and has produced only half of the expected amount of written work.

The difficulties are greatly alleviated if the pupil has gained peer acceptance. Too often he finds he is in conflict not only with the teacher but also with the rest of the class. Peer group acceptance emerged as the most significant factor in my research with secondary age pupils in determining the child's motivation and attitude towards school. The child should be placed in groups according to his intellectual ability, which at first may be difficult to judge if indecipherable written work is used as a criterion. If the child is placed inappropriately he will not be motivated by the lesson content, and behavioural difficulties will emerge.

Try to involve the pupil in organised lunch-time activities. Dyspraxic children who are not accepted by their peers can easily become the victims of bullying. Many pupils gain great benefits from a homework club because:

- they are able to discuss classwork which has caused concern;

- they are with other pupils who require additional adult help and they view themselves less as being the only child with difficulties;

- it is easier to establish relationships within a small group.

Subject teachers covering topics which require good spatial awareness, for example map reading and technical drawing, should be made aware of the additional support requirement for a pupil with motor learning difficulties. In other subjects where dictated material is presented to the group the dyspraxic child should be allowed to record the information on tape as he is unable to listen and write at the same time.

The exercise programme proved most effective with pupils of secondary age. Most encouraging results were achieved when dyspraxic pupils were paired with other youngsters from within the school who were responsible for completing the record sheet. Their profile in the school was raised and peer group acceptance achieved. Close liaison between parents and school is essential to ensure that any difficulties are addressed quickly before unnecessary distress is caused to the pupil.

Dyspraxic students: post-16

Provision for students in colleges of further education is available if they are identified as having special educational needs. Increased access to computer-assisted learning reduces the quantity of work recorded manually. The environment can be adapted more easily for older pupils, who can identify for themselves the parts of the curriculum causing particular difficulties.

It is helpful if students can make taped recordings in some lessons to alleviate concerns that important aspects of the course may be missed. The student should be offered open access to a word-processor so that he is able to produce assignments which are legible and which reflect his ability in the subject. Tutors should ensure that additional time is allocated to dyspraxic students for the production of their work and special consideration should be given for examinations.

Recently-developed voice-processing packages will enable students to prepare course work with up to 98 per cent accuracy in presentation. Details of the programmes available are discussed in Chapter 9 under the heading 'Recording information'.

Dyspraxic youngsters usually adapt well to the less structured environment in college when non-contact time is allocated to all students for research into their subjects and work preparation. The areas which had previously presented so many difficulties are, by choice, no longer part of the curriculum. Although access to motor-skill programmes will alleviate some of their presenting problems, students should concentrate on working on their strengths.

Some of those interviewed had already discussed the possibility of obtaining qualifications to enable them to work with 'special needs' children and adults. They said that personal experience had given them some understanding of the anxieties suffered when learning difficulties are not diagnosed and appropriate support is not available.

9 Adults with dyspraxia

During the past two years I have been involved in working on intervention programmes and supporting 27 dyspraxic adults. The group comprised 14 males and 13 females. Initially 43 adults were referred via local colleges, universities, GPs, parents or themselves. Following a detailed assessment, those presenting characteristics associated with developmental dyspraxia were invited to take part in the study. The resulting 27, aged between 16 and 31, agreed to attend six weekly sessions which were followed up at monthly intervals for a period of twelve months to monitor home-based intervention programmes.

Group composition

The male/female split within the sample was not representative of the ratios expected in the general population. In the school population there had been four times more boys than girls referred for assessment. In the adult population, factors such as personal motivation and access to appropriate support networks have to be considered. There were five adults referred from local colleges and three from university (six were female). Already there is evidence of a significant difference between males and females who decide to move on to further education. Of the remaining adults, 12 referred themselves, five were encouraged to seek help by their parents and two were referred by local GPs. In the group, six had been given a diagnosis of developmental dyspraxia, 21 had not.

Children with dyspraxia who do not have access to appropriate intervention become adults with dyspraxia who in addition display a host of comorbid conditions. The following case studies are representative of the adults in the study and their stories give an insight into their difficulties.

Simon aged 18

Simon had just finished his final year in comprehensive education. He had hoped to transfer to a college but his examination results had not been as good as he had expected. The predictions of teachers had been quite accurate, but Simon believed he should have done better.

The school careers advisor had suggested that Simon explore possibilities of entering an apprenticeship on leaving school but he was determined to follow a more academic course. As a result of his disastrous performance in the examinations he was forced to consider other options. For several months he continued to be extremely resistant to any suggestion other than that he should re-sit the following year and try again for a college place. It was evident he had not really come to terms with the difficulties he had experienced throughout his school career.

He described himself as a friendly youngster who felt more comfortable in the company of adults than his peer group. He attributed his poor academic performance to long periods of absence from school in his infant years when he had been prone to recurring chest infections and severe bouts of eczema. The eczema disappeared when he entered his teens and his health had generally improved. He felt that by then the damage was done and his failure to establish good relationships with his peers in the primary school meant he could not expect to have any successful relationships in the secondary school environment. It was almost a self-fulfilling prophecy: Simon did not expect other youngsters to like him and so his general demeanour had given the impression of indifference and unwillingness to socialise.

Simon could not remember having had any particular speech difficulties, but his parents stated that he had been the victim of some teasing while in the nursery and reception class environment because of his poor pronunciation. There was still evidence of some hesitancy in Simon's language, and although his articulation was now competent he visibly processed the words before speaking. This gave the listener the feeling that he was not being totally open in his verbal responses and in group sessions this was certainly the impression he gave to other members.

Simon had accepted from a relatively early age that he would always be a 'loner'. He believed that it was his preference to spend time at home playing on the computer rather than engaging in physical activity such as cycling and playing football with other youngsters. By the time he was 13 he felt so incompetent in his development of gross motor skills that he regularly complained of illness when he was due in school for a PE lesson.

Simon's reluctance to consider an apprenticeship was based on his anxiety when remembering his work-experience placement. He had been given several options which included supporting a group of 7-year-old pupils in a local primary school, working with customers in a local video shop and working in the local library. Both his personal tutor and the careers officer felt that the library placement would be most acceptable because of his keen interest in books. Simon had always been a competent reader and the technology was such that he would have access to computerised equipment to exchange books at the counter.

Simon had been anxious to test his initiative and made a personal approach to a local firm of insurance brokers. He gave details of his curricular subjects and convinced the manager that it would be of benefit to them both if he could spend two weeks with the firm. Simon's responsibilities included answering the telephone and taking messages, filing the necessary paperwork, addressing letters to clients, and making the tea.

Simon had problems with his short-term auditory memory and found it difficult to retain more than two pieces of information. He was competent at recording the client's name but could not remember the address, telephone number or details of the enquiry. The staff believed that directing him towards the filing would lose less business and he was required to match incoming post with the client's name and produce the documentation for action. Simon worked industriously and at the end of his first afternoon every letter had been successfully filed. Unfortunately, he had not remembered to remove the files from the cabinets and there was no other record of post arriving that morning. It then became the responsibility of the other staff members to search through every file in turn to see whether it had been linked with any post.

The manager, keen to support youngsters in education, agreed to allow Simon to return the next day. He was asked to write the names and addresses on the front of 80 envelopes. The details may well have been entered correctly but they were completely illegible. In desperation he was directed to make the tea. Simon did not have much experience of making hot drinks. His parents were anxious to minimise any possible risk and he was encouraged to have fresh orange, and milk. Anxious to redeem himself for the previous day's misdemeanours, Simon did not ask for assistance and prepared four cups. It did not occur to him to bring them in separately and he loaded all four beakers on the top of a large table mat. Needless to say the tea never arrived in the front office. That afternoon he was requested to leave the placement and a letter of complaint was sent to his personal tutor.

Simon was anxious that information regarding his difficulties should not be given to the employer. This was his choice, not the recommendation of the school. In discussion with the tutor, the business manager said that, had he been aware of Simon's problems, he would have ensured that more appropriate tasks were set.

Although the events described amount to a 'comedy of errors', Simon's unrealistic expectation of himself caused further damage to his diminishing self-esteem. It was impossible within such a short time-scale to be offered alternative work experience which could have been more appropriate. Simon had made a decision then that the workplace was not for him in the near future. With the removal of this option Simon felt he had to pursue his educational studies, hence his application to college.

Simon's assessment had highlighted particular strengths in his visual ability and major deficits in his perceptual and auditory sequencing skills. He was committed to work towards improving these skills and he completed his exercise programme daily for a period of 12 weeks. Re-assessment identified significant improvements in his co-ordination, balance and handwriting. He was encouraged to develop an interest in outside activities and he started to attend an evening class for developing IT skills.

Part of the intervention involved considering the improvement of social skills, and Simon was given strategies and targets to achieve on a weekly basis. He developed a close relationship with another member of the computer group, who was significantly older than himself but gave him the confidence to ask questions and request support from the tutor when necessary. Simon re-applied for a college course which placed a heavy emphasis on computing skills and has just finished his third term.

Caitlin aged 27

Caitlin was a self-referral and she had amassed some information about dyspraxia from newspaper and magazine articles. During her first interview she spoke almost continuously for 40 minutes. Although I attempted to encourage her to answer specific questions, she wanted to begin the story of her life at a stage as far back as she could remember and talked through her perceptions of its progress up to the present.

Caitlin initially was quite reluctant to make eye-contact and this was compounded by her high level of excitability. Whenever there was a movement outside the door or traffic visible through the window in my office she immediately gave it her attention. In school she had achieved the equivalent of six Grade C GCSEs and two 'A' levels, although she had taken four years to achieve the acquired results in the latter. Her hands, and quite often her feet, moved continuously as she spoke and I found this quite exhausting to observe.

Caitlin had received some support in school for her identified learning difficulties but attention had been given exclusively to her handwriting and spelling problems. The wider picture of her high level of excitability and limited concentration had not been addressed.

Caitlin did not feel that she had always presented as emotional and excitable: she felt that these traits had developed in her later teenage years. She was accepted within her peer group but said that she felt that she was very different from everyone else. She said that, because she knew she was different, she tried to make herself even more so, by dressing bizarrely and making up stories about holidays she had had and people she had met.

At the age of 18, she was referred via her GP to a psychiatrist and was described as suffering from manic depression. She was prescribed daily medication for this condition.

Caitlin's employment history was brief. She had gone through a series of temporary contracts in a variety of jobs, including stacking shelves, receptionist to a travel agents, mobile co-ordinator for a book company and a private tutor of English for a GCSE student.

She had entered into relationships with a number of different partners, but felt that she always became too deeply involved, too quickly.

As I developed a greater understanding of Caitlin, it became evident that whenever anyone disagreed with her she perceived it as a complete rejection. This caused her to move from one partner to another or seek alternative friendships.

Caitlin tried to be a perfectionist, which is an impossible ideal to reconcile with dyspraxia. She was unable to accept praise and constantly changed it to criticism. One day I commented on her jewellery. She said: 'Well, don't you like the jacket as well? That's new.'

During the third interview, Caitlin said that the reason for coming was to find out whether an intervention programme would 'cure her depression'. It took many further sessions to unravel what was currently affected by her specific learning difficulty, and its part in what had developed into a significant psychological problem.

Assessment using the Wechsler Adult Intelligence Scales indicated that she had an extremely high verbal ability with scaled scores in many sub-tests at 14 or above. There was evidence of problems with her short-term auditory memory but it was apparent that she had attentional difficulties and was unable to focus herself to listen appropriately. Caitlin's non-verbal ability was significantly depressed and although her visual sequencing was competent her perceptual skills were extremely depressed.

Her handwriting was barely legible, but she had developed competency in word-processing. We discussed the purpose of the intervention programme, namely to improve co-ordination, perceptual skills and concentration. After what I thought had been a reasonable discussion, we agreed to set some short- and long-term targets.

I expected, given Caitlin's educational background, that she would want to further her studies and obtain a professional qualification to give her greater access to the employment market, and that in addition she would seek permanent housing. Her lists of targets were as follows:

Short-term targets	**Long-term targets**
To have her hair cut at least monthly	To be a top model
To have a good memory	To own a riding school (she had
To learn to ride a bike	never been anywhere near a horse)
To buy some new shoes	To emigrate to Australia

The content of the list shows a mixture of trivia combined with totally unrealistic expectations. Some of the achievable short-term targets could be met with relatively little effort and no intervention. The others were virtually impossible. From this, the outcome of any professional involvement would be: 'I could have done that myself anyway. It hasn't made any difference. I didn't achieve what I wanted.' This would reinforce Caitlin's already low opinion of herself.

Caitlin attended for nine sessions in total and didn't complete any of the suggested programmes. I could see why she thought they were irrelevant. What she really needed was involvement in a support network which would give her access to structured sessions on an individual basis with a therapist. Perhaps we went a little way along that path but the provision she really required was not available.

Caitlin's dyspraxia had at this stage become one of the least of her difficulties.

Amanda aged 31

Amanda had two older brothers and had been brought up by her mother. Her father left the family when she was 5 years old. She said she had 'little memory of him', although 'professionals' had attributed many of her educational and psychological difficulties to his departure.

Amanda was referred by her GP who felt that alternatives to permanent daily medication for anxiety and depression should be explored.

Amanda had positive early recollections of her school days. She spoke of friends she had made and she could remember the names of 12 children in her nursery.

The departure of Amanda's father coincided with transfer to a class where she had a difficult relationship with the teacher. She remembered a very structured, formal classroom where children were discouraged from speaking. She remembered finding the work very hard and being unable to answer questions.

One day she was asked to read her story to the rest of the class. She hadn't been able to put a single word on the paper and she found handwriting very difficult. She stood at the front of the class and held her sheet as though she was reading from it. She felt she had told a good story.

Amanda became distressed as she remembered how the paper had been snatched from her hands and shown to the class. She was publicly humiliated.

By the age of 7, Amanda had become extremely withdrawn within her class group, and assumptions were made that this related to the emotional distress caused by her father. Attention had not been paid to the difficulties she was experiencing with learning. She dreaded the threat of the Friday 'test' which she knew would be another humiliation. They alternated: one week it was spelling, the next week mental arithmetic. Despite her attempts to master the sequences of letters or remember her tables under pressure, in exam conditions her mind went completely blank.

The pressure was too great and she developed an eating disorder. She resorted to food whether she was happy, sad, anxious or settled. At the age of 10 she weighed 9 stones and as well as criticism regarding her poor attainments she was name-called by several members of her class. During the summer holidays before transfer to secondary education she attempted suicide, but this was felt by the professionals involved to be an attention-seeking act rather than a serious attempt. Her situation deteriorated in secondary school and whenever possible she made excuses to stay away. Her symptoms had become so extreme by the age of 12 – severe headaches, violent sickness, pains in her joints and severe sleeping problems – that she was referred to a family centre for psychological and psychiatric input. Following a two-week assessment in the unit she was admitted to the ward of a psychiatric hospital where she remained until she was 16 years old. She received daily medication but felt that she had never really been allowed to address her problems.

Amanda was 31 when I saw her and she presented as a woman with the appearance of being much older than her years. Her clothing comprised several layers of cardigans with sleeves pulled down over her hands. She invariably wore trousers as she felt they 'covered her up better'. Neuro-psychological assessment indicated that Amanda had many strengths which are well above the level expected for her age. When she opted out of school and exchanged it for placement in a psychiatric unit she concentrated on developing her musical talent. She was an exceptionally competent flautist and said that there had been many times when her fingers blistered because of the requirement of so much repetition to develop her skills. She had always felt that she should have been able to achieve something academically but believed that was no longer a possibility. After leaving hospital she spent virtually all of her time at home. She had lost all of her friends and did not feel sufficiently socially competent to go out and make new ones.

Observational assessment of Amanda's movements indicated that she was extremely unco-ordinated and her in-turned feet hampered her ability to walk in a straight line without tripping. She said that if there was anything that she could possibly trip over she would find it. She preferred to eat alone because of the mess that remained on the table and floor after finishing a meal. Amanda identified her poor co-ordination skills as her main cause of distress.

Amanda was extremely committed to working on the intervention programme and meticulously recorded her achievements. Within six weeks she was able to walk, hop and jump along a straight line, 5 metres in length, without tripping or falling over. In the beginning she had been unable to complete a simple 12-piece jigsaw; within six months she was timing herself for the completion of those in excess of 200 pieces. Her perceptual skills were improving but her uncorrected vision was quite poor and she had significant problems with left/right tracking.

Within 12 months Amanda's perceptual, motor and cognitive skills had improved significantly. I do not believe that at the age of 12 she had significant psychological and psychiatric problems. Her difficulties at that time could have been explained with an understanding of the educational, emotional and social consequences of having developmental dyspraxia. With so many of the adults the root of their problems, dyspraxia, had long been overtaken by the incidents of diagnosed psychiatric conditions. In Amanda's case, it was insufficient simply to diagnose developmental dyspraxia, offer a treatment programme and then assume that all would be well. In the end she required intensive weekly sessions of professional therapy which lasted for almost five months. She has now enrolled on an access course which will enable her to register for study at degree level. She believes that almost 19 years of her life have been wasted.

Attainments

The adults presented a profile of achievement which differs significantly from the rest of the group. As highlighted earlier in the chapter, I thought that the sample was skewed towards adults who in some cases had achieved academic success and were trying to gain access to appropriate support services. Verbal skills were good and 82 per cent of those assessed were competent readers. Spelling presented problems in 68 per cent of cases and mental arithmetic was identified as an area of weakness in 77 per cent.

Assessment

The psychometric profile obtained in the WAIS highlighted strengths in many areas of verbal and non-verbal development.

Average values for each sub-test were:

Verbal scores		Performance scores	
Information	10.5	Picture completion	10.3
Similarities	10.1	Digit symbol (coding)	6.1
Arithmetic	7.6	Picture arrangement	10.2
Vocabulary	11.7	Block design	7.0
Comprehension	9.1	Object assembly	11.1
Digit span	9.8		

Attentional problems were evident in timed sub-tests. Although tasks were usually completed quickly, when a timed component was introduced this had a significant impact on the result: heightening anxiety in the adult was evident.

Most tests were completed with the adult offering high levels of verbal reinforcement to himself. There were occasions when I had to force myself to keep listening to continuous speech for periods of up to an hour. Conversations were at times difficult to follow. I tried to break into some of the monologues but my questions remained unanswered. Some of the adults asked questions of me, but then gave the expected answer themselves before giving me time to reply. Listening skills needed to be practised.

A small proportion of adults were reluctant to say much. They had become so socially withdrawn and isolated that verbal communication was difficult. At some time all had been prescribed medication for depression.

The picture painted by many of the adults in the study was one of school failure, virtually non-existent self-esteem, feelings of total exclusion from society and, in some cases, extreme loneliness. As there has been raised awareness of the difficulties encountered by dyspraxic adults, there is increasing access to support.

Responses to a questionnaire I circulated to dyspraxic adults highlighted strengths and weaknesses within the systems which are currently available. I received 223 completed responses with 161 males and 62 females in the sample. Ages ranged from 16 to 58 with the majority aged between 25 and 39. Figure 9.2 is a sample of the questionnaire to adults.

Survey results

The breakdown into age groups was:

16–19	17
20–24	42
25–29	54
30–39	79
40+	31

Forty-eight per cent of those aged 29 or under had been given a diagnosis, and 23 per cent of those aged 30 and above had been given a diagnosis. The breakdown in terms of percentages as to the origin of the diagnosis is:

	%
General practitioner	17
Psychologist	23
Psychiatrist	12
Occupational therapist/Physiotherapist	31
Teacher	6
Other	11

In response to the question 'When was the diagnosis made?', the earliest recorded was 1979.

Newspaper and magazine articles and radio and television programmes were identified as the first information given about dyspraxia in 46 per cent of the responses. Information from professionals was responsible in 19 per cent of the cases, friends and relatives 21 per cent, and other sources 14 per cent.

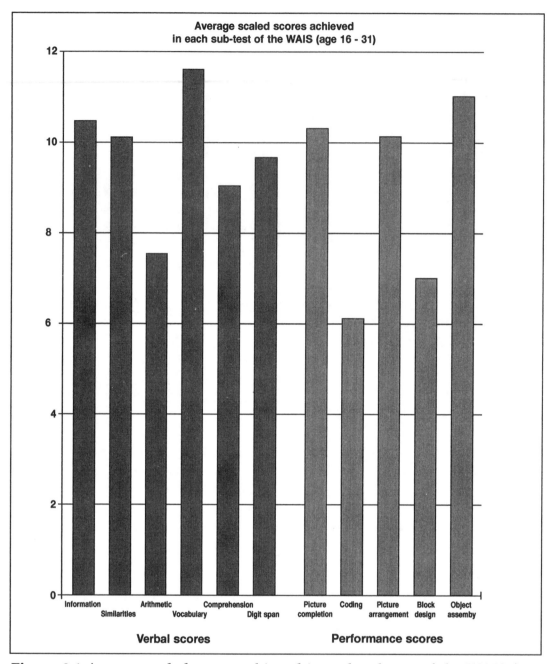

Figure 9.1 Average scaled scores achieved in each sub-test of the WAIS (age 16–31)

In the sample, 92 per cent had been educated within the state mainstream environment for part or all of their education; 4 per cent had attended only a special school. Many of those beginning in mainstream education were transferred to special schools or private schools, usually following failure within the mainstream system; 32 per cent of the total population had been offered alternative 'special' educational provision; 11 per cent had some private education.

Sixty-two per cent of responses indicated a stable childhood, 38 per cent unstable.

Sex: Male ☐   Female ☐

Age: 16–19 ☐   20–24 ☐   25–29 ☐   30–39 ☐   40+ ☐

Have you been given a diagnosis of dyspraxia? Yes ☐ No ☐

If 'Yes' who gave the diagnosis?

General practitioner   ☐

Psychologist   ☐

Psychiatrist   ☐

Occupational therapist   ☐

Physiotherapist   ☐

Teacher   ☐

Other specialist (please state)   ☐

When was the diagnosis made?   Date:.......................

Where did you first hear about dyspraxia?

Newspaper   ☐

Magazine   ☐

Television/Radio   ☐

Professional – who?   ☐

Friend   ☐

Other (please state)   ☐

What type of school did you attend?

State mainstream   ☐

Unit in mainstream   ☐

State special school   ☐

Private school   ☐

Other (please state)   ☐

Figure 9.2 Adult questionnaire

Would you describe your childhood as	Stable	☐
	Unstable	☐

Was your time in school:

Very happy	☐
Fairly happy	☐
Neither happy nor unhappy	☐
Unhappy	☐
Very unhappy	☐

Did you receive any additional support in school?	Yes ☐ No ☐
Have you ever been offered specific treatment for dyspraxia?	Yes ☐ No ☐
Have you ever had any incidence of psychiatric illness? (includes depression)	Yes ☐ No ☐
Are you taking any form of regular medication?	Yes ☐ No ☐
Are you currently in employment?	Yes ☐ No ☐

If yes, please state occupation...

Please indicate level of educational attainment:

No formal qualifications	☐
Subjects in GCSE grades A–F	☐
Subjects in GCSE grades A–C	☐
'A' level examinations	☐
NVQ or further educational qualifications	☐
Degree	☐

Additional qualifications (please state)...

Do you currently have access to appropriate levels of support? (e.g. health, social services)	Yes ☐ No ☐

Figure 9.2 (continued)

The responses to questions about school were:

	%
Very happy	9
Fairly happy	5
Neither happy nor unhappy	21
Unhappy	42
Very unhappy	23

37 per cent had been given additional support in school
17 per cent had been offered specific treatment for dyspraxia
51 per cent had incidence of psychiatric illness
29 per cent were taking regular medication

39 per cent were employed (some responses indicated part-time work)

8 per cent had degrees
13 per cent had 'A' levels or NVQ
19 per cent had GCSE (or equivalent) grades A–C
21 per cent had GCSE (or equivalent) grades A–F
39 per cent had no formal qualifications

Percentages indicate highest level of achievement as some adults had obtained GCSEs, 'A' levels, and a degree.

88 per cent did not believe they had access to appropriate levels of support.

Conclusions

The survey suggests that until the past few years diagnosis and any form of intervention have been very difficult to access by those who have left the educational system. There is a much higher incidence of diagnosed psychiatric illness than would be expected, and a relatively high proportion of adults resorting to medication to ameliorate their difficulties. Levels of educational attainment do not reflect those expected from tables representing national norms, and therefore it has to be concluded that this sample population is underachieving. Less than half the dyspraxic population is employed and many have short-term or temporary contracts.

The response to the question 'Do you currently have access to appropriate levels of support? (e.g. health, education, social services)' was a convincing 88 per cent 'No'.

Adults are concerned that there is limited awareness among professionals about dyspraxia. After leaving the education system support, networks break down.

Adults who have been successful in achieving a diagnosis and referral to the appropriate specialists have usually had access to a supportive GP. The GP can refer patients to neurologists, clinical psychologists, psychiatrists, physical and occupational therapists and counsellors/therapists.

In further and higher education additional support is available if the problems have been identified. Colleges and universities have structures in place to help students overcome the pressures of producing course work on time and preparing for examinations.

However, most dyspraxic adults have to help themselves and rely on the support of carers, close friends and sympathetic employers. Many potential problems can be overcome if those involved have an understanding of the difficulties experienced by dyspraxic adults.

Characteristics of dyspraxic adults

- Attentional problems – poor concentration
- Very quick and loud speech
- Obsessional characteristics developing because of a need for routine
- Lack of co-ordination
- Poor handwriting
- Very low self-esteem
- Unrealistic expectations
- Inability to remember verbal instructions
- Constant lateness for appointments
- Anxiety to complete tasks quickly
- Decisions constantly altered
- Depression
- Considerable excitability with evidence of associated hand movements
- Difficulty maintaining relationships with peers
- Sleeping difficulties
- High comorbidity with ADHD and psychiatric illness.

Employers must be aware that verbal instructions should carry only two or three pieces of information. Sufficient time must be given to complete the task in an un-pressured environment. The employee must be open and not try to 'cover up'. Accommodation cannot be made if the employer does not know.

Recording information

Whether in the workplace, college, or at home, students and adults are required to produce written documentation. This could involve the preparation of records, course work or communicating with outside agencies and friends. Manual recording is laborious and stressful, producing an outcome that is usually illegible.

Word-processing has been helpful to some students, but it is still time-consuming. Voice-processors have achieved limited success, with students and adults having problems if their speech patterns are inconsistent. Regional accents have been problematic. Varying voice tone and pitch, a characteristic of dyspraxia, has rendered some systems inoperable.

IBM have worked extensively on their ViaVoice software and the 98 Executive edition is available, priced £139.00. A home version has been produced at a much lower cost (£49.99) which performs most of the functions a home user would require.

The executive version holds more than 64,000 words and is 95–98 per cent accurate when the speech patterns of the user are installed correctly. Problems emerge when the enrolment script is not processed properly.

The script has been prepared for use with secondary age pupils and adults: consequently its readability is set at a level which is higher than the capability of many students with specific learning difficulties. This can be overcome if the script is read to the student who repeats it word by word.

This voice-processing facility is ideal for dyspraxic students and adults. It enables Microsoft Word to be run by voice. The user can give verbal commands and move quickly between applications.

A report can be processed and instructions given to change font and size. Bullet points, paragraph indentations, underlining and colour changes can be made by verbal command. The document can be read back to the user.

The program has a multiple-user facility and the enrolment script must be read by each. Between 1 and 3 megabytes of hard disk are required for each of up to 500 users.

Some parts of the manual are difficult to follow and, in agreement with IBM, I have produced a separate manual for students with specific learning difficulties. This includes a pre-recorded tape of the enrolment script which can be repeated by the user. It is available from the Dyspraxia Foundation and the address is listed in Appendix B.

The minimum system specification to run the program is:

- PC with 166Mhz Pentium processor with MMX and 256K L2 cache

- Windows 95/98: 32MB RAM (48MB if dictating into MS Word)

- Windows NT: 48MB RAM (64MB if dictating into MS Word)

- Hard disk space: 250MB

- 16-bit Soundblaster or MWave compatible sound card.

IBM recommend 3.5GB disk space for optimum performance. The ViaVoice 98 Executive program is available in English, US English, French, German, Italian and Spanish.

Other programs with a speak-back facility have been produced, and a project in Pennsylvania assessed the effectiveness of translating the pages of the driving manual. It was extremely popular with adults with specific learning difficulties. (Any help to pass a driving test has to be appreciated!)

In any system, whether it is health, education or social services, there is always greater demand for provision than is available. With increasing awareness among professionals, and the producers of technological aids working closely with the groups they are trying to support, children and adults with specific learning difficulties are beginning to achieve some equality of provision.

10 Epilogue

The research evidence examined in previous chapters confirms that many factors influence the way the brain develops and over some we have little control. We can, however, identify children who are likely to be 'at risk' for reasons such as:

- concern during pregnancy

- low birth weight

- pre- or post-maturity

- assisted delivery

- hyper- or hypo-activity from birth

- feeding difficulties

- food intolerance

- failure to achieve expected developmental milestones in the acquisition of early motor skills.

When one child in three born prematurely is likely to have some neurological immaturity, everything that is possible to improve their development should be done.

Early identification and intervention is important and home-based programmes are very effective in the pre-school years. Parents who know their children better than anyone else must have the support of outside specialists who acknowledge their concerns.

A child who cannot be breast fed, and the reasons are manifold, should be given the advantage of a formula milk which has had added the long-chain polyunsaturated fatty acids crucial for the development of the brain. Examine the packet and find the listed ingredients.

If the child is having difficulties acquiring motor skills, break the movement pattern down into smaller, achievable steps. Teach the child to crawl, walk independently, balance, jump and hop. These co-ordinated movements reinforce the appropriate transmission of messages in the cortex and improve thinking skills.

Self-help skills, such as dressing, feeding and toilet training are not acquired 'naturally' and must be taught. Feeding problems are exacerbated if the child has difficulty with textured foods: try a desensitisation programme. Problems with bowel control may be the result of food intolerance or difficulties with the processing of the planned series of movements: i.e. sensation in the bowel, feedback to the brain and the co-ordination of appropriate muscles.

The child may have severe articulation difficulties. Despite high levels of input, many youngsters continue to have problems planning the subtle changes in movement of the lips, tongue and palate until they are 8 or 9 years old. Don't despair: it is a developmental process and appropriate speech sounds emerge when the co-ordination of the required movements matures.

Parents and teachers need to be aware of the relationship difficulties likely to be encountered by a youngster with dyspraxia. A prescriptive environment at home or in the classroom where the child is encouraged to engage in structured 'play' can be very beneficial.

The child can be identified from a very early age as being different from the group. If this is not 'managed' appropriately, the child becomes a victim of more assertive pupils and the 'loner' observed as being peripheral to all activities in the playground and in the classroom.

If the child's abilities can be promoted, he is less likely to suffer the loss of self-esteem which often leads to educational failure.

Previous chapters have examined recent research into dyspraxia and considered ways of identifying from an early age children who have the condition. Motor learning difficulties, the research tells us, are evident in a large proportion of youngsters who have failed in the educational system and find themselves placed in residential institutions for those experiencing emotional and behavioural difficulties or clinical depression. If preventative measures can be introduced which provide remediation programmes for those youngsters, the population currently requiring alternative, and often very expensive, provision will be reduced.

All disciplines in health, education and social services must work co-operatively with parents to ensure that these children are correctly diagnosed. Too frequently their difficulties are dismissed as being the result of:

- behavioural problems
- poor diet
- bad parenting
- frequent changes of school, or
- attention seeking.

A detailed assessment of the child and subsequent access to specified remediation programmes can bring about dramatic social, emotional and educational improvements.

Resources available for children with special educational needs are finite whether that means access to professional time or specialised equipment. If we say constantly that there is not time and insufficient expertise to provide treatment then we are undervaluing ourselves and the commitment of parents.

Programmes which have been successful are described in detail. The sources of materials are listed in the appendices and some identified outside agencies which can offer support have been provided. The contents of the appendices are free from copyright and may be reproduced.

In addition to the remediation programmes, the environment in school and at home must be examined. The following factors are important:

- remove stress from the child
- always find something positive to acknowledge
- set personal attainable targets
- allow sufficient time for the completion of work
- integrate the child within his peer group
- always match the curriculum to ability: even though the child exhibits poor attentional skills he will have good understanding
- give the child time every day to discuss his anxieties
- decide which behaviours are evidently because of the condition and which are not: do not use dyspraxia as an excuse.

Intervention is also appropriate for juveniles identified in the criminal justice system. The programmes already developed for secondary age pupils can be delivered through peers which will be financially very cost-effective. The relevant support systems would be responsible for monitoring their implementation.

There is no doubt that an increasing number of children and adults are being identified as having specific learning difficulties and behaviours described as 'on the autistic spectrum'. I do not believe that this can be explained solely by making the assumption that we are better diagnostic clinicians.

We have to consider the wider picture of our environment and activities within it. Our dietary habits have changed dramatically during the past 50 years and we must look carefully at the implications of inadequate and inappropriate nutrition.

Regardless of the child's age, he should be encouraged to develop his gross and fine motor skills. Generally, society is becoming less physically active and many children spend a large part of their time watching television, videos and glued to the computer screen.

Whatever the reasons for increasing numbers of identified dyspraxic children and adults, they continue to represent a significant educational underclass, largely misjudged, frequently maligned and extensively ignored. They do, indeed, have 'special needs'.

Research is constantly providing us with explanations and greater understanding of conditions such as developmental dyspraxia. We must continue to update our knowledge and offer the best possible advice on strategies to overcome the social, emotional and educational difficulties the condition frequently generates, and work towards restoring the self-esteem of all these individuals.

Appendix A

Record sheets and prepared intervention material

Parental questionnaire

Background information

Is X your first child? If not, what is his position in the family?.................................

How old were you (mother) at the time of birth?...

Is there any family incidence of learning difficulty, e.g. dyslexia, dyspraxia, autism, ADHD or diagnosed genetic condition?..

....

Personal details

Can you remember whether you had any illness during your pregnancy?..............

Did nausea persist beyond the third month?...

How did your weight progress?..

When did you have your scan and was it repeated later during pregnancy?...........

....

Were there any concerns?...

Was there anything unusual about the last trimester (6–9 months in utero)?.........

....

Did you maintain a good diet?..

Did you smoke during pregnancy?...

Birth details

At what stage of pregnancy was X delivered, e.g. 34 weeks, 42 weeks?...............

Was X induced and if so what was the method of delivery?..................................

Was there any indication of foetal distress before the birth?................................

How long was the labour? Obtain additional information regarding the second stage if possible...

....

Were there any concerns immediately after the birth?...

What was the birth weight?..

Figure A.1

Parental questionnaire

Developmental profile

Child presentation within the first four weeks

• Levels of activity (e.g. hyper-, hypo-active)

• Feeding – was weight gain appropriate? Any evidence of lactose intolerance?

• Sleeping – settled quickly or very irritable with very short periods of sleep?

Motor skills

• Sitting independently at –

• Crawling at –

• Walking independently at –

Social skills

• Finger feeding at –

• Co-ordinating a knife and fork at –

• Toilet trained at –

Language

• Able to say 20+ distinguishable words at –

• Used 3+ words to construct simple phrases at –

Were there any other difficulties during the first 12 months?

Suggestions may be:

a) raised temperature/convulsion

b) jaundice

c) infections

Is there anything else you can remember that was of concern?

Has your child been assessed by anyone, e.g. paediatrician, speech therapist, physio- or occupational therapist?

Additional Information

Name.. DoB..................

Reading Age	CA	Date

Spelling Age	CA	Date

Numeracy Attainments	CA	Date

Perceptual Skills	CA	Date

Comments

Figure A2

Motor Skills Screening		
Name.................................... Date............................ Age...		
Activity	**Behaviour**	**Date**
1. Walking on toes forwards and backwards		
2. Walking on heels forwards and backwards		
3. Walking on insides of feet		
4. Walking on outsides of feet		
5. Recognising fingers touched when obscured from view. Right hand then left		
6. Finger sequencing – right then left		
7. Wrist rotation		
8. Balancing on each foot		
9. Touching end of nose with index finger of each hand (eyes closed)		
10. Jumping: feet together		

Figure A.3

Baseline motor assessment

Name .... DOB .... Date ....

Laterality			
	Hand	RH	LH
	Foot	RF	LF
	Eye	RE	LE

Activity		Indicators
Crawling		
Balance	Right leg	
	Left leg	
Parallel lines	Soles – heel/toe	
	toes	
	heels	
	side steps	
Running		
Jumping		
Hopping	Right foot	
	Left foot	
Rope turning	Right hand	
	Left hand	
Clapping		
Finger sequencing	Right hand	
	Left hand	

Figure A.4

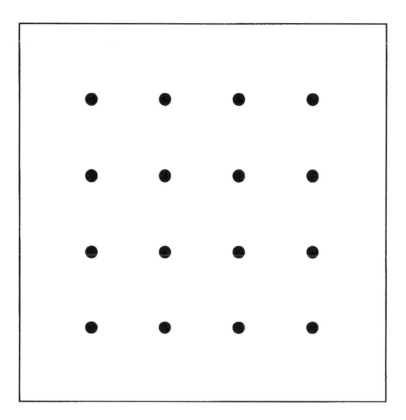

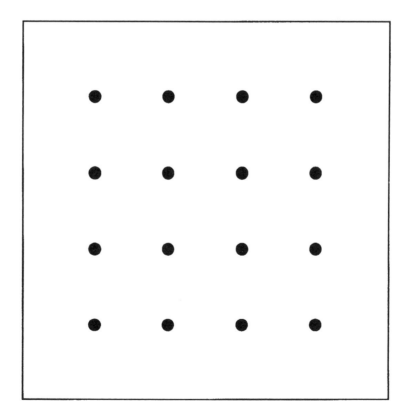

Figure A.5

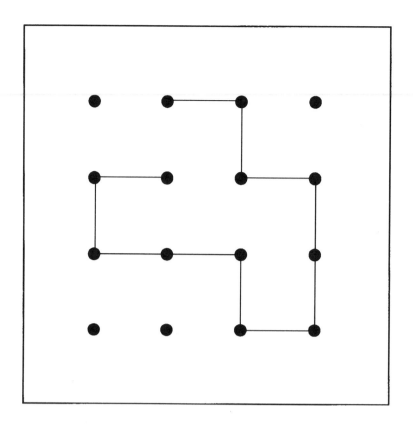

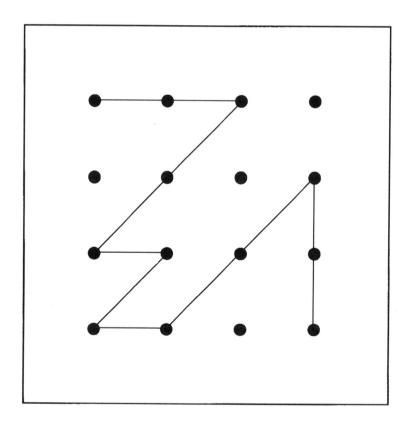

Figure A.6

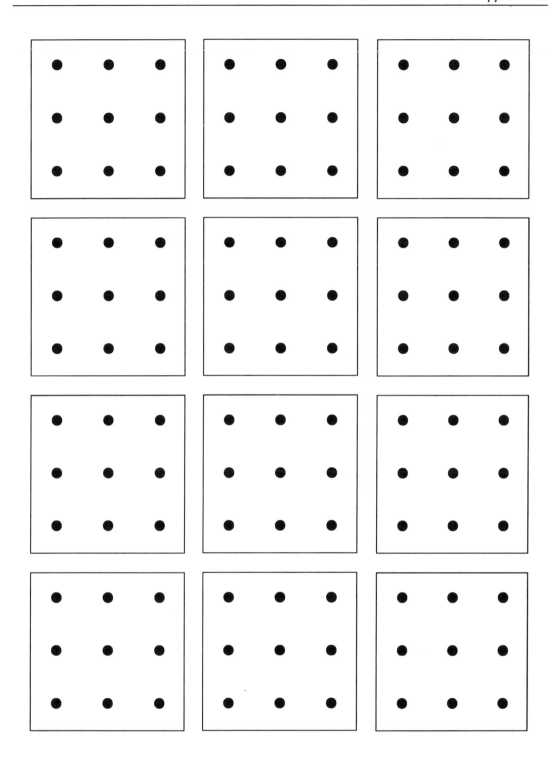

Figure A.7

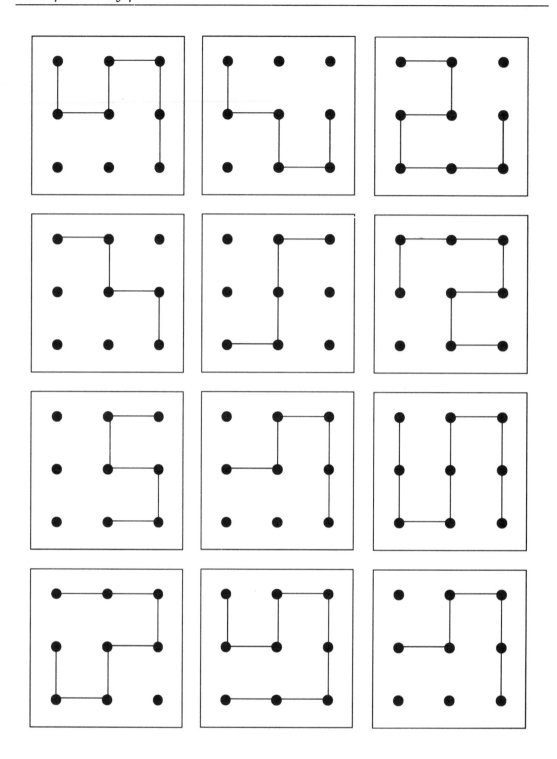

Figure A.8

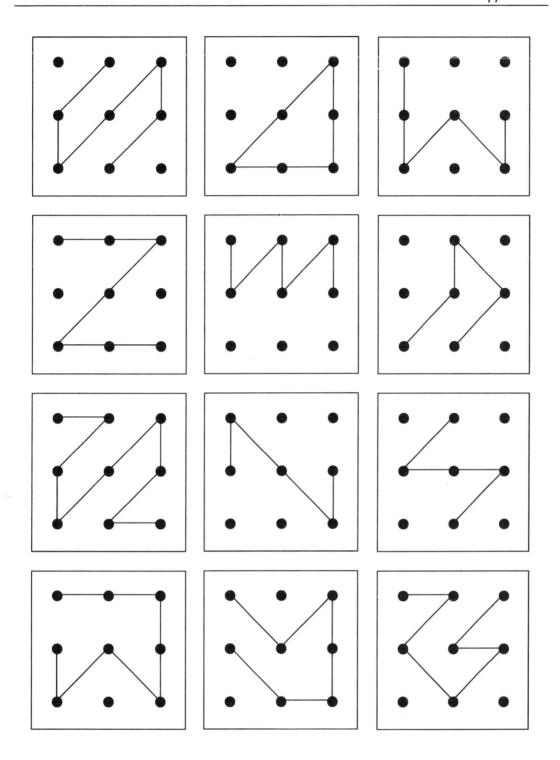

Figure A.9

Name: _____ Class _____ Co-ordinator _____ Date ____					
Activity	Mon	Tue	Wed	Thu	Fri

Figure A.10 Programme record sheets

A11.1 Computer

A11.2 Co-operative play

A11.3 Snacks

A11.4 Sand

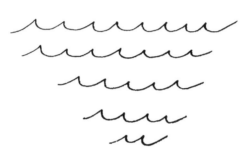

A11.5 Water

A11.6 Story

A11.7 Outdoor play

A11.8 Construction

A11.9 Drawing

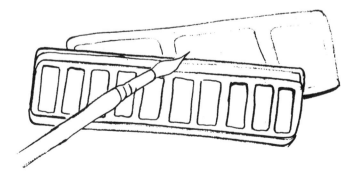

A11.10 Painting

A11.11 Home corner

A11.12 Cloakroom

A11.13 Creative play

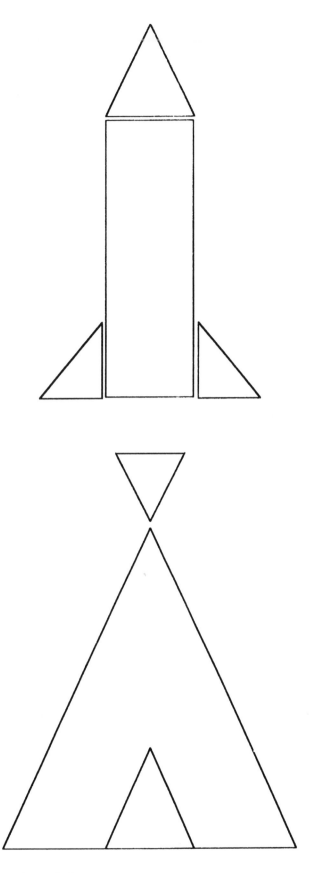

Figure A.12 Picture templates

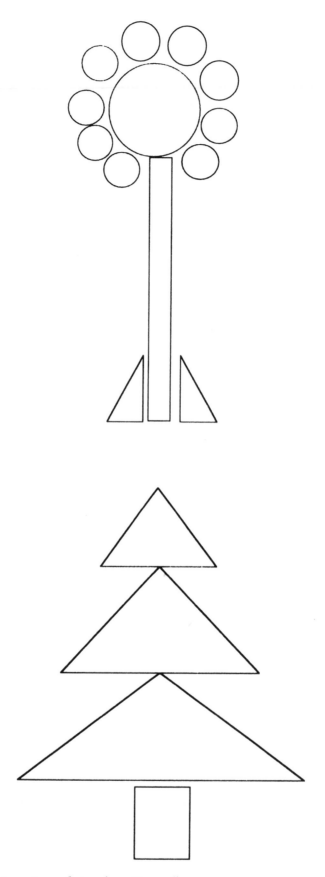

Figure A.12 Picture templates (continued)

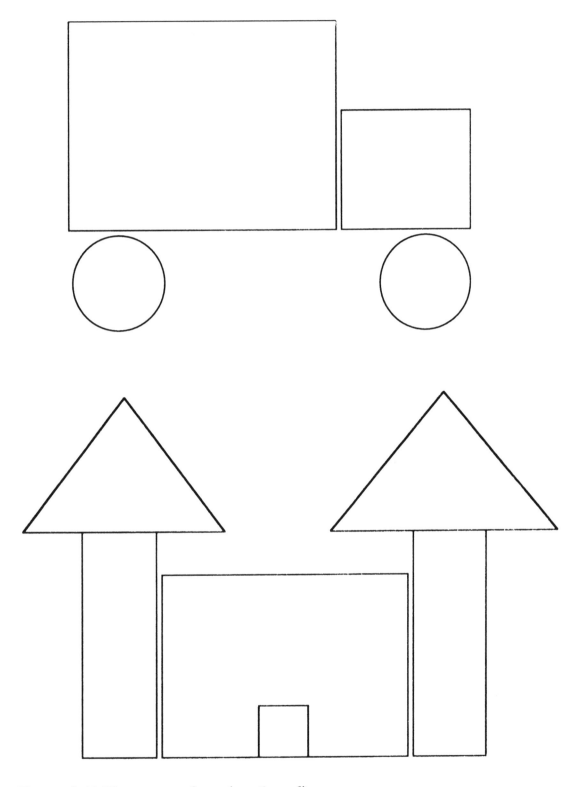

Figure A.12 Picture templates (continued)

Figure A.12 Picture templates (continued)

Appendix B

Useful names and addresses

The Dyspraxia Foundation
8 West Alley
Hitchin
Herts
SG5 1UU
Tel: 01462 455016
Helpline: 01462 454986
Fax: 01462 455052
http://www.emmbrook.demon.co.uk/dysprax/homepage.htm

Tumble Tots Licensees

London and the South East

Sarah Field	0181 944 8818	Fulham, Wimbledon, Barnes
Lorraine Harrison	0181 959 4261	Finchley, Highbury, St John's Wood, Muswell Hill, Golders Green
Lesley Oliver	0181 777 4332	Clapham, Dulwich, Blackheath, Streatham, Bromley, West Wickham, Beckenham
Tracy Harding	0181 777 8110	Orpington, Sevenoaks, Westerham, Petts Wood
Lesley Burnand	01732 359688	Tunbridge Wells, East Grinstead, Oxted
Sue Atkinson	01634 686182	Ryarsh-West Malling, Walderslade, Maidstone, Sutton Valence
Pauline Mcintyre	01634 726314	Gravesend, Strood, Longfield
Karen McGee	0181 406 5200	Kenley, South Croydon, Thornton Heath, Coulsdon
Helen Jutting	01932 568263	Twickenham, Kingston, Kew, Hampton, New Malden, Chiswick

Anne Kapoor	0181 440 0634	Palmers Green, Bush Hill Park, Wormley, Hertford Heath, Enfield East
Beverley Regan	0181 958 6579	Harrow, Edgware, Ruislip, Hatch End, Enfield West, Goff's Oak, Barnet, Potters Bar
Rona Sparrowhawk	0181 559 0617	Harold Wood, Buckhurst Hill, Theydon Bois, Chigwell, Chingford
Gill Sayers	01727 824259	Chorleywood, Bushey, St Albans, Elstree, Watford
Nora Shipley	01737 352375	Epsom, Banstead, Cheam, Sutton
Nicola Spink	01932 564512	Addlestone, Walton on Thames, West Moseley, Thames Ditton, Shepperton, Byfleet, Weybridge, Sunbury, Hersham
Gillian Smith	01372 273649	Dorking, Leatherhead, Woking, Cobham
David Barker	01276 62438	Camberley, Farnham, Yately, Fleet, Mychett
Sue and John Knight	01483 420741	Cranleigh, Godalming, Guildford, Haslemere
Ann Clapham	01730 267596	Petersfield, Southsea, Copnor, Fareham, Waterlooville, Havant
Janet Standley	01264 353377	Salisbury, Andover, Thatcham
Steve Milton	01983 528149	Isle of Wight
Jane Bayden	01344 452083	Bracknell, Crowthorne, Windsor, Slough
Geoff Beech	0118 978 5481	Reading, Wokingham, Sindlesham
Beverley Davis	01494 443113	Chalfont St Peter, Amersham, Maidenhead, Beaconsfield, Marlow, Great Missenden, High Wycombe, Chesham
Sharon Owen	01908 374895	Bletchley, Buckingham, Milton Keynes, Stony Stratford
Amanda Stephenson	01296 394709	Berkhamsted, Aylesbury, Leighton Buzzard, Hemel Hempstead, Tring
Carole Shackell	01438 369848	Hitchin, Letchworth, Stevenage, Welwyn Garden City, Royston
Sue Dobson	01235 868119	Kidlington, Bicester, Witney, Wallingford, Wantage, Oxford, Faringdon, Swindon, Didcot

Linda Aspel	01234 838883	Flitwick, Bedford, Sandy, Newport Pagnell, Clapham
Lorraine Puttock	01273 883782	Horsham, Crawley, Horley, Redhill, Reigate
Veronika Anderson	01424 850265	Hastings, Eastbourne, Uckfield, Bexhill on Sea, Hailsham, Heathfield
Julie Fuller	01273 723511	Hove, Brighton, Hassocks and Cuckfield, Worthing
Rosemarie Herring	01621 891948	Witham, Brentwood, Chelmsford, Malden, Ingatestone, Billericay
Chris Maidman	01371 850431	Harlow, Bishops Stortford, Great Dunmow, Braintree
Susan Slow	01268 699222	Canvey Island, Carrington, Rayleigh, Southend on Sea, Leigh on Sea.

South West

Helen Priest	01452 750242	Cirencester, Tewkesbury, Gloucester, Cheltenham
Graham Middle	01934 417550	Bristol, Westbury-on-Trym, Stoke Gifford
Lorraine Exley	01202 749249	Poole, Ferndown, Bournemouth
Nicola Sloan	01752 348484	Plympton, Saltash, Ivybridge, Plymstock, Hartley
Tumble Tots Head Office	0121 5857003	Exeter, Tiverton, Exmouth, Honiton.

East Anglia

Sylvia West	01223 263 412	Cambridge, Cherry Hinton, Fowlmere, Bar Hill, Linton
Kim Mackay	01787 228151	Sudbury, Bury St Edmunds, Halstead, Hadleigh
Jan Smith	01493 750520	Loddon, Great Yarmouth, Gorleston, Lowestoft, Ringsfield, Mutford
Denise Sadler	01603 419074	Taverham, Norwich, Wymondham, North Walsham, Dereham.

East Midlands

Pat Partington	01778 590225	Stamford, Peterborough, Market Deeping, Oundle, Eye
Carran Stevenson	01332 544958	Derby, Littleover, Belper, Oakwood

Irene Jones	01664 444555	Oakham, Market Harborough, Melton Mowbray, Leicester
Jayne Cragg	0115 981 5731	Radcliffe on Trent, Keyworth, Long Eaton, Nottingham South
Adrian Allsopp	01327 706586	Northampton, Banbury, East Hunsbury, Daventry, Rugby
Tumble Tots Head Office	0121 585 7003	Newark, Mapperley, Ravenshead.

West Midlands

Sandra Crofts	01527 854287	Bournville, Bromsgrove, Kings Heath, Redditch, Alcester
Karen Pincher	01922 643109	Solihull, Bentley Heath, Harborne, Shirley
Jennifer Cromie	01902 338320	Wolverhampton, Stafford, Cannock, Wednesfield, Penn
Anne Bartram	01827 66318	Sutton Coldfield, Tamworth, Lichfield
Diann Tanser/ Lisa Pugh	01905 796111	Kingswinford, Hagley, Kidderminster, Halesowen
Zeeta and John Dowsey	01952 433391	Bridgnorth, Dawley, Ironbridge, Shrewsbury, Wellington
Ellen Braham	01926 674039	Warwick, Kenilworth, Leamington Spa, Stratford upon Avon, Southam
Linda Hill	01283 716499	Whitwick, Loughborough, Ashby, Burton upon Trent, Swadlincote.

York/Humberside

Sue Courture	01453 563731	Harrogate, Otley, Wetherby
Peter and Jane Harrison	0113 260 5494	York, Acombe, Selby, Pocklington
Christine and Peter Chilton	01845 522712	Richmond, Thirsk, Northallerton, Malton
Monique Brennan	01484 689467	Huddersfield, Halifax, Holmfirth, Grenoside.

North West

Hillary Bernstein	0151 722 0618	Childwall, Formby, Maghull, Liverpool, Crosby
Sarita Collins	01706 648128	Shaw, Oldham, Bury, Rochdale
Catherine Cotton	0151 428 3710	Warrington, St Helen's, Runcorn, Widnes

Karen and John Irving	01253 795021	Bispham, Blackpool, Poulton-Le-Fylde, Andsell (near Preston)
Megan Kneale	0189 741921	Chester, Frodsham, Wrexham, Caldy Valley
Karen Hickson	01606 833393	Alsager, Sandbach, Middlewich, Holmes Chapel, Northwich
Val Jackson	01298 816100	Poynton, Marple, New Mills, Buxton, Glossop
Martin Lawson	01625 876505	Bramhall, Wilmslow, Macclesfield, Stockport
Sue Livesey	0151 645 7212	West Kirby, Wallasey, Heswall, Bebington, Great Sutton
Jane McDowell	0161 499 3699	Lymm, Hale, Sale, Knutsford, Timperley.

North

Maria Barker	01661 871870	Washington, Gosforth, Ponteland, Morpeth
Sheila Boyes	01642 321243	Stockton on Tees, Middlesbrough, Guisborough, Stokesley, Marske by the Sea
Anna Linford	01325 377576	Stockton, Bishop Auckland, Darlington, Durham
Rose Thompson	01539 824036	Kendal.

Scotland

Jo Letelier Lobos	01592 873287	Kirkcaldy, Dunfermline, Glenrothes, St Andrews, Kinross, South Queensferry, Edinburgh, Linlithgow
Paula Tatters	01343 545294	Elgin
Tumble Tots Head Office	0121 585 7003	North Glasgow, Bearsden, Milngavie, Helensburgh, Kirkintilloch

Northern Ireland

Norma Wylie	01849 479701	Belfast, Antrim, Newtownabbey, Carrickfergus, Antrim
Claire Ogg	01247 888432	Ballynahinch, Carryduff, Hillsborough, Newtownards, Bangor, Dundonald

Appendix C

Names and addresses of support agencies and educational suppliers

Ayres Collection for Development (A.C.)
Ayres and Co. Ltd
Unit 1 Turnoaks Business Park
Burley Close Chesterfield
S40 2HA   Tel: 01246 551546

Early Learning Centre (E.L.C.)
South Marston Park
Swindon
SN3 4TJ   Tel: 01793 444844

Educational Co. Ltd. (EDCO)
Freepost BE281
Newtonabbey
Northern Ireland
BT36 6BR   Tel: 0800 243087

Galt Education (G.E.)
Culvert Street
Oldham
OL4 2ST   Tel: 0161 627 5086

Mr. J. Jacob
Howden-Le-Wear Primary School
Howden-Le-Wear
Bishop Auckland
Co. Durham

Mr. A. Potts
Howden-Le-Wear
Bishop Auckland
Co. Durham   Tel: 01388 763350

ROMPA
Chesterfield
Derbyshire   Tel: 0800 056 2323
www.rompa.co.uk

N. E. S. Arnold Ltd. (N.E.S.)
Ludlow Hill Road
West Bridgford
Nottingham
NG2 6HD   Tel: 0115 945 2201

Tumble Tots Equipment (T.T.)
Blue Bird Park
Bromsgrove Road
Hunnington
Halesowen
West Midlands
B62 0JW   Tel: 0121 585 7003

*Note the supplier codes alongside their names
and after each product.*

Actipack –
practical activities to develop mathematical
skills with 8- to 13-year-olds.
N.E.S.

Adjustable wobble boards –
wooden base screw attachment for adjustable
height.
J. Jacob

Assorted foam balls –
lightweight, varying sizes and colours.
N.E.S., E.L.C.

Basketball net –
forms an early introduction to ball skills.
Adjustable height – ball included.
G.E.

Bean bags –
set of 12 in assorted colours.
G.E., T.T.

Catchball –
pronged ball with numbers on each stem
EDCO

Chime bars –
8 coloured chimes which can be removed
from tray. Comes with 3 pairs of hammers.
N.E.S., G.E.

Climbing frame –
wooden hardboard frame with two platforms
of variable height.
N.E.S. G.E.

Creepie-crawlie puppets –
hand puppets designed to make the fingers
appear to form the legs of the insects. 2 sizes:
adult and child. Finger puppets are also
available.
G.E.

Cutting fruit –
apple, pear and lemon. Pieces attached with Velcro. Comes with a wooden knife.
G.E.

Cutting vegetables –
11 different fruits and vegetables attached with Velcro. Special plastic knife provided.
E.L.C.

Desk music stands –
inexpensive plastic stands which will hold reading material in an angled position.
N.E.S.

Diagnostic development frames –
progressively extends eye-hand co-ordination which is essential for the development of a range of physical and intellectual skills. Actual activities are suggested in Training Aids, produced by Galt Educational.
N.E.S.

Dot to dot pictures –
simple pictures for young children to develop pencil control skills. Maximum of 20 dots.
E.L.C.

Easel –
adjustable drawing easel, various attachments.
G.E., E.L.C.

Easihold rulers –
designed to enable the child with poor co-ordination to hold ruler more securely. Flat surface with handle attachment.
A. Potts

Finger puppets –
12 characters from nursery rhymes, and children's stories.
N.E.S.

Foam dart board –
Velcro-tipped darts and colourful felt target, encourages number skills and eye–hand co-ordination.
E.L.C.

Foam fishing –
fun game to play in the bath, develops eye–hand co-ordination.
E.L.C.

Geo nuts and bolts –
a set of giant nuts and bolts which can be twisted together. Matched for shape and colour. Designed for small fingers to gain dexterity.
N.E.S.

Geo-board –
a sorting board with 4 different shapes.
N.E.S.

Geometrix –
a 2-dimensional game based on colour, shape and form matching. Patterns progress from very simple shapes to more complex abstract figures.
N.E.S.

Gym equipment under-7s –
slide, ladders, stepping stones, balancing beams, Meccano walkway.
N.E.S., T.T., G.E.

Hand and foot-prints –
provide a directional pathway for movement giving the child cues for placing feet and hands.
N.E.S.

Hand looms –
2 sizes: small – nursery & reception class, large – 6+.
A. Potts

Happy matrix –
3 different themes. Each pack contains 5 sets of illustrated coloured cards, a laminated matrix board and computer software which enables the game to be played on the table top or on the computer screen.
A.C.

Hedgehog balls –
for massage, hand and finger exercises or for throwing and catching. Available in 3 sizes.
A.C.

Hoops –
assorted colours and sizes.
G.E.

Inset boards –
large handled: fruit, everyday objects.
N.E.S., G.E., A.C.

Lacing fruit –
large holes allow the big wooden threader to pass through. Ideal for developing basic co-ordination skills.
N.E.S.

Letter shapes –
26 boards – one for each letter – incorporating a series of graded letter grooves. As the letter sizes decrease, children gradually acquire more controlled motor skills to help them form the letters correctly.
N.E.S.

Logic materials –
sorting activities and introduction of logic. Comprises assortment of plastic pieces with P.V.C. templates.
N.E.S.

Magnetic fish game –
suitable from 3+. Designed to develop hand and eye co-ordination.
N.E.S.

Magnetic playdesk –
magnetic angled board with 37 numbers, 40 upper case and 40 lower case letters.
E.L.C.

Magnetic shapes –
Piky decor and mosaic. Magnetised pieces in various shapes and sizes. Develops understanding of shape.
N.E.S

Math safari –
highly motivating scheme to teach mathematics from age 4. Pupils can use it individually or play competitively. Angled board for easy viewing. Scheme reduces the amount of handwritten recording.
N.E.S.

Mega Bloks –
large bright building blocks which develop co-ordination skills.
G.E., Woolworths.

Mini hurdles –
4 hardwood hurdles – height 11.5 cm.
G.E.

Modelling clay and Play Doh –
modelling material that is easy to manipulate. Assorted colours.
G.E.

Mounted chime bars –
development of rhythm and extension of hand movements.
A.C.

Multi-link –
fractions, exploring angles and algebra through structures. Suitable for youngsters aged 7–11. Develops understanding of mathematical concepts with emphasis on practical activities.
N.E.S.

Multi-link pattern cards –
3 sets of pattern cards designed to be placed on the Multi-link grid tray under the transparent grid. Cubes may then be put down on to the grid to match the pattern underneath. Develops skills in colour matching, making patterns and language development, and extends a child's perceptual skills and recording ability.
N.E.S.

Pedal-go – wheeled activity –
designed to improve balance, co-ordination and motor control skills.
G.E.

Pegboards –
boards and pegs are available in different sizes. Designed to improve hand–eye co-ordination.
G.E.

Picture Lotto –
6 wooden boards with 54 matching pieces. Designed to encourage language development.
N.E.S.

Play Tunnel –
heavy duty reinforced plastic.
N.E.S., E.L.C.

Pre-writing –
2 wooden panels with cut-out tracks of different degrees of difficulty. The aim is to pull the bead/knob along the predetermined track. Develops pre-writing skills and assists with eye–hand co-ordination.
A.C.

Pre-writing skills worksheets –
30 re-usable worksheets which provide a series of finely graded exercises to encourage left-to-right tracking skills and basic letter patterns.
N.E.S.

Reward chart –
laminated write-on/wipe-off surface: records activities on a weekly basis. Includes pens, stars and reward coupons.
T.T.

Rol 'n' Write –
a steel ball slowly traces the letter in the correct sequence. Alternatively the children can follow the groove with their fingers. In addition there are 48 photocopy masters to complete. Develops fine motor control, hand–eye co-ordination, fluency and flow of hand and letter formation.
N.E.S.

Sand shapers –
5 differently shaped moulds.
G.E.

Self-opening scissors –
designed for small hands or children with a weak grip. They allow the strength in all the fingers to be used when cutting. A spring is incorporated into the handles to pull open the blades.
G.E.

SENSO –
a lotto game which focuses on the development of tactile skills as well as stimulating visual language and simple counting skills.
N.E.S

Sequential colour cards –
12 14-step sequences. Easy-to-understand concepts in familiar domestic scenes.
A.C.

Sequential thinking cards –
each sequence shows familiar situations such as getting ready for bed, crossing the road etc. Through sets 1–5 the sequences become visually and logically more complex. Stimulates imagination and language development. Set 1: 3 × 2 card, 4 × 3 card, 3 × 4 card sequences.
A.C.

Short tennis racquets –
large surface heads and short handles. Ideal for youngsters learning to co-ordinate movements between bat and ball.
N.E.S.

Stampabouts –
improves balance: cords held taut while feet are lifted.
N.E.S.

Star-stack –
available in 2 sizes: 6-pronged shapes fit together to form increasingly complex structures.
N.E.S.

Stirex scissors –
designed to help children who have a weaker grip. Operated using the whole hand rather
than the forefinger and thumb.
G.E.

Tactile letters –
letter template and soft shiny colourful P.V.C letters. Extends language.
G.E.

Tactile touch cards –
34 cards to demonstrate a range of different tactile sensations such as smooth and rough, thick and thin, etc.
G.E.

Targets –
wooden design 50 cm². Inner target 15 cm diameter, outer target 35 cm diameter.
N.E.S., E.L.C.

Threading butterfly –
easy-to-thread shape.
A.C.

Training aids –
designed specifically to develop perceptual, motor, manipulative and language skills. Blocks are manoeuvred around a wire frame and it is a test of eye–hand co-ordination. A precursor to writing skills.
G.E.

Training scissors –
double-handed to teach youngsters with poor motor skills.
G.E.

Trampoline –
steel frame complete with handrail. Suitable for 2 years+.
N.E.S., E.L.C.

Triangular pencils –
chunky pencils designed to help children develop drawing and writing skills. The grip gives better control, improved comfort and less writing fatigue.
N.E.S.

Waffle blocks –
36 blocks in assorted colours. Easy to manipulate.
G.E.

Bibliography

American Psychiatric Association, Category 315.40 Developmental Co-ordination Disorder (1994) *Diagnostic and Statistical Manual*, 4th edition. Washington D.C.: A.P.A.

Barber, M. A., Milich, R., Welsh, R. (1996) 'Effects of reinforcement schedule and task difficulty on the performance of attention deficit hyperactivity disordered and control boys', *Journal of Clinical Child Psychology* 25, 66–76.

Barkley, R. A. (1997) 'Behavioural inhibition, sustained attention and executive functions: constructing a unified theory of ADHD', *Psychological Bulletin* 121(1), 65–94.

Barkley, R. A., Murphy, K. R., Kwasnik, D. (1996) 'Psychological adjustment and adaptive impairments in young adults with ADHD', *Journal of Attention Disorders* 1, 41–54.

Bruininks, R. H. (1978) *Bruininks-Oseretsky test of motor proficiency*. Circle Pines, CA: American Guidance Service.

Carramazza, A. (1986) 'On drawing inferences about the structure of normal cognitive systems from the analysis of patterns of impaired performance: the case for single-patient studies', *Brain and Cognition* 5, 41–66.

Carramazza, A. *et al.* (1976) 'Right-hemisphere damage and verbal problem solving behaviour', *Brain and Language* 3, 41–6.

Chu, S. (1991) *The Diagnosis of Dyspraxia 1991*. Hitchin: The Dyspraxia Foundation.

Code, C. (1987) *Language, Aphasia and the Right Hemisphere*. Chichester: John Wiley.

Colombo, J. (1993) *Infant Cognition: Predicting Later Intellectual Functioning*. Newbury Park, CA: Sage Publications.

Coltheart, M. (1983) 'The right hemisphere and disorders of reading', in Young, A. W. (ed.) *Functions of the Right Cerebral Hemisphere*. London: Academic Press.

Cratty, B. J. (1994) *Clumsy Child Syndromes: Descriptions, Evaluations and Remediation*. Langhorn, PA: Harwood Academic Publishers.

Crawford, M. A. (1996) 'The rationale for pre-pregnancy supplementation in high risk women of reproductive age', *Asia Pacific Journal of Clinical Nutrition* 5(4), section 3.

Damasio, A. R. and Benton, A. L. (1979) 'Impairment of hand movements under visual guidance', *Neurology* 29, 170–78.

Department for Education and Employment (1997) *Excellence for all Children*. London: The Stationery Office.

Dewey, D. and Kaplan, B. J. (1992) 'Analysis of praxis task demands in the assessment of children with developmental motor deficits', *Developmental Neuropsychology* 8, 367–79.

Edelman, G. M. (1989) *Neural Darwinism. The Theory of Neuronal Group Selection*. Oxford: Oxford University Press.

Edelman, G. M. (1992) *Bright Air, Brilliant Fire on the Matter of the Mind*. London: A. Lane Publishers.

Edwards, B. (1979) *Drawing on the Right Side of the Brain*. Los Angeles: Tarcher.

Ellis, A. W. (1982) 'Spelling and writing (and reading and speaking)', in Ellis, A. W. (ed.) *Normality and Pathology in Cognitive Functions*. London: Academic Press.

Ellis, A. W. (1983) 'Syndromes, slips and structure', *Bulletin of the British Psychological Society* 36, 372–4.

Ellis, A. W. (1987) 'Intimations of modularity, or, the modularity of mind', in Coltheart, M., Sartoria, G., Job, R. (eds) *The Cognitive Neuropsychology of Language*. London: Lawrence Erlbaum Associates.

Ellis, A. and Young, A. (1988) *Human Cognitive Neuropsychology*. Hillsdale, NJ: Lawrence Erlbaum Associates.

Farquharson, J., Cherry, E. C., Abbasi, K. A., Patrick, W. J. A. (1995) 'Effect of diet on the fatty acid composition of the major phospholipids of infant cerebral cortex', *Archives of Disease in Childhood* **72**, 198–203.

Florey, C. Du V., Leech, A.M., Blackhall, A. (1995) 'Infant feeding and mental and motor development at 18 months of age in first born singletons', *International Journal Epidemiology* **24**, S21–26.

Fog, E. and Fog, M. (1963) 'Cerebral inhibition examined by associated movements', in Bax, M. and Makeith, R. (eds) *Minimal Cerebral Dysfunction. Clinics in Developmental Medicine No. 10.* London: SIMP/Heinemann.

Fox, A. M. and Ho, H. (1990) 'Use of methylphenidate for attention deficit hyperactivity disorder: Canadian Paediatric Society Statement'. *Canadian Medical Association Journal* **142**(8), 817–18.

Frith, U. (ed.) (1980) *Cognitive Processes in Spelling*. London: Academic Press.

Frostig, M. (1964) *Developmental Test of Visual Perception*. Palo Alto, CA: Consulting Psychological Press.

Gilberg, I. C., Gilberg, C., Groth, J. (1989) 'Children with pre-school minor neuro-developmental disorders *v.* neurodevelopmental profiles at age 13', *Developmental Medicine and Child Neurology* **31**, 14–24.

Goodman, R. A. and Carramazza, A. (1986) 'Aspects of the spelling process: evidence from a case of acquired dysgraphia', *Language and Cognitive Processes* **1**, 1–34.

Gordon, N. and McKinlay, I. (1980) *Helping Clumsy Children*. New York: Churchill Livingstone.

Gorman, K. S. and Pollitt, E. (1996) 'Does schooling buffer the effects of early risk?', *Child Development* **67**, 314–22.

Griffiths, R., (1973) *Griffiths Mental Development Scales*. High Wycombe: Test Agency.

Gubbay, S. S. (1975) 'Clumsy children in normal schools', *Medical Journal of Australia* **1**, 223–36.

Gubbay, S. S. (1985) 'Clumsiness', in Vinken, P., Bruyn, G., Dlawans, H. (eds) *Handbook of Clinical Neurology*. New York: Elsevier.

Hack, M. *et al.* (1992) 'The effect of a very low birth weight and social risk on neurocognitive abilities at school age', *Journal Development Behaviour Paediatrics* **13**, 412–20.

Hécaen, H. and Marcie, P. (1974) 'Disorders of written language following right hemisphere lesions', in Dimond, S. J. and Beaumont, J. G. (eds) *Hemisphere Function in the Human Brain*. London: Elek.

Hellgren, L. *et al.* (1994) 'Children with deficits in attention, motor control and perception (DAMP) almost grown up: psychiatric and personality disorders at age 16 years', *Journal of Child Psychology and Psychiatry* **35**(7), 1255–71.

Henderson, S. E. (1993) 'Motor development and minor handicap', in Kalverboer, A. F., Hopkins, B., Geuze, R. (eds) *Motor Development in Early and Later Childhood: Longitudinal Approaches*. Cambridge: Cambridge University Press.

Henderson, S. E. and Hall, D. (1982) 'Concomitants of clumsiness in young school children', *Developmental Medicine and Child Neurology* **24**, 448–60.

Henderson, S. E. and Sugden, D. (1992) *Movement Assessment Battery for Children*. New York: Harcourt Brace/The Psychological Corporation.

Hier, D. B. and Kaplan, J. (1980) 'Verbal comprehension deficits after right hemisphere damage', *Applied Psycholinguistics* **1**, 279–94.

Hinshaw, S. P. (1992) 'Externalizing behaviour problems and academic underachievement in childhood and adolescence: causal relationships and underlying mechanisms', *Psychological Bulletin* **111**, 127–55.

Hotopf, W. H. N. (1980) 'Slips of the pen', in Frith, U. (ed.) *Cognitive Processes in Spelling*. London: Academic Press.

Hulme, C. and Lord, R. (1986) 'Clumsy children: a review of recent research', *Child: Care, Health and Development* **12**, 257–69.

Kaplan, E., Fein, D., Morris, R., Delis, D. (1991) *Manual for WAIS-R as a Neuropsychological Instrument*. San Antonio, TX: The Psychological Corporation.

Keller, E. and Gopnik, M. (eds) (1987) *Motor and Sensory Processes of Language*. Hillsdale, NJ: Lawrence Erlbaum Associates.

Kimura, D. and Archibald, Y. (1974) 'Motor functions of the left hemisphere', *Brain* **97**, 333–50.

Lang, J. (1995) 'The emotion probe: studies of motivation and attention', *American Psychologist* **50**, 372–85.

Lanting, C. I. *et al.* (1994) 'Neurological differences between 9-year-old children fed breast-milk or formula-milk as babies', *Lancet* **344**, 319–22.

Laszlo, J. I. and Bairstow, P. J. (1986) *Perceptual Motor Behaviour*. New York: Holt, Rinehart and Winston.

Lee, M. G. and Smith, G. N. (1998) 'The effectiveness of physiotherapy for dyspraxia', *Physiotherapy* **84**(6), 276–84.

Lobascher, M. (1995) *Praxis Makes Perfect*. Hitchin: The Dyspraxia Foundation.

Losse, A. *et al.* (1991) 'Clumsiness in children – do they grow out of it? A ten year follow up study', *Developmental Medicine and Child Neurology* **33**, 55–68.

Lucas, A. *et al.* (1989) 'Early diet in pre-term babies and developmental status in infancy', *Archives of Disease in Childhood* **64**, 1578.

Lucas, A. *et al.* (1992) 'Breast milk and subsequent intelligence quotient in children born prematurely', *Lancet* **339**, 261–4.

Luria, A. R. (1976) *Basic Problems in Neurolinguistics*. The Hague: Mouton.

Mcgee, R., Williams, S., Feehan, M. (1992) 'Attention deficit disorder and age of onset of problem behaviours', *Journal of Abnormal Child Psychology*, **20**, 487–502.

Makrides, M., Neumann, M. A., Byard, R. W., Simmer, K., Gibson, R. A. (1994) 'Fatty acid composition of brain, retina and erythrocytes in breast- and formula-fed infants', *American Journal Clinical Nutrition* **60**, 189–94.

Makrides, M., Neumann, M. A., Gibson, R. A. (1996) 'Effect of maternal docosahexanoic acid (DHA) supplementation on breast milk composition', *European Journal of Clinical Nutrition* **50**, 352–57.

Margolin, D. I. (1984) 'The neuropsychology of writing and spelling: semantic, phonological, motor and perceptual processes', *Quarterly Journal of Experimental Psychology* **36A**, 459–89.

Miceli, G., Silveri, C., Carramazza, A. (1985) 'Cognitive analysis of a case of pure dysgraphia', *Brain and Language* **26**, 187–212.

Missiuna, C., Bushby, C., Rupert, C. (1994) *Management of Children With Developmental Co-ordination Disorder: at Home and in the Classroom*. Hamilton, Ontario: Cheryl Missiuna.

Nadeau, K. (1995) *Attention Deficit Hyperactivity Disorder in Adults: A Handbook*, New York: Brunner/Mazel.

Narhi, V. and Ahonen, T. (1995) 'Reading disability with or without attention deficit hyperactivity disorder: do attentional problems make a difference?', *Developmental Neuropsychology* **11**, 337–49.

Neuringer, M. *et al.* (1988) 'The essentiality of n–3 fatty acids for the development and function of the retina and brain', *Annual Review of Nutrition* **8**, 517–41.

Neuringer, M. (1993) 'Cerebral cortex docosahexanoic acid is lower in formula-fed than in breast-fed infants', *Nutrition Review* **51**, 238–41.

Patterson, K. E. and Besner, D. (1984) 'Is the right hemisphere literate?', *Cognitive Neuropsychology* **1**, 315–41.

Patterson, K. and Kay, J. (1982) 'Letter-by-letter reading: Psychological descriptions of a neurological syndrome', *Quarterly Journal of Experimental Psychology* **34A**, 411–41.

Pennington, B. F. and Ozonoff, S. (1996) 'Executive functions and developmental psychopathology', *Journal of Child Psychology and Psychiatry* **37**, 51–87.

Polatajko, H. J. *et al.* (1995) 'Clinical trial of the process-oriented treatment approach for children with developmental co-ordination disorder', *Developmental Medicine and Child Neurology* **37**(4), 310–19.

Portwood, M. M. (1996) *Developmental Dyspraxia – a Practical Manual for Parents and Professionals*, 1st edn. Durham Co. Council.

Posner, M. I. *et al.* (1982) 'Neural systems control of spatial orienting', *Philosophical Transactions of the Royal Society* (London) **B298**, 187–98.

Posner, M. I., Cohen, Y., Rafal, R. D. (1985) 'Inhibition of return: neural basis and function', *Cognitive Neuropsychology* **2**, 211–28.

Regehr, S. M. and Kaplan, B. J. (1988) 'Reading disability with motor problems may be an inherited subtype', *Paediatrics* **82**, 204–10.

Revel, C. (1998) 'Research and development', interim report for the Dyspraxia Foundation Adult Group. Hitchin: The Dyspraxia Foundation.

Rogan, W. J. and Gladen, B. C. (1993) 'Breast-feeding and cognitive development', *Early Human Development* **31**, 181–93.

Rudel, R. G. and Denckla, M. B. (1974) 'Relationship of forward and backward digit repetitions to neurological impairment in children with learning disabilities', *Neuropsychologia* **12**, 109–18.

Russell, J. (1988). *Graded Activities for Children with Motor Difficulties*. Cambridge: Cambridge University Press.

Saffran, E. M. (1982) 'Neuropsychological approaches to the study of language', *British Journal of Psychology* **73**, 317–37.

Sandler, A. *et al.* (1992) 'Neurodevelopmental study of writing disorders in middle childhood', *Journal of Developmental and Behavioural Paediatrics* **13**, 17–23.

Schachar, R. J. *et al.* (1995) 'Deficient inhibitory control in attention deficit hyperactivity disorder', *Journal of Abnormal Child Psychology* **23**, 411–38.

Searleman, A. (1983) 'Language capabilities of the right hemisphere', in A. W. Young (ed.) *Functions of the Right Cerebral Hemisphere*. London: Academic Press.

Seidman, L. J. *et al.* (1995). 'Effects of family history and comorbidity on the neuropsychological performance of children with ADHD: preliminary findings', *Journal of the American Academy of Child and Adolescent Psychiatry* **34**, 1015–24.

Shaffer, D. *et al.* (1985) 'Neurological soft signs: their relationship to psychiatric disorder and intelligence in childhood and adolescence', *Archives of General Psychiatry* **42**, 342–51.

Shaley, R. *et al.* (1993) 'The acquisition of arithmetic in normal children: assessment by a cognitive model of dyscalculia', *Developmental Medicine and Child Neurology* **35**, 539–601.

Shalice, T. (1981) 'Neurological impairment of cognitive processes', *British Medical Bulletin* **37**, 187–92.

Stevens, L. J. *et al.* (1995) 'Essential fatty acid metabolism in boys with attention deficit hyperactivity disorder', *American Journal of Clinical Nutrition* **62**, 761–68.

Uauy, R. and Andraca, I. (1995) 'Human milk and breast feeding for optimal mental development', *Journal of Nutrition* **125**, 2278S–2280S.

Wechsler, D. (1992) *WPPSI–R. UK., WISC–III, WAIS*. New York: The Psychological Corporation/Harcourt, Brace.

Wechsler, D. (1996) *Wechsler Objective Reading Dimensions (WORD)*. New York: The Psychological Corporation/Harcourt, Brace.

White, M., Bungay, C., Gabriel, H. (1994) *Guide to Early Movement Skills*. Slough: NFER-Nelson.

Williams, L. V. (1983) *Teaching for the Two-Sided Mind*. New York: Simon and Schuster.

Index